Church of England Record Society

Volume 25

THE FIRST WORLD WAR DIARIES OF THE RT. REV. LLEWELLYN GWYNNE JULY 1915–JULY 1916

This is possibly the photograph of Bishop Gwynne referred to in the diary entry for 5 August 1915. A copy is held in the Museum of Army Chaplaincy and is reproduced by permission of the Trustees.

THE FIRST WORLD WAR DIARIES
OF THE RT. REV. LLEWELLYN GWYNNE
JULY 1915–JULY 1916

EDITED BY

Peter Howson

THE BOYDELL PRESS

CHURCH OF ENGLAND RECORD SOCIETY

First published 2019

A Church of England Record Society publication
Published by The Boydell Press
an imprint of Boydell & Brewer Ltd
PO Box 9, Woodbridge, Suffolk IP12 3DF, UK
and of Boydell & Brewer Inc.
668 Mt Hope Avenue, Rochester, NY 14620–2731, USA
website: www.boydellandbrewer.com

ISBN 978–1–78327–396–6

ISSN 1351–3087

Series information is printed at the back of this volume

A CIP catalogue record for this book is available
from the British Library

The publisher has no responsibility for the continued existence or accuracy
of URLs for external or third-party internet websites referred to in this book,
and does not guarantee that any content on such websites is,
or will remain, accurate or appropriate

This publication is printed on acid-free paper

Printed and bound in Great Britain by
TJ International Ltd, Padstow, Cornwall

Contents

Acknowledgments

It was Canon Professor Michael Snape who first suggested to me that the Gwynne diaries, covering the time Bishop Gwynne spent as a member of the Army Chaplains' Department in France during the First World War, might prove a useful addition to the published documents that cover the conflict. He also suggested that an approach to the Church of England Record Society might prove the way forward for publication. As with all interested in the study of chaplaincy in the British army, I can never fully repay him for his interest and encouragement.

The Museum of Army Chaplaincy at Amport House contains a substantial amount of archive material relating to the First World War. Along with many others, I must express my thanks to David Blake, the Curator, for his willingness to share his knowledge of the collection and the Chaplains' Department's history in general. It was good to have been able to point him to a source within the Gwynne archive in the Special Collection at Durham University Library that has increased our awareness of the posting of chaplains, during the period August 1915 to December 1916, both to and within the British Expeditionary Force.

The National Railway Museum are thanked for their help in trying to identify the Ambulance Train mentioned by Gwynne in March 1916. The staff of the Army Medical Services Museum are thanked for their assistance in identifying members of the Royal Army Medical Corps.

The Special Collection at Durham University Library contains a wealth of material relating to Gwynne's service during the First World War. Some of it has enabled entries in the diaries to be better understood. They have also provided alternative spellings for names that otherwise would have been unidentified. I am grateful to the reprographic staff for their ready and expert completion of the requests for digital copies of the diary entries and other holdings. I am grateful, too, for the willingness to answer questions of other members of the library staff at Palace Green. The visits that I have made to the Special Collection have also been met with unfailing kindness and professionalism. I am grateful to Francis Gotto for guidance on the reproduction of the diary entries held in the Special Collection.

The wartime diaries are split between Durham University and the Cadbury Research Library at the University of Birmingham. I am grateful to the librarian and staff of the latter institution for their willingness to meet my queries about the holding and to allow access to material in the collection. I am also grateful for permission to reproduce the entries in the diaries held in the library.

I am grateful to the Lambeth Palace Library for permission to quote from the papers of Archbishop Randall Davidson.

The Gwynne material in both libraries was deposited by the Church Missionary Society. I am grateful to Ken Osborne, the archivist at the Society's present headquarters in Oxford, for his guidance in allowing access to the Gwynne material. I am also grateful to him for his advice on helping to understand entries in the diaries that related to members of the Society. I am also grateful for permission to use the Gwynne material.

My researcher, Mrs Yvonne Kidd, used her experience of genealogical sites to provide much of the information about the Gwynne family. She was also able to provide additional information about some of the other people mentioned by Gwynne during his visits to London. I am grateful to the Librarian at Westminster Abbey for information relating to the services at the Abbey which Gwynne either attended or in which he participated. I am also grateful for information about members of the Abbey staff, especially Canon Pearce with whom Gwynne stayed several times between July 1915 and July 1916. The Librarian at St Paul's Cathedral provided information about the service held on 4 August 1915 that marked the first anniversary of the outbreak of the war. The archivist of the diocese of New Westminster in Canada provided information about Bishop A. de Pencier who served as a chaplain with the Canadian Forces, and with whom Gwynne came into contact.

As with so many others I am grateful to the staff at The National Archives at Kew for their professionalism in providing documents.

My brother, Professor John Howson, read and commented on the draft of the introduction. I am grateful that he took the time to do so during a busy schedule. As ever, his comments were insightful.

Grant Tapsell, in his first year as the Editor of the Church of England Record Society has been unfailingly helpful. I am grateful for the time that he has devoted to bringing the manuscript into line with the style used by the Society, especially as he has had to do this in a year which has been exceptionally busy in his own academic life. Many thanks to Linda Randall who helped me through the process of final editing. Her eye for details and willingness to put up with my idiosyncrasies at a particularly difficult moment for my family have made working with her a pleasure.

Abbreviations

AChD	Army Chaplains' Department (from February 1919 'Royal' and thus RAChD)
ACG	assistant chaplain general
ADC	aide de camp
AG	adjutant general
ANZAC	Australia and New Zealand Army Corps
ASC	Army Service Corps
ASR	Army Scripture Readers
BEF	British Expeditionary Force
Bde	Brigade
CA	Church Army
Cav Div/Bde	Cavalry Division/Brigade
CC/CCS	Casualty Clearing/Casualty Clearing Station
CEMS	Church of England Men's Society
CG	chaplain general
C of E	Church of England
CMS	Church Missionary Society
CO	commanding officer
CRA	Commander Royal Artillery
CWGC	Commonwealth (formerly Imperial) War Graves Commission
DCG	deputy chaplain general
Div	Division
FA	Field Ambulance
GHQ	General Headquarters
GOC	General Officer in Command (or Commanding)
HC	Holy Communion
HLI	Highland Light Infantry
IEE	Indian Ecclesiastical Establishment
KHC	king's honorary chaplain
LPL	Lambeth Palace Library
MC	Military Cross
NZ	New Zealand
QMG	quartermaster general
RAMC	Royal Army Medical Corps
RC	Roman Catholic
RFC	Royal Flying Corps
SCF	senior chaplain to the forces
SChap	senior chaplain to the forces
TF	Territorial Force
TNA	The National Archives (Kew)
VC	Victoria Cross
WO	War Office
YMCA	Young Men's Christian Association

Introduction

Llewellyn Gwynne was an inveterate diarist. For almost every day of his adult life, he wrote about what he saw and did. The sixty-nine volumes in the Cadbury Special Collection of the University of Birmingham[1] together with the eight volumes in the Special Collection at Durham University,[2] along with a considerable amount of other material that have survived, have provided an invaluable insight into the life of a Church of England cleric, army chaplain and colonial bishop in the first half of the twentieth century. The diaries also represent an almost unrivalled example of reflection on the First World War by someone who served in France continuously between late August 1914 and February 1919.[3] The entries reproduced in this work cover just over a year whilst Gwynne was serving as a member of the Army Chaplains' Department (AChD) with the British Expeditionary Force (BEF) in France and Flanders. These entries, from the start of July 1915 to the end of July 1916, spanned the second year of the First World War. It was a period that was to see great changes in the British army.[4] It was also to see a change in the way chaplains of the Church of England were administered in the BEF, and Gwynne's *rôle* in overseeing them.

The importance of Gwynne's diaries to the understanding of army chaplaincy in the First World War

Few of the men who went to France with the initial deployment of the BEF in August 1914 returned to Britain in 1919 having remained in the same post throughout. There was one such, the Reverend Dr J. Simms, an Irish Presbyterian army chaplain. He had been about to retire at the end of a career in army chaplaincy[5] when, in August 1914, he was appointed to be the principal chaplain to accompany the BEF on its initial deployment. His post was the only one for a chaplain that was specified in the mobilization tables for the BEF.[6] The precise reasons for this situation are now lost but it was likely that they were the result of the unresolved tensions that existed

---

[1] Cadbury Research Library Special Collection of the University of Birmingham, CMS/ACC/18F1 Bishop Gwynne diaries.

[2] Special Collection of Durham University, SAD 34/10/1 – 120 diary of Bishop Gwynne for May 1915 to May 1916.

[3] For comments on other First World War diaries kept by chaplains, see P. J. Howson, *Padre, prisoner and pen-pusher: the World War One experiences of the Reverend Benjamin O'Rorke* (Solihull, 2015), esp. ch. 6 and bibliography.

[4] See, for instance, Anon., *The Times history of the war 1914–1920* (22 vols., London, 1920).

[5] National Army Museum, NAM 2006-12-65, minutes of the Presbyterian Advisory Committee to the WO held on 30 July 1914.

[6] TNA, WO 33/611.

within the army about the organization and function of the chaplains.[7] Simms's task
was to provide administrative oversight for such members of the AChD as were
to accompany the troops as chaplains. It was that *rôle* he continued to fulfil until
February 1919, when he was demobilized and returned to the United Kingdom.
He then took his retirement from the army and returned to his home in Ulster. He
was to reappear as the Member of Parliament for North Down, elected in 1922 to
replace Field Marshal Sir Henry Wilson, whose death at the hands of members of
the Irish Republican Army had caused a by-election.[8] There was one important
alteration to Simms's *rôle* in the supervision of chaplains. In July 1915, during the
period covered by this volume of Gwynne's diaries, the chaplains serving with the
BEF who belonged to the Church of England were placed into a separate administrative category, one to which Gwynne was appointed to be head. It is not possible
to record what Simms thought about that change, or indeed any other event during
his period in France. None of his personal papers appear to have survived. This
gap has been made worse by the fact that no papers from his branch at the General
Headquarters (GHQ) of the BEF appear to have been retained. The disappearance
of branch records concerned with chaplaincy from the files of the War Office (WO)
that covered the period of the war, destroyed in the bombing of London during the
Second World War that was responsible for the loss of a significant part number of
army records, has only added to the problem for scholars who wanted to discover
the experience of chaplaincy on the Western Front.

Those losses make the survival of Gwynne's diaries even more important as a
source to understand not only Church of England chaplaincy, but in some measure,
all chaplaincy, in the BEF. This is especially true for the opening entries. At the start
of the period reproduced in this volume Gwynne was a chaplain to the forces class
4, the lowest of the ranks in the AChD. The entries have thus given an insight into
the life of a chaplain in the BEF at the level at which the majority of chaplains oper-
ated. It was, for both Gwynne and the AChD, a position of some oddity. This was
reflected in the way in which the chaplain general (CG), the Right Reverend John
Taylor Smith*, had dealt with Gwynne's application to serve as an army chaplain.[9]
When, in August 1914, Gwynne made his request to be commissioned as a chaplain
with the British army, he was already the bishop of Khartoum.[10] It was by chance
that, on the day that war was declared with Germany, he was in London, on leave
from the Sudan.[11]

---

[7] The organization of chaplains in the British army has been examined in M. Snape, *Clergy under
     fire: the Royal Army Chaplains' Department 1796–1953* (Woodbridge, 2008); J. Smyth, *In this
     sign conquer* (London, 1968); P. J. Howson, *Muddling through: the organisation of British army
     chaplaincy in World War One* (Solihull, 2013).
[8] Information supplied by the Museum of Army Chaplaincy.
[9] SAD 28/5: letter Gwynne to Taylor Smith, 4 Aug. 1914.
[10] H. C. Jackson, *Pastor on the Nile* (London, 1960).
[11] *Ibid.*

Gwynne's life before 1914

Gwynne, in August 1914, was already fifty-one.[12] He had been born on 11 June 1863, at Foxholes, Lamsamlet Lower in the Kilvey valley on the outskirts of Swansea, the fourth of the six sons who –together with two daughters – made up the family of Richard Gwynne, the local schoolmaster, and his wife Charlotte. One of his brothers was Howell Arthur Gwynne who was later to have a noted career as a newspaper editor. There are many references to Howell at various points in the wartime diaries. Two other brothers were to be ordained and a further brother to be commissioned into the army. Gwynne was educated at Swansea Grammar School and, after a short spell as a teacher in Beverley in Yorkshire, he received his ordination training at St John's Hall, Highbury.

Gwynne was ordained deacon in 1886, and then appointed curate at St Chad's, Derby.[13] He came to the notice of large crowds in the town when he played association football as an amateur for Derby County. His prowess in sports was also shown when, in 1891, he moved to Nottingham to serve as a curate to the Reverend Frank Woods at the parish of St Andrew's.[14] A year later, he became the incumbent of the neighbouring parish of Emmanuel.[15] Among those whom he prepared for confirmation in that parish was a teenager, Benjamin O'Rorke.[16] They were to meet again during the First World War. Whilst studying for the ministry, Gwynne had been influenced by the stories of the final days, and death, in Khartoum, of Major General Charles Gordon. As a result, when the Church Missionary Society (CMS) appealed for volunteers to work in the Sudan, Gwynne applied.[17] Selected to serve in Khartoum, he left London in November 1899 and arrived a month later. At that point, General Kitchener was coming to the end of his time as governor-general of Sudan and was unenthusiastic about Gwynne working with the local, and largely Islamic, community. He was, however, prepared to permit him to minister among the military. Following the battle of Omdurman in 1898, the British had retained a significant military presence in the Sudan. Thus began a long association with the British army that was likely to have been one of the factors that influenced Gwynne's decision to offer his services as a chaplain in 1914. There are numerous references in the diaries to those members of the army whom Gwynne had met previously in the Sudan.

It was in 1905 that Gwynne was appointed to be the archdeacon of the Sudan. His energetic style attracted attention, and in 1911 he was consecrated as the first suffragan bishop of Khartoum in the diocese of Jerusalem and assistant to Bishop G. F. P. Blyth, the Anglican bishop of Jerusalem (1887–1914). One of Gwynne's early tasks was to oversee the construction of a permanent church building in Khartoum. It was decided that it would contain a chapel which would serve as a memorial to General Gordon and would be larger than was needed for the Christian population of the city. The foundation stone was laid on Sunday 7 February 1904. It was an

---

12   *Ibid.*
13   *Ibid.*
14   *Ibid.*
15   *Ibid.*
16   Howson, *Padre, prisoner and pen-pusher.*
17   Jackson, *Pastor.*

appropriate church to serve as a cathedral and the partly completed structure was consecrated, on 26 January 1912, as All Saints by the bishop of London.[18]

Kitchener was succeeded, at the end of 1899, as governor-general of Sudan, by Sir Reginald Wingate. Gwynne came to know him well. It happened that Wingate was also on leave from the Sudan, and in London, in August 1914. It was thus possible for Gwynne to raise with him the question as to whether he should offer to serve in the AChD.[19] It was undoubtedly a delicate subject. Gwynne had discussed the matter with the CG, who, not unnaturally, thought that Gwynne was too old, at fifty-one, to be commissioned as a chaplain. There was also the question of leave of absence from his duties in the Sudan. Taylor Smith suggested that Gwynne consult the arch-bishop of Canterbury, Randall Davidson, perhaps hoping that the plan would thus go no further. Davidson, however, gave his blessing, and Gwynne was thus granted a commission as a chaplain to the forces class 4, being gazetted on 29 August 1914 along with fifty-one others.[20] It is interesting that Davidson should have agreed to Gwynne seeking a commission at a time at which he was involved with other African bishops, mediating in the row that had broken out over the 1913 Kikuyu Conference.[21] The archbishop also had to deal with requests from other, British, bishops who were seeking approval to take up full-time chaplaincies, as a result of their commissions in the Chaplains' Department of the Territorial Force (TF). On 12 August 1914, Davidson had replied to Alfred Edwards, the bishop of St Asaph, about whether he might accompany the regiment to which he was the chaplain. The archbishop had advised strongly against such a course of action, arguing that the place of a bishop was in his diocese. He commented in a postscript, 'I have said the same to the Bp. of London, but much more strongly in his case.'[22] The archbishop gave the same advice to several incumbents from parishes within his diocese who had sought his counsel about applying to become a chaplain. Before deploying to France, Gwynne had written, on 18 August 1914, to the archbishop about his posting.

> I write to you to tell you that the Adjutant General is sending me out as acting chaplain to the Expeditionary force which I join on Friday. I am not due back in the Sudan until November. Please God the war will be over before then … I am placing myself so entirely under the orders of the Chaplain General that even my moustache has to be sacrificed at his command.[23]

It might have been the feeling that the war would last no more than a few months at most that had allowed the archbishop to agree to Gwynne's request when others were denied. The only bishop to serve as a combatant was Frank Weston of Zanzibar, a central figure in the Kikuyu crisis. He raised, in 1916, and commanded, the Zanzibar Carrier Corps.[24]

---

[18] *Ibid.*

[19] *Ibid.*

[20] *London Gazette*, 3rd Supplement, 29 Aug. 1914, p. 6881.

[21] For a discussion of the *rôle* of Davidson, during Aug. 1914, in handling the aftermath of the 1913 Kikuyu Conference, see David Law, 'Frank Weston, the Kikuyu Controversy, and the necessity of episcopacy', *International Journal for the Study of the Christian Church*, 15 (2015), 214–43.

[22] Lambeth Palace Library (LPL), Davidson papers, vol. 343, fo. 4: Davidson to Edwards, dated 12 Aug. 1914.

[23] *Ibid.*, fo. 20: Gwynne to Davidson, dated 18 Aug. 1914.

[24] C. Beresford, *The Christian soldier: the life of Lt. Col. The Rev. Bernard William Vann, VC MC and bar, Croix de Guerre avec palme* (Solihull, 2017), p. 284.

The AChD in August 1914

Amongst Gwynne's papers in the Special Collection of Durham University are various items of correspondence with Benjamin O'Rorke. The teenager, whom Gwynne had prepared for confirmation in Nottingham, had also become a priest, and had since 1901 been serving as a member of the AChD. O'Rorke was, in August 1914, stationed at Bordon in Hampshire and was preparing to go with the BEF as a chaplain, serving with 4 Field Ambulance (FA) of the Royal Army Medical Corps (RAMC).[25] Not unnaturally, Gwynne went to him for advice about the practicalities of service as an army chaplain.

The AChD into which Gwynne was commissioned as initially an acting chaplain, and then, when the WO rapidly reorganized the complicated range of commissions in the Department, as a temporary chaplain, was different from its post-war successor. After the end of the First World War, not only was the Department to be granted the prefix 'Royal',[26] but was also to undergo a reorganization that was to see its administrative structure changed. Furthermore, it also acquired a new understanding of the *rôle* of a chaplain in the army. Chaplains were no longer to be based at a garrison church acting as a quasi-parish priest, with a captive congregation each Sunday for the compulsory church parade. By the end of the war, they had become identified with individual units. Few, in the field, had taken a service in a consecrated building for years. The processes by which the AChD had evolved during the conflict, and in which Gwynne participated, contributed to both the need for the reorganization and the solution that was eventually produced. The need for these changes was reflected at several places in the diaries.

The AChD in August 1914 was a collection of men – there were to be no women serving as a chaplain in the regular army until the twenty-first century – who acted as the priests and ministers to the military garrisons to which they were posted.[27] The Department had been created by Royal Warrant in 1796.[28] It sought to replace the system of regimentally employed chaplains that, by the end of the eighteenth century was failing to provide the spiritual support for troops deploying on overseas operations. It was the creation of the secretary of state for war, apparently without any consultation with either the archbishop of Canterbury or any other church leader. It can be considered to have been an attempt by the military authorities to create for the army a system similar to the one provided by the Admiralty for the Royal Navy. Events rapidly showed that there were a number of essential differences between the army and the navy that meant that the naval model of chaplaincy came under strain in the army. During the early nineteenth century, it came to be recognized that the chaplaincies at the army fortresses within the United Kingdom, such as Fort George near Inverness and the Tower of London, needed to be included in the organization. It also became obvious that whereas the Royal Navy might argue for a homogeneity that included a unified approach to religious practice, and that such practice should be that of the Church of England, the army was formed of many units some of which had distinct affiliations to individual nations within the United

---

25 Howson, *Padre, prisoner and pen-pusher.*
26 Army Order, 19 Feb. 1919.
27 *Army List* for July 1914 contained the names and stations of army chaplains.
28 For the history or army chaplaincy since 1796, see Snape, *Clergy under fire*; and Smyth, *In this sign conquer.*

Kingdom. Regiments of Scots, such as the 93rd Foot, who prided themselves on their Presbyterian character, were unimpressed by the lack of government provision for their spiritual welfare by ministers of their own ilk.[29] Equally, Irish soldiers, not only in regiments that traditionally recruited in Ireland but also in the considerable numbers who joined other units, were in many cases Catholic.[30] Even as early as the wars of the Napoleonic period, unofficial arrangements were being made to employ Catholic priests to meet the spiritual needs of their soldiers. The total number of full-time chaplains employed before 1815 remained low. They were mostly used in the hospitals and the question of their status does not appear to have arisen. With no major deployment of the British army until the Crimean War started in 1854, the AChD had withered in much the same way as other branches of the army that were mostly required in any number only in a time of war. The experience in the Crimea showed that unlike the navy, where a chaplain aboard one of Her Majesty's ships was likely to be easily identifiable to the crew as such, and thus would not need any rank insignia to show entitlement to quartering and messing, the same was not true in the vastly larger and more complex situation of a battlefield. A chaplain might be known in a particular headquarters or unit but would be a stranger elsewhere. As such, he might find it difficult to obtain the resources he needed to carry out his ministry.

So it was that in 1858, following the end of the Crimean War, the Royal Warrant was amended. The recognition that had been gained, during the war, by Presbyterian ministers from Scotland[31] and Catholic priests was formalized.[32] More importantly a system of ranks was introduced into the AChD. It was done in such a way as to recognize that chaplains were appointed by their several churches and whilst administered by the army once they were in uniform remained a priest or minister. Thus, the rank of chaplain to the forces was created.[33] It was divided into four classes, with the class 4 being the most junior. To provide some indication of what that signified in the main rank structure of the army, and thus to indicate appropriate status, the chaplain to the forces class 4 was equated to a captain. The higher classes thus equated to major, lieutenant colonel and colonel. The system, with its inherent likelihood of confusion, has continued to the present. The CG was excluded from the structure and given the equivalent rank of a major general.[34]

The appointment of CG was one that had continued, with a brief change of title to principal chaplain in the 1830s, from the 1796 creation of the AChD. The position remained, in 1914, as it always had been, solely responsible for those chaplains recruited from the Church of England. Presbyterians and Catholics, when, after 1858 they received commissions, were not placed under the authority of the CG. Church relations would never have permitted such an arrangement. They were the administrative responsibility of a civil servant. Since, in peace there were relatively

---

[29] D. Reid, *The kirk of the 93rd: a short history 1808 to 1968* (Plymouth, 1968).

[30] M. Snape, *The redcoat and religion: the forgotten history of the British soldier from the age of Marlborough to the eve of the First World War* (London, 2005).

[31] See A. C. Dow, *Ministers to the soldiers of Scotland* (London, 1962), for discussion of Church of Scotland chaplains.

[32] See T. Johnstone and J. Hagerty, *The cross on the sword: Catholic chaplains in the forces* (London, 1996), for details of Catholic chaplaincy in the army.

[33] Snape, *Clergy under fire*, p. 102.

[34] For an explanation of the AChD rank structure and how it related to appointments held during the First World War, see Howson, *Muddling through*, pp. xi–xii.

small numbers, and they were widely spread serving garrisons across the United Kingdom and the Empire, administration was minimal. Nobody, even in the WO, fully understood the complexity of the AChD and it remained a cause for concern to those who longed for a tidy structure.

None of these issues were far from the surface when, in August 1914, the AChD began to tackle the provision of spiritual care for the first expeditionary force being sent by Britain to mainland Europe for a century. Indeed, in various ways questions about the nature and shape of chaplaincy in the army had caused problems during the previous ten years. Following the end, in 1902, of the Second Anglo-Boer War, there had been an exchange of letters between Archbishop Bourne, the Catholic archbishop of Southwark, and the person responsible for the oversight of Catholic clergy in the forces, and the WO. It concerned the ability of a local hierarchy, in this case in South Africa, to bar the ministry of an army chaplain whom the WO intended to post there. Partly because of this case, Bourne, by now archbishop of Westminster, renegotiated the terms of service under which future Catholic chaplains would serve in the army. It included a provision that all such chaplains would remain at the same rank, effectively as a chaplain to the forces class 4.[35] The immediate effect of this decision was masked by another decision taken after the end of the Second Anglo-Boer War. In this case, it was the decision of the WO that chaplains, not on operations, would not wear uniform. They were instead to wear clerical dress.[36] Again, it mirrored a practice in the Royal Navy, where until the Second World War most chaplains wore a suit with a clerical collar, even when aboard ship. Whatever the effect in the navy, the result in the army was to emphasize the garrison *rôle* of the chaplain in peacetime. Chaplains were not identified with individual units. They do not appear to have had any *rôle* in the exercises of the period except to conduct the compulsory church parades required by the regulations.

The AChD of 1914 was also required to recognize another dynamic. It was one that was to have an immediate and profound influence once war was declared and the expansion of the army started, with the immediate appeals for new recruits. It concerned the needs of those who did not belong to the Anglican, Catholic or Presbyterian communities. During the second half of the nineteenth century, there had been a growing desire amongst other religious groups for recognition of the spiritual needs of those soldiers who belonged to such groups. The best organized had been the Wesleyan Methodists.[37] With a committee to oversee their work, they had eventually obtained, in 1881, the right for their members and adherents to declare themselves as 'Wesleyan' on their army documents. The number of soldiers who claimed a connexion with the Wesleyan Methodist Connexion, or Church as it retitled itself in the 1890s, was sufficiently large that it could not be discounted. Most other groups had so few members in the forces that their needs could usually be ignored. The exception was the Jewish community. Jewish soldiers were identified as such from 1886. Neither group had commissioned chaplains in the regular army prior to 1914. In the case of the Jewish community, it was because the total number was small and spread throughout the army, a situation that would have made the task of a chaplain almost impossible. The presence of local synagogues meant that those based in Britain could attend worship should they so desire. The Wesleyans had

---

35 *Ibid.*, pp. 21–5.
36 TNA, WO 32/6624.
37 Howson, *Muddling through*, pp. 25–8.

no commissioned chaplains for a different reason; the controlling conference had
decided that they did not wish those ministers who were set aside for work with the
forces to receive commissions. It was feared that to allow commissions would tip
the delicate balance of control away from the church and towards the army. Having
negotiated a financial arrangement with the WO in respect of those ministers whom
it directed to work with the forces, the Wesleyan Conference felt no inclination to
accept commissions into the AChD for its ministers, when the offer was renewed
after the end of the Second Anglo-Boer War.[38]

Curiously, the Wesleyan Conference appeared to have no such disinclination
when it came to their ministers being commissioned as members of the AChD in the
newly formed TF. This had become a possibility once the old confusion of militia,
yeomanry and volunteer units had been reorganized, in 1908, into the new structure
of the TF.[39] Among the many changes was the creation of a branch of the AChD
into which chaplains would be commissioned. With prior service being accredited
towards the rank granted, it resulted in several chaplains in the TF holding ranks
above chaplain to the forces class 4, including a number who were appointed chaplain to the forces class 1 solely on the time served. The creation of the TF AChD
also allowed formal recognition for a number of religious communities that did not
have commissioned chaplains serving the regular army. Locally raised units could
well have a religious concentration unknown in the regular army. It was this that had
resulted in commissions for Wesleyan ministers. It also allowed the Welsh Calvin-
istic Methodist Church, distinct from the Wesleyans in their adoption of Calvinism
rather than Arminianism, to appear in the list of chaplains. The opportunity was also
taken to commission the first rabbi into the army. The Reverend Michael Sadler
was commissioned into the AChD of the TF in 1912. His appointment was not to a
single unit, but centrally, although it was expected that his duties would mostly be
with London units.

By the summer of 1914, the chaplains serving with the TF had developed a
different ethos from their regular counterparts. On occasion, this brought them into
conflict. This should not have been a surprise. TF chaplains were recruited locally to
serve men whom they might know in daily life. Their requirement was to be with the
unit at its regular drill nights and when on its annual camp. Their ministry thus had
an overwhelmingly operational context, in contrast to the regular chaplains whose
ministry centred on the conduct of worship in garrisons. Whilst this involved an
element of pastoral concern that would have included the families of the units in the
garrisons to which they were posted, it lacked the pastoral focus on the needs of the
soldier that came to characterize the work of the TF chaplain. Unsurprisingly then
it was the TF chaplains who reacted to the restriction on the wearing of uniform.
They needed to be seen as part of the organization of the army when they appeared
at camp. Uniform was thus essential to them to achieve this degree of identification. In 1911, the Army Council was forced to reverse the decision on the wearing

[38] J. H. Thompson, 'The free church army chaplain, 1830–1930', Ph.D. thesis, University of Sheffield, 1990.
[39] For a discussion of the AChD in the Territorial Force, see P. J. Howson, *Ministry to Saturday
night soldiers: the formation of a Chaplains' Department for the new Territorial Army of 1907*,
United Board History Project (n.p., 2016).

of uniform, at least in so far as TF chaplains were concerned, by the unearthing of a claim that King Edward VII had personally allowed it.[40]

There was one other issue that came to the fore when the consequences of the creation of the AChD for the TF came to be recognized. It centred on the position of bishops within the new organization, and thus might be thought to have had some bearing on the position of Gwynne when, in August 1914, he was seeking to be commissioned into the AChD. There would appear to have been a tradition in a few dioceses that the bishop would be the chaplain to one of the voluntary units.[41] Since such units had no liability for full-time military service, other than possibly within the United Kingdom if invasion threatened, this imposed no exceptional expectation upon them. The formation of the TF did not require any different liability, although those who understood the military scene in the first decade of the twentieth century might well have foreseen that the reorganizations taking place were a response to the shambles that had accompanied the need to put together a credible force to assist the regular army in South Africa, and which might thus be required to do the same in any forthcoming European war. Since the rule for what rank a chaplain would have in this new branch of the TF was based on time served with previous units, several bishops found themselves in the rank of chaplain to the forces class 4. Notable amongst these was the Right Reverend A. Winnington-Ingram, since 1901 bishop of London. At that point, he had also become chaplain to the London Rifle Brigade (Bde), a volunteer unit. Thus, with the formation of the TF, he had less than the ten years required service for promotion, and was commissioned, on 13 July 1909, as a chaplain to the forces class 4. The same list also included the bishops of Liverpool and Kensington, again commissioned as chaplain to the forces class 4.[42] There must have been some concern that this would not adequately recognize the status of the bishops. Thus, on 26 June 1912, the *London Gazette* recorded that the bishop of London, along with four other diocesan bishops, Liverpool, St Asaph, Bath and Wells, and Southwark, together with the suffragan bishops of Colchester and Hull, and the dean of Westminster, would now rank as chaplains to the forces class 1.[43] The rationale behind the decision was set out in a letter that the CG wrote, in October 1914, to the archbishop of Canterbury. It was, he wrote, 'To prevent absurdities – e.g. a bishop who takes up chaplaincy having as his senior officer a curate who has only served a few years.'[44] This gave them the equivalent status of a colonel and explains why when Winnington-Ingram appeared, in the early days of the war, in photographs wearing uniform he had the badges of rank of a colonel.[45]

The detailed mobilization proposals for the TF included some 250 serials that referred to chaplains. Since the official doctrine for the TF was that its *rôle* was to defend the United Kingdom, many of the posts earmarked for chaplains were in association with the fixed defences around the coasts. The tables for the regular army contained only one specific post for a chaplain. The Expeditionary Force headquarters that deployed had a post for a chaplain to the forces class 1 to serve as

---

[40] TNA, WO 32/6624.
[41] This is reflected in names in the list of 'Honorary Chaplains' contained in *Army List* for July 1914.
[42] *London Gazette*, 13 July 1909, p. 5387.
[43] *Ibid.*, 26 June 1912, p. 5535.
[44] LPL, Davidson papers, vol. 343, fo. 57: Taylor Smith to Davidson, 15 Oct. 1914.
[45] As in A. Wilkinson, *The Church of England and the First World War* (London, 1996 edn).

principal chaplain. His task would be to administer the chaplains who were to be deployed with the BEF. Exactly how many chaplains there would be, and in what posts, was not made clear. The introductory remarks to the table simply referred to chaplains being deployed, 'as required'.[46] It might have been this to which the Reverend H. Blackburne, a regular chaplain who served in the BEF throughout the war and who appeared regularly in the diary entries, was referring, in remarks, made after the war was over, that the Chaplains' Department had been unprepared for war. They were, however, comments made by someone who at that time was not in the WO, and have more than a little sense of hindsight about them.[47]

The deployment of the AChD to France

Whatever the apparent lack of planning among the diverse elements of the organi-zational structure in the WO that oversaw the AChD, it was able to provide chap-lains for the BEF. At the same time, however, as it was finalizing the plans for deployment, there were other headaches for the chaplaincy oversight in the WO. The CG had to deal with applications from numerous clergy who felt that they were exactly what the army was looking for to serve as a chaplain. The civilian staff who administered the non-Anglican chaplains were shielded from that problem. The Catholics, in the person of the by then Cardinal Bourne, the Presbyterians with a committee co-ordinating the work of the four main churches that provided chaplains – the Church of Scotland, United Free Church of Scotland, Presbyterian Church of Ireland and Presbyterian Church of England – and the Wesleyan Methodist Church with a committee that oversaw their involvement with the forces, were responsible for recruiting men to serve as chaplains. The WO was only required to indicate the number of men that were needed and then to undertake the paperwork that went with their being commissioned. This had increased because the Wesleyan Methodist Church Committee on Chaplains to the Royal Navy and Army had, immediately following the declaration of war, decided to accept the outstanding offer of commis-sions for those of their ministers who were to accompany the BEF.

The first decision that had to be made was the name of the principal chaplain who would be a member of the headquarters of the BEF. As was noted at the start of this introduction, the choice fell on the Reverend Dr J. Simms. He was a chaplain from the Presbyterian Church of Ireland who was about to retire after a career that had taken him to the battle of Omdurman and the war in South Africa. He had been one of the four chaplains who had conducted a memorial service for Gordon after the capture of Khartoum. There is no indication as to why he was chosen for this post. It might have been that his Sudan service had brought him to the attention of Kitch-ener, the secretary of state for war,[48] and thus made him an acceptable candidate. He was also by some margin the most senior of those who held the rank of chaplain to

---

[46] Anon., *War establishment, Great Britain, army*, Part I, The Expeditionary Force (London, 1912).

[47] H. W. Blackburne, 'Existing organisation and work of the Royal Army Chaplains' Department', *RUSI Journal*, 67 (1922), 421–33.

[48] Field Marshal Lord Herbert Kitchener was credited, in 1898, with winning the battle of Omdurman and securing control of the Sudan for which he was made Lord Kitchener of Khar-toum.

the forces class 1, and who were available to be deployed. Again, whilst there is no evidence that he had any input into the acceptance of Gwynne for a commission, it is possible that the shared experience of life in the Sudan would have encouraged him to support the application.

The second decision to be made was how the limited numbers of chaplains were to be used. Within the regular army, there were few close links between regiments and chaplains. There were in any case only some 160 regular chaplains to meet the needs of the whole army outside India. It was another of those oddities that marked chaplains out from the rest of the army that the AChD had no responsibility for the spiritual care of British troops in India. Their needs were provided for by chaplains of the Indian Ecclesiastical Establishment (IEE).[49] Its chaplains were to accompany the Indian Corps to France where their administration remained partially separate from that of the British chaplains. The IEE also provided chaplains for the Indian army-led deployment to Mesopotamia. Gwynne was involved with IEE chaplains from the start of his time as DCG. On 25 August 1915, he was recording conversations with 'Horwood', an IEE chaplain at Calais, about his relationship with a clergyman working for the Young Men's Christian Association (YMCA). That issue, the relationship between clergy serving with the YMCA and those commissioned as chaplains, was to be one of the major themes in his first months in office as DCG.

The decision that was made, at the start of the war, was to attach chaplains to medical units. In such contexts, the chaplains would be able to provide spiritual comfort to those who were at the point of most need. In the light of the experience of chaplains during the protracted fighting in the Second Anglo-Boer War, where many of the casualties had been the result of sickness rather than wounding, there was some sense in this as the hospitals handled the sick as well as the wounded. The RAMC had used the years before 1914 to work out a strategy for how to handle the casualties of battle. The treatment started at the Regimental Aid Post, where the unit doctor and his team of medical orderlies would provide immediate care and then decide which of the casualties would benefit from further treatment where there were more facilities.[50] It was the responsibility of the FAs, attached to each brigade, to collect the casualties from the Regimental Aid Post, provide further treatment and then to arrange for those that needed still more treatment to be sent to General Hospitals based in the rear areas. The plan that was devised was for two chaplains to be posted to each of the FAs and for either two or three chaplains to be attached to the General Hospitals. Amongst the documents in The National Archives (TNA) at Kew is an envelope, marked SECRET, which contained the plans for the location of the hospitals should the BEF deploy to France. The chaplains had to be attached to a unit as there were no chaplaincy units on the establishment of the army.[51]

As Gwynne's diary for August 1914, together with diaries kept by other chaplains deployed with the BEF, and memoirs written by still others, showed, the deployment went well.[52] All the FAs and hospitals deployed to France with their complement of

---

49   M. Snape, 'The First World War and the chaplains of British India', in *The clergy in khaki: new perspectives on British army chaplaincy in the First World War*, ed. M. Snape and E. Madigan (Farnham, 2013).

50   TNA, WO 106/49A/8 (details of mobilization of medical units).

51   *Ibid.*

52   Howson, *Padre, prisoner and pen-pusher*; see ch. 6 for a discussion of other diaries covering the deployment of the BEF in Aug. 1914.

chaplains. Not all the FAs had been expecting chaplains to be posted to them before they deployed, and there were some issues about what equipment was available. Since the chaplains were 'attached' to the FAs rather than part of the establishment of the unit, there were varying attitudes as to how much they were part of the unit. Most of the chaplains attached to the FAs soon proved their worth. As the BEF engaged the German army at Mons and then began its long strategic withdrawal to the Marne, the number of casualties that needed to be treated rose with each of the delaying battles that were fought. Two Church of England chaplains, including Gwynne's acquaintance the Reverend B. G. O'Rorke, were captured. O'Rorke with members of 4 FA[53] and the Reverend J. T. Hales, who was taken prisoner when he stayed with wounded under the care of 7 FA. Other chaplains, including the Wesleyan, the Reverend O. Spencer Watkins,[54] and the Reverend D. F. Winnifrith, an Anglican,[55] also recorded being heavily engaged in the fighting in which the BEF was involved.

It was at that moment that the carefully worked out evacuation chain that was to take the casualties back to Britain failed. The depth of the German thrust alarmed the military leaders who had command of the base areas to the British rear. It was in these areas that the hospitals were located. With the possibility that there might be a break through, much as was to happen in the Second World War, the decision was taken to move the hospitals to the west coast of France. Having recently disembarked from the ships that had carried them across the channel the personnel and equipment were re-embarked and moved to the Atlantic ports around St Nazaire. The hospitals were to be based around Nantes. Whilst the decision might have saved the bases and preserved the hospitals, it had an unintended consequence. With the German thrust held at the battle of the Marne and then pushed back, the hospitals were badly placed and received few casualties. It was easier to transport them back to Britain through the channel ports.[56]

For two months, the hospitals were thus divorced from the battles taking place in the east of France and had little to do. As a result, the chaplains allocated to them also found themselves with little call for their services. The dichotomy between the two groups of chaplains could not have been more striking. Two things followed, a blame game to seek to show who was responsible for the underuse of the chaplains, and a sense that the chaplains would have been better used by being deployed in a different manner. As Gwynne's diary for 1 September 1914 showed, he was not above taking part in the unhappiness that spread through the staff of the hospitals.[57]

The decision to deploy chaplains with the medical units was undoubtedly a sensible one. It was also the most logical one given both the number of chaplains available to accompany the BEF and their experience of ministry in the peacetime army. The result was, however, that the front line units rarely saw a chaplain once the fighting had begun at Mons. There appear to have been few services taken with units. Those who looked for chaplains who could serve in the *rôle* of priests

---

53 *Ibid.*
54 O. S. Watkins, *With French in France and Flanders* (London, 1915).
55 D. F. Winnifrith, *The church in the fighting line: experiences of an army chaplain* (London, 1915).
56 J. E. Edmonds (ed.), *The official history of the war military operations France and Belgium 1914*, I (London, 1933).
57 CMS/ACC/18F1: Gwynne diary entry for 1 Sept. 1914.

by providing personal absolution for men about to go into battle and anointing for those who fell on the battlefield were inevitably frustrated. That frustration began to find its way back to Britain and to be expressed in the church newspapers.[58] The expression took various forms. A campaign began to increase the number of Catholic chaplains so that there would be enough to attach one to each battalion that had a significant proportion of Catholic soldiers. Although this took time to implement, it was broadly successful. A second movement was among the English nonconformist churches that had previously not been represented among the regular army chaplains. That movement was to culminate, in early 1915, with the recognition by the WO of a United Board to represent those Christian communities. A third movement was among some influential leaders of the high church tradition within the Church of England.

The position of the Church of England in respect of its service to the British army was more complicated than that of any other church. At one level, it appeared to be simple and to its advantage. The CG was an Anglican. With his appointment within the WO, having oversight of Anglican chaplains, the Church of England thus seemed in a strong position. This strength was, though, allied to an equally singular weakness. Uniquely among the churches, the Church of England lacked, within its own structures, either an individual or a committee that was responsible for creating policy for chaplaincy work in the forces. The archbishop of Canterbury might have some overall care for chaplains but, in 1914, he had neither the time nor the staff to manage that responsibility. This lack of focus for debate within the Church of England meant that, as with other matters, arguments were too often played out in public through the medium of the church press. In the autumn of 1914, one of the complaints was that the Anglican part of the AChD was under the direction of a CG who was only selecting evangelicals to serve as temporary chaplains. Numerous letters to the *Church Times* attested to the lack of opportunity to receive the sacraments in the BEF.[59]

One of the leading critics of the Church of England's ability to provide army chaplains and their organization was the 4th marquess of Salisbury. He argued, during much of late 1914 and early 1915, that a change was needed in the way in which Anglican chaplains were administered. The outcome of discussions that resulted from his interventions was, eventually, to have a direct influence on what happened to Llewellyn Gwynne. More immediately, it resulted in a committee being appointed to offer guidance to the WO on matters to do with Anglican chaplaincy in the army. This committee was to exist alongside a similar one for the Presbyterian churches that had been created in 1906.[60] Since the CG was Anglican, it was not clear whether the advice was to him, to the wider WO or to the archbishop of Canterbury as the person with oversight for Anglican chaplains. Its formation saw one of those mistakes that could probably only ever occur in England. Kitchener as secretary of state for war had sanctioned the creation of the committee, and Lord Salisbury had agreed that he would be one of the small number that was to form the committee. The clerk who was responsible for the administration of the committee

---

58 There were debates about the experiences of individual soldiers and the nature of the policy in operation in the church press throughout the late summer and autumn of 1914. Notable examples are to be found in the *Church Times* and the *Tablet.*
59 See editions of the *Church Times* throughout Sept. 1914.
60 National Army Museum, NAM 2006-12-65.

received a list that included 'Salisbury' in it. Perhaps unsurprisingly he interpreted this to mean that he was to send the *pro forma* letter of invitation to the bishop of Salisbury, the Right Reverend Frank Ridgeway. The bishop duly replied that he was surprised, having heard nothing of the plan to form the committee, but was delighted to accept. A second letter had then to be sent to him, apologizing for the mistake as it was *Lord* Salisbury who was the intended recipient. The bishop replied in courteous but somewhat strained tones, pointing out that his diocese, which included Salisbury Plain, had the greatest concentration of soldiers of any part of England and he might have been considered a suitable candidate for membership of the committee.[61]

On 4 August 1915, Sir Reginald Brade, the permanent under-secretary at the WO wrote to the archbishop of Canterbury informing him that the committee would comprise Lord Salisbury as Chair, the bishops of Winchester and Ripon, Field Marshal Lord Grenfell and himself, with the secretary to be appointed. A week later, Brade wrote to the CG indicating that he had had a meeting with Lord Salisbury in an attempt to discover how the committee might work. He reported that there was a lack of clarity and that a preliminary meeting might be necessary. Salisbury obviously intended the committee to cover the whole range of subjects connected with the recruitment, status, organization and establishment of Anglican chaplains. He was, in fact, proposing that a small group of very busy men carry out the tasks that other churches delegated to much larger chaplaincy committees with some form of secretariat. It would also appear that he was envisaging something more than an advisory *rôle*.

Brade foresaw problems and, on 2 September 1915, wrote to Macready, the adjutant general (AG) to the British army in France expressing his concerns.

The eternal Chaplains' question is again prominently before us. The Advisory Committee which Lord Kitchener has appointed is going over the ground so far as the C of E Chaplains are concerned and we are about to be faced with two problems. First it is being claimed that the Establishment is too small, there is no margin for sickness and the numbers allowed give roughly 2,000 to each man's charge which is alleged to be too many and in the case of Divisional troops the charge is about 4,000 to a man. I don't endorse these figures.

Secondly, the proposals to meet this insufficiency are either (a) a pool from which to supply marked deficiencies and (b) the provision of one Chaplain per battalion or similar unit.

Thirdly the administration is centralised in the DCG and there is no graduation of representatives of his in the Armies and the Army Corps – as in other Departments.[62]

He believed that the last point had been met as the situation that had prevailed when the Advisory Committee had been created had been altered by Gwynne's appointment to be deputy CG to the BEF. Brade then sought a military view on whether there would be enough work for increased numbers. He argued that point (b) was

[61] TNA, WO 32/5636.
[62] *Ibid.*

plausible, 'on the analogy of a precedent of the RCs'. He then wanted to know answers to the following questions:

1. Has the newly approved establishment from the Spring been reached and is it sufficient. If not what would be? And would this be better met by a Pool or one per battalion?

2. Any opinion on clergy selected as chaplains?

3. Are there enough senior chaplains to guide younger ones?

4. Are there sufficient staff to administer chaplains properly?

5. Any points from hospitals and bases as against fighting troops?[63]

Brade needed to be well informed because the Advisory Committee immediately set out to produce reports on the work of the Anglican chaplaincy in the army. The first report was presented to the Advisory Committee in mid-September 1915. It concluded that,

1. The Chaplain General's Department was unduly centralised

2. There were 2 Assistant Chaplain Generals (ACGs) needed for Commands and Training Centres

3. Devolve admin to ACGs

4. Staff Officers for these posts (i.e. chaplains) should be selected as able to work with dioceses and parishes.

5. Bishop's recommendation needed for candidates for chaplains

6. Bishops be asked to help in recruiting best men

7. Reduce service from 1 year to six months

8. Recruit churchman of high standing to Chaplain General's staff.[64]

These were general comments that were designed to deal with the needs of the whole army. It is of interest that the report recommended that the contract for service as a commissioned chaplain within the AChD be reduced from a year to six months. This was likely a reflexion on the problems that were faced by incumbents who wished to retain their living and who were thus responsible for the provision of services during their absence at the front. This difficulty almost certainly influenced the decision of some with limited means as to whether they should offer to serve. An interesting side-light on this problem can be noted in the Free Churches. When in May 1916 the Reverend W. J. Coates, Baptist pastor of the Bunyan Meeting in

[63] *Ibid.*
[64] *Ibid.*

Bedford, requested permission of the elders to continue as a chaplain when his year was completed, this was denied. He then returned to civilian ministry.[65]

The creation of an Anglican AChD within the BEF

One reason that the Anglican Advisory Committee had been formed was the belief that the establishment figure for Church of England chaplains needed to be increased. With additional Catholic chaplains having been approved, and with the new style of fighting forcing the limited number of chaplains with the BEF to choose either to work with the casualty evacuation chain or to visit the front line troops, there was general agreement within the church that the establishment figure should be increased. Davidson's papers demonstrate that there was another matter that was raised during the first part of 1915, and which was to have a direct bearing on the work of Bishop Gwynne. It was one that was resolved even before the Advisory Committee had been formed.

The difficulties concerning the numbers, placement and *rôles* of chaplains in the BEF that had been identified in the autumn of 1914 had resulted, in December 1914, in the creation of 'senior chaplains' to advise the principal chaplain on specific denominational matters. These were to include the posting of chaplains to units. A regular chaplain, the Reverend E. G. F. Macpherson, was appointed as the senior Anglican, with the Reverend W. Drury to assist him. As early as February 1915, the archbishop had received a note of a meeting between the Reverend H. R. L. Sheppard, vicar of St Martin-in-the-Fields, and the Reverend H. Blackburne, a regular army chaplain on leave from France, in which the latter had noted that the system for administering chaplains in the BEF was not working as well as the one used in the South African war, where each denomination was responsible for its own organization.[66]

In the spring of 1915, Bishop Furze of Pretoria had spent some time visiting the BEF. He reported back to the archbishop of Canterbury.[67] Whilst his first point dealt with the number of chaplains he believed were needed, the second was headed, 'Organisation'. In his report, Bishop Furze commented, 'I submit that the present system of organization, which is merely an adaptation of the Peace organisation of the army, is totally inadequate.'[68] He believed that the BEF could be seen as parallel in shape and size to a diocese and that it needed its own bishop. Such a leader would be both a 'Father in God' to chaplains but also have the ability to decide where the limited number of chaplains might best be placed. In his view the need was urgent:

> The feeling amongst Army Chaplains, and I can speak with absolute certainty regarding those of the six Army Corps at the Front, is that they have no one to back them: that the organisation of their Department is a bye-word in the Army:

---

[65] N. A. Sherhod and N. E. Allison (eds.), *Bunyan history: Padre W. J. Coates' letters from the front* (Bedford, 2015).

[66] LPL, Davidson papers, vol. 343, fo. 144: memo 22 Feb. 1915.

[67] *Ibid.*, fo. 200: memo on visit to Church of England chaplains at the front by the bishop of Pretoria, covering letter, 20 June 1915.

[68] *Ibid.*

that they have no one to give them a helping hand, and nobody cares: and from what I have myself seen I believe, that there is a good deal to justify this feeling.[69]

For the bishop, the remedy was close at hand.

> The Bishop of Khartoumn [*sic*] is working as an ordinary Chaplain to a Brigade in the First Army, he takes confirmations, and his work, I know, is greatly appreciated: but it is pure chance that he happens to be a Bishop so far as the Army organisation is concerned.[70]

It is not clear whether by 'the Army organisation' the bishop was referring to the general WO staff or specifically to the CG.

This report was to cause a considerable amount of activity at Lambeth over the next month. The archbishop came under pressure from various quarters within the church not only to make the case for an increased establishment for Anglican chaplains but also to obtain a revision of the administration of chaplains within the BEF. The bishop of Pretoria had briefed the archbishop of York as the latter wrote to his fellow archbishop on 24 June 1915 about a discussion of the findings of the visit to the BEF. Lang was concerned, not only about the numbers issue, but also about wider problems of how the chaplains could be helped in their work, and how there could be more mobility in the system. The answer was a bishop, both because he would have a better-defined status within the church rather than a 'senior chaplain', which was merely a military appointment with no civilian equivalent, and that he would be available to take confirmation services. More importantly yet:

> Is it not involved in the principles of an Episcopal church that the supervision of the work of such overwhelming opportunity and importance should be in the hands of one who has received episcopal consecration? He ought to be more than an administrative officer; but a Father in God to both the Chaplains and also to the Officers and men.[71]

He went on to propose that the best man for the post would be the bishop of Kensington, the Right Reverend John Maud. Since he was unlikely to be available, he believed that either the former bishop of North Queensland, the Right Reverend George Frodsham – who in 1915 was a residentiary canon at Gloucester Cathedral, or the bishop of Thetford, the Right Reverend John Bowers might be approached.

Having received the archbishop of York's letter, Davidson asked the CG to meet him at Lambeth Palace to discuss the situation and possible ways forward. Without specifically referring to either the archbishop of York or the bishop of Pretoria, Davidson put forward the case for a bishop to oversee Anglican chaplains in the BEF. The CG was unenthusiastic. In a lengthy note of the conversation, Davidson recorded the arguments on both sides.

> I pressed the point that the Chaplain General has too much on his hands ... and that it would seem right that (he) should have a Deputy who should be in command of the Chaplains at the Front and preferably he should be in episcopal Orders. I

---

[69] *Ibid.*
[70] *Ibid.*
[71] *Ibid.*, fo. 205: Lang to Davidson, 24 June 1915.

related, in my own way, the contents of Ebor's letter to me. The Chaplain General said this was all based on a misapprehension. There is no need for anything of the kind … With regard to the work in general, Macpherson as Senior Anglican Chaplain, does it admirably. It is no doubt unfortunate that the Brigadier General Senior Chaplain should be Simms, a Presbyterian. But he is an excellent man who works entirely in harmony with Macpherson, and as regards our Chaplains, is simply the means of formal communication, conveying Macpherson's wishes or orders. No other Senior Chaplain appointed either permanently or *ad hoc* could properly take Macpherson's place.[72]

The CG followed the meeting by asking whether the archbishop believed there to be either a weakness or a breakdown of the machinery in the BEF.[73] The archbishop replied that he knew nothing of either being present but that everyone was 'under strain'. He suggested a conversation once he had had time to consult those who had written independently to him.[74]

With concern over the need to increase the number of chaplains growing among the bishops, the argument over the need for a bishop in the BEF was unlikely to go away. The bishop of London suggested to Davidson, at the beginning of July 1915, that the whole subject of the AChD in the WO could be raised at the forthcoming meeting of the Convocation of Canterbury.[75] Davidson was less than enthusiastic, not being able to see what the answer was and asked Winnington-Ingram if he could 'throw any light on this that would be helpful'.[76]

Others were more certain of the way forward. On 5 July, the editor of the *Morning Post* wrote to the archbishop ostensibly about the problems his brother, Bishop Llewellyn Gwynne, was having in France with obtaining transport. Howell Gwynne concluded his letter,

No doubt your Grace knows that the Chief Chaplain attached to the British Expeditionary Force is a Presbyterian, and that this is in spite of the fact that according to the statistics, the members of the Church of England form an overwhelming majority of the troops, to the extent of some 75%. This is a matter which primarily concerns the military authorities but it is also a matter in which the Church authorities should have a say.[77]

The archbishop was well aware of the statistics. On 16 June 1915, the archbishop had asked a question, in the House of Lords, about army chaplains. For the government, Lord Newton provided a detailed analysis of the denominational allegiance of the chaplains serving with the BEF. This showed that Anglicans comprised 213 of the total of 425, almost exactly half.[78] Howell Gwynne had written on *Morning Post* notepaper, the paper of which he was the editor. The implication was that here might be a subject that the press would find of interest.

[72] *Ibid.*, fo. 210: memo of meeting between archbishop of Canterbury and Bishop Taylor Smith, chaplain general, held on 28 June 1915.
[73] *Ibid.*, fo. 212: Taylor Smith to Davidson, 29 June 1915.
[74] *Ibid.*, fo. 213: Davidson to Taylor Smith, 1 July 1915.
[75] *Ibid.*, fo. 217: Winnington-Ingram to Davidson, 1 July 1915.
[76] *Ibid.*, fo. 225: Davidson to Winnington-Ingram, 3 July 1915.
[77] *Ibid.*, fo. 229: letter from Howell Gwynne to Davidson dated 5 July 1915.
[78] *House of Lords debates*, 16 June 1915.

Over the next few days, the archbishop received letters from the bishop of Pretoria, which included a scheme to reorganize the chaplains with a bishop,[79] and from the bishops of Chelmsford and Wakefield arguing for a bishop to be appointed for the BEF. These coincided with the meeting of the Convocation of Canterbury at which the bishop of London proposed a motion, on 7 July 1915, in the House of Bishops.

> The Bishops of the Province request the Archbishop of Canterbury, in conjunction if it may be with the Archbishop of York, to make arrangements if possible for a private conference between the War Office and certain representatives of the Bishops upon the whole question of Religious Ministrations to the Army at the present time, both at home and abroad, with a view to securing the best help available, both from Chaplains as from the Parish Clergy at home.

As a result, the archbishop wrote to Kitchener on 10 July 1915 enclosing a copy of the resolution and proposing that a conference be held. As he noted,

> I am certain that some of the difficulties (and they are real) could be removed by such a friendly conference as is suggested. The Chaplain General, whom I saw yesterday and to whom I have given a copy of the Resolution, agrees with me in thinking that such a conference would be desirable.[80]

Plans for the conference moved forward. Several conversations took place and letters were written. Davidson had, on 12 July, travelled across London from the Charterhouse to the House of Lords with the bishop of London. In a memo of their conversation, he noted that the bishop of London had been in favour of a bishop being appointed at the front and had strongly urged the case for the appointment of Gwynne.[81] Not everyone was so certain. The archbishop of York, having been informed by Davidson on 3 July of the proposed meeting, indicated that he intended to be present. He also commented, 'All I know of Gwynne is in his favour. But I doubt very much whether he would meet the need … I wonder whether he would take the episcopal office sufficiently seriously.'[82]

Davidson was quick to reassure him.

> I think myself Gwynne is a stronger and bigger man than you perhaps realise. I know him pretty well, and though his learning is scant and his ecclesiastical traditions are not what would be called strong, his personal piety, his delightfulness as a man, and his unassuming modesty have made him a success wherever he has been.[83]

The conference was to take place at Lambeth Palace on Monday 19 July 1915.

The CG and Sir Reginald Brade, permanent under-secretary of state for war, met with the two archbishops and the bishops of London, Winchester, Southwell and Southwark. The archbishop of Canterbury noted in his memo of the meeting that the bishop of Chelmsford had hoped to be present but was ill. Having set out the background to the meeting, the archbishop of Canterbury then initiated a discussion

---

79 LPL, Davidson papers, vol. 343, fo. 238: letter from Furze to Davidson dated 9 July 1915.
80 *Ibid.*, fo. 258: Davidson to Kitchener, 10 July 1915.
81 *Ibid.*, fo. 269: memo of meeting between Davidson and Winnington-Ingram, 12 July 1915.
82 *Ibid.*, fo. 279: Lang to Davidson, 6 July 1915.
83 *Ibid.*, fo. 282: Davidson to Lang, 17 July 1915.

about numbers. Eventually, Brade spoke, acknowledging the usefulness of the Advisory Committee that was being created. He then turned to the subject of a bishop for the BEF. He indicated that Kitchener had been impressed with Gwynne and that he had summoned him to London. His next statement ended all discussion on the matter: 'and Bishop Gwynne is to be definitely appointed Deputy Chaplain General over all the Chaplains in France with the rank of Major General. The announcement to be sent to the papers tonight.'[84] It was a *fait accompli.*

Arguably, this decision, taken by the army authorities, meant that the archbishop of Canterbury and the other bishops who had been debating the issue of episcopal authority over Anglicans in the BEF, could avoid answering any question about the status of any other bishop appointed as a chaplain. It would not be until 1948 that a bishop was given specific oversight for the armed forces. Even then his title was, as it has remained, the archbishop's episcopal representative to the armed forces. It is also arguable that the decision, taken in the WO, solved another problem for the archbishop.

As has been noted above, Randall Davidson counselled bishops against becoming full-time chaplains, whatever their status within the TF. He also had to deal with requests for guidance from clergy who wished to enlist as combatants. Studying, in general, the experience of such men, and that of Lieutenant Colonel the Reverend Bernard William Vann VC MC*[85] in some detail, Beresford noted that on 2 September 1914, Davidson had commented that a combatant *rôle* 'was incompatible with the position of one who has sought and received Holy Orders'.[86] Some 500 Anglican clergy, however enlisted, other than as chaplains, with over 300 serving in combatant units. Vann was commissioned into the 8th (Territorial) Battalion of the Sherwood Foresters. The battalion was part of 139 Bde in 46 (North Midland) Div. There were frequent references to the division in the diaries. Gwynne, with his connexions with the East Midlands, appeared to have an interest in its activities and to have visited it on a frequent basis. The diaries made several mentions of the Reverend J. P. Hales, brother to the Hales taken prisoner in August 1914 and the chaplain to 8th Battalion, but none to Vann. Since, as Beresford has shown, Vann carried a portable chalice, and conducted services, the episcopal oversight for his activities appears to have been non-existent. The earlier desire for a 'diocese', which would have included all clergy, was not pursued. Gwynne did not appear to consider that his task, as deputy chaplain general (DCG), extended beyond the oversight of chaplains and the episcopal duty of confirmation services. It appeared easier not to deal with any disciplinary outcome that resulted from clergy defying the archbishop's understanding of ordination.

No thought appeared to have been given to informing the other churches of the unilateral change made by the creation of the post of DCG. Gwynne recorded in his diary entry that it was on the evening of 16 July that he had received a message telling him to report to the CG. Two days later, he recorded that he had been informed by the CG that Kitchener had appointed him to be the DCG for the BEF with the equivalent rank of major general. Gwynne was thus promoted overnight from chaplain to the forces class 4 (captain) and would outrank not only all other Anglican chaplains in the BEF but also the principal chaplain, the Reverend

---

[84] *Ibid.*, fo. 285: memo of meeting of bishops and WO held on 19 July 1915.
[85] The use of an asterisk denotes the second award of the medal or decoration.
[86] Beresford, *The Christian soldier.*

Dr J. Simms, who remained with the equivalent rank of brigadier general.[87] It did not, as Edward Madigan has suggested, make Simms 'technically subordinate to Gwynne',[88] any more than Bishop Taylor Smith, as CG, despite being the most senior member of the AChD, had any responsibility for other than Anglicans. What it did mean was that a new era for Anglican chaplaincy in the BEF had begun.

The Church of England section of the AChD

The diary entries for the following days and months show, first, how Gwynne came to terms with the sudden change in his position, and secondly, how he then went about creating the structure that was needed to allow him to carry out the task that he had been given. As has been described in *Muddling through*, the decision to remove the Anglican chaplains from the unified administrative structure and place them under a DCG was greeted with considerable opposition, both within the headquarters of the BEF and from the other churches. Particularly angry were the leaders of the Church of Scotland who saw the move in terms of being both a slight to Simms, a fellow Presbyterian, and of creating a status for one national church that was denied to another.[89] The move was not replicated in the other expeditionary forces, except for that in East Africa, and initially in Italy. Elsewhere, the unified structure remained in place under a single principal chaplain who might come from one of a variety of denominations. It may have been that the size of the BEF made such a reorganization a useful way of ensuring that administrative efficiency was achieved but, if so, it was a by-product rather than the intention.

A chart showing the organization within the AG's office at the end of 1915 did not differentiate between the two branches. 'Chaplains' appeared under the third sub-division of AG(b). That was headed by an assistant AG, Colonel B. E. W. Childs, of whom several mentions were made in the diaries. This sub-division, one of six in the AG's office, was without its own head. The chart merely indicated, 'AAG.' The list of responsibilities was:

Discharges of NCOs[90] and men.

Chaplains.

Graves Registration Commission.

Questions emanating from the French Mission.

Chaplaincy thus had a low profile within the AG's area of responsibility.[91]

As well as the diaries, the Durham University Special Collection holds other material in the Gwynne collection that shed light on the period immediately after his

---

[87] TNA, WO 95/23/3: war diary for the AG of the BEF, which included a General Routine Order for 1 Nov. 1914, 'The Revd J M Simms DD KHC, Principal Chaplain to the Expeditionary Force, has been granted relative precedence as a Brigadier General whilst so employed.'

[88] E. Madigan, *Faith under fire: Anglican army chaplains and the Great War* (Basingstoke, 2011), p. 54.

[89] Howson, *Muddling through*, pp. 89ff.

[90] Non-commissioned officers.

[91] TNA, WO 95/25: war diary of AG BEF.

appointment as DCG.[92] Gwynne noted, as his first entry, in the book that recorded his approach to the new post, that he faced several difficulties.

Difficulties

    1. Two [*sic*] many RC and Presbyterians.

    2. Two [*sic*] few C of E.

The mistake of (1) was brought about by politics or extreme pressure. The result is that the C of E Officers and man have not the same advantages of spiritual ministrations as other denominations enjoy.

Can this be altered?

    1. By ascertaining the number of different Denominations in each Brigade or Division and distributing accordingly.

    2. Calculating spreading over New Divisions the superfluous Presbyterian and RC Chaplains so as to make them equal in proportion to the Church of E.[93]

He had a belief that he could persuade the chaplains from the other denominations to work through a Church of England representative in the field. He was unaware of the hostility that his appointment was to arouse in Scotland.

Whilst in London, Gwynne continued to think about the issues that would face him when he took up his post in France. He reflected that the position of chaplains from India, and also those with Territorial Commissions, needed to be addressed. More serious was the question of the use for services by chaplains who were not Catholic, of Catholic churches in France and Belgium. Two pages of jottings set out his thoughts.

The Use of RC Churches in France for British Troops.[94]

    (i)α. Experiences last winter. Wet and cold. No place except for small numbers in barns and sheds.

    β Now and then, at first, Services allowed in the Churches.

    γ In one or two cases the Chaplains forced their way wh. was a mistake. It may be that our Commanding Officers advised it at the instigation of French military authorities.

---

92 Durham University Special Collection, Gwynne Collections, SAD 28/5 contains jottings from the first three months following his appointment as deputy chaplain general. SAD 28/1 contains lists of chaplains and postings from Aug. 1915.

93 SAD 28/5/1–2.

94 The use of Catholic churches for worship by other denominations was an issue throughout the war. After a limited number of cases, the Catholic hierarchy refused permission for this to take place. Outside base areas chaplains were thus forced to use whatever accommodation was available.

δ In some cases French priests seemed willing, on the condition pulpits, altars, not used, viz. Essars.

ε It appears as if the English Roman Catholics were using pressure on the Cures to refuse.

ζ In some cases this caused great bitterness between our soldiers and the priests, e.g. Philosophe, Mazangarb.

(ii) Out of this war we all pray for great unity. At present it looks like coming out with great enmity.

(iii) How to avoid the experiences of last year and get hard covering for the troops.[95]

The final part of the entry is unclear. It appeared to recommend that the matter be taken up with the pope, ending, somewhat enigmatically, 'Give him the chance of refusing or going on leave.'

Immediately before starting back to France to begin in his new post, Gwynne wrote himself a note as to what his work was to be.

Definite aims in my work as DCG.

1. That the C of E officers and men shall have the privilege of spiritual ministrations.

2. To encourage and inspire by every means in my power the Chaplains in their work.

3. To try and know them, love them – to bear patiently in all their difficulties and complaints.

4. To be a Father in God to them all.

5. To foster the unity of Spirit, the bond of peace and to make our Chaplains in France an example of united band of workers – differing only in non essentials but bound together in the holiest bonds of Xtian love.

6. To work for the unity of the churches, the RCs, the Presbyterians and our own separated parts.

7. To win for Christ and to establish in the Faith our officers and men in France.

8. To arouse in our Chaplains a spirit of intercession for the war – that they may exercise that important part of their sacred office.[96]

Gwynne then included the following prayer, 'before crossing over.'

---

[95] SAD 28/5/3.
[96] SAD 28/5/7.

O God my Father unasked, unsought, Thou has called me to this work. I feel helpless as a little child. I therefore look to Thee for strength, grace, love, wisdom, humility enough to do it. My one ambition is to do it entirely for Thee, Thy Glory and the good of the troops, expecting as my greatest reward, 'Well done', from Thee. I ask this in the Name of Jesu my Lord and Master. Amen.[97]

Once in France, most of Gwynne's time appears to have been taken up with the routine of organizing the Church of England chaplains. The issue of the use of French churches remained on the agenda and, prior to a visit to the bishop of Arras, Gwynne wrote out again the arguments that he wanted to use in the forthcoming meeting.

Bp of Arras.

1. Last winter's experiences of the religious worship for troops.

2. War almost certain to last this winter. The Army must make provisions (75% of the troops being C of E) The Question is how to do it – 1,000,000 this winter. Lord Kitchener of Kt general concerned, as I am, about the providing of places of worship.

In an interview with him when I told him of last year's experience, he expressed an opinion that this could be put right by offering himself to approach the Government.

I stopped him doing that until I see the Bp of Arras.

What is the Bishop prepared to do?

Last winter 250,000

This winter 1,400,000

Kitchener would rather we settle this with the Church. If we cannot he will take it out of my hands. Make our position clear to the Bp of Birmingham. Proud to use Church and the Garage.

You say your people would be upset if our argument is granted. But what about our 1,400,00 who might be now upset if it were not given?[98]

Despite Gwynne's best efforts, the bishop of Arras remained unmoved. The policy of the Catholic church remained that their churches were not to be used for services by Church of England chaplains.

At the end of August 1915, Gwynne received a letter ordering him back to the WO for a meeting with the CG. He evidently found this summons difficult, for he confided a prayer to his notebook, in which he asked that he might be 'loyal to and plumb straight with T.S. That I might be a true friend to him and a comfort and cheer to him.'[99] Gwynne also noted that the Catholics, probably inspired by his own appointment, had asked for a CG. He reflected that such a move could lead to

[97] *Ibid.*
[98] SAD 28/5/20ff.
[99] SAD 28/5/24. 'T. S.' was a reference to the Rt Rev. John Taylor Smith, chaplain general.

the Wesleyans, Presbyterians and Baptists making the same request. He noted that he believed that those groups were more numerous in the Empire than the Catholics, although he would need to verify the figures. He also reflected that Catholic recruiting was falling behind that of the other denominations. Finally, he believed that the position of CG reflected the position of the established church. Although prepared to concede that the situation would be different in Austria, France or Italy, where the position could be held by a Catholic, he apparently ignored the claims of the Church of Scotland to be a national church.[100]

By the middle of September, Gwynne's notebook had become an aide-memoire for the meetings that were taking up more and more of his time as the amount of administration needed to oversee the Anglican chaplains increased. Specific matters have been indicated against the relevant meeting. There were, though, many continuing issues, and the notebook ended with a list. Gwynne confided to the final page of the book.

Things to keep in mind to do

1. Promotions

2. Reinforcement camps, etc.

3. Uniform for A[rmy] Scripture Readers.

4. Authority to pay for Residential Chaplains.[101]

5. Book for Rewards, etc.

6. Book for Chaplains fitness and knowledge of different units.

7. What to ask 'K' for.[102]

8. Seven motor cars[103] for SChaps Armies, Bases.[104]

By the end of October 1915, the main features of his *rôle* had become clear and his ministry had settled into a pattern that was to continue for the remainder of the period covered by the diary entries in this volume.

One of the features of Gwynne's ministry was that of preaching. It would have been part of the normal weekly parade service. A sermon would almost certainly have formed part of the confirmation services which he conducted, possibly as advice to the candidates. Given that these were men being presented, not in some cathedral or parish church in England, but in whatever makeshift accommodation might be available for the service, it would be useful to know what Gwynne said on such occasions. Sadly, he has left no record in these diary entries. Indeed, whilst referring to the services that he conducted, he made almost no reference to the sermons that he preached in France. He was, apparently, happier recording infor-

---

[100] SAD 28/5/24.

[101] Probably a reference to the Anglican clergy serving the congregations at various points on the north coast of France.

[102] Field Marshal Horatio Herbert Kitchener, 1st Earl Kitchener.

[103] These would be for the senior chaplains of the armies and the bases.

[104] SAD 28/5/47.

mation about the sermons he preached, and those he heard, whilst in England, than doing so for addresses to the soldiers in France.

Gwynne was to continue as DCG until February 1919, when he left the army and returned to the Sudan. His relationship with Simms appears to have been cordial. He came to be regarded as a good leader by the Church of England chaplains. His diary entries showed something of what he believed they should do – a matter of considerable significance since those who were posted to the BEF as chaplains initially received no training. Gwynne's time in France was the subject of a single chapter in his biography, *Pastor on the Nile*.[105] In it, Jackson summarized the experiences of four and half years in twenty-eight pages. He quoted an unreferenced letter, that Gwynne had written to the Reverend H. Blackburne,[106] possibly towards the end of the war, in which he had indicated that he had intended to serve only for a single contract of one year and then return to the Sudan, but that Kitchener had appointed him DCG, 'entirely off his own bat and without any hint of suggestion from anyone made me take on this job'.[107]

This selection of entries from the diaries thus covers the moment at which Gwynne ceased to be a chaplain serving with front line troops and became responsible for the oversight of all Church of England chaplains in the BEF. Since December 1915, he had been serving with front line troops in the static line of trenches that had come to symbolize the fighting on the Western Front. He had transferred from his original post with a General Hospital and found the ministry at the front to be more rewarding. It is of significance that his diaries make no mention of any restriction being placed upon chaplains visiting front line troops in the trenches. He paid frequent, and apparently welcome, pastoral visits to soldiers from the units of the brigade to which he had been attached. If there was ever an order forbidding all chaplains, or even just Anglicans, from visiting the trenches, he appeared to be unaware of it as he made no comment either about it or about any lifting of such a restriction.[108] Whether such a restriction existed has remained unclear; there is still more to learn about the nature of chaplaincy on the Western Front. The entries from Gwynne's diaries have provided valuable evidence towards a better understanding of that ministry. They will, hopefully, reveal more when other volumes from his First World War service are made available.[109]

[105] Jackson, *Pastor*.
[106] The Rev. H. Blackburne, regular army chaplain and sometime ACG of First Army in the BEF.
[107] Jackson, *Pastor*, p. 152, unreferenced letter to the Rev. H. Blackburne.
[108] L. Parker, *The whole armour of God: Anglican chaplains in the Great War* (Solihull, 2009).
[109] Diary entries exist for the whole of the war except for the period between Mar. and Nov. 1918.

Comments on the diary entries

Bishop Llewellyn Gwynne belonged to that category of clerical diarists who have left an invaluable record of their generation. In his case, the diaries cover his long period of service in Sudan and Egypt between 1884 and 1957, with one interlude, his years as a member of the AChD during the First World War. It is part of that period, between the start of July 1915 and the end of July 1916 which is reproduced here. The original diaries were deposited, by the CMS, in the Special Collections of two different university libraries, Birmingham and Durham. There is no apparent logic as to how the dairies were divided between the two institutions. The entries reproduced here are taken from originals in the holdings of both. Since Durham University has concentrated on material connected with the Sudan, this volume and some other items relating to Gwynne's military service sit rather oddly with the rest of its collection. The Special Collection at the University of Birmingham has a larger collection of material dating from the First World War, and since this includes the volumes covering almost the entire remainder of the period from August 1914 to February 1919, it would more convenient if some arrangement could be made for it to provide easy access to the missing volume from the war period.

The diaries are written in notebooks. For the months reproduced here, there are entries for every day with the exceptions of 22 September and 15 November 1915. The entries usually either occupied a full page or were two to a page. Occasionally, as when Gwynne was suffering from a heavy cold in March 1916, the entries were reduced to a few lines. From time to time, he noted, 'wrote up diary', as he did on 13 February 1916, suggesting that he did not complete it every day. There were also frequent entries that chronicled late night conversations. It would have been possible that he would not then have written up his diary for that day.

Whilst the handwriting is usually easily legible, it did deteriorate on a few occasions, such as 5 August 1915, when he was attempting to end the entry for that day at the bottom of a page. The reader is however, presented with two difficulties: the interpretation of the names of individuals and of places. The names have been deciphered using a variety of cross-referencing. For members of the AChD, the initial starting point was the index of Medal Cards held at TNA at Kew and accessed in the WO 339 series. Where a name was rare it would normally be possible to identify an individual. Where a name was common – such as Smith, Lewis or Griffiths – there were often too many options to offer any meaningful suggestion. For chaplains, the next method of identification was the card index of interviews conducted by the CG. Accessed through www.chaplains-museum.co.uk/search, the digitized cards provided information on many of those who were temporary Church of England chaplains. The names of those who were posted to the BEF after August 1915 have then been cross-referenced with the entries in SAD 28/1. This notebook, held as part of the Gwynne archive, in the Durham University Special Collection, contained the names of those posted, as chaplains, to, within and from the BEF. Two other sources of information, *Crockford's* and *Army Lists,* were also used to try to identify chaplains. These were sometimes a help in considering alternative possible spellings to those used in the diaries. *Crockford's* also provided details of civilian Anglican churches, and the clergy serving them, in the various ports on the coast of northern France.

The process of identifying other individuals in the army has proved more difficult. Again, the starting point was the WO 339 series of Medal Cards in TNA. On occasions, this provided an identification. For some, it suggested a possible cap badge. In some cases, the individual could then be identified using either *Hart's Army List* or the official *Army List*. For members of the RAMC, assistance was received from the Museum of Military Medicine. However, the destruction, during the 1920s, of the records of temporary officers made the identification of such officers more problematical. The 1915 edition of *Hart's Army List* identified names under their unit, whereas the official *Army List* provided details of individuals according to their seniority. The former was more useful for members of the regular army; it did not, however, include temporary officers. The latter was more useful for tracing senior officers, as the number was more limited. In each of the books, there were references to service with the Egyptian army that indicated those who might have served in the Sudan. Gwynne made numerous mentions in the diaries of those whom he had met in the Sudan. In some cases, especially in July 1915 when Gwynne was acting as a chaplain at brigade level, the use of war diaries has proved a considerable help. These diaries, contained in the WO 95 series at TNA, were required to be maintained by units on active service. Not all were retained after the end of the war. Most notably, one only war diary kept by any army chaplaincy branch in the BEF, that for Church of England chaplains in 18 Div, during the battle of the Somme in 1916, has survived.[1] This may well have been due to decisions about what material would be needed for the Official War History. No official record of the work of chaplains during the First World War was written. There is no evidence that a volume covering their work was, indeed, ever contemplated. If that were so, there would be no requirement to keep the war diaries that would undoubtedly have been kept by the Church of England chaplains' branch headed by Gwynne.

The rapid expansion of the army meant that some people received frequent promotion in rank. Using the sources available, it has not always been possible to be exact about the rank held at the time of the diary entry. In the case of a lieutenant colonel, it would be normal to refer to the individual as 'colonel', and Gwynne does so in the diaries. The substantive rank could be at least two grades below an acting or a temporary rank. The tradition of 'brevet' rank, still in use during the First World War, complicated the subject of rank. It implied selection for the next higher rank but that no vacancy was available. Such vacancies would be on the peacetime establishment of a regiment and would thus have no relation to the needs of the regiment during the war.

For civilians, and especially for members of the Gwynne family, use was made of a variety of genealogical programmes. In a few cases, these also helped identify individuals living in the same area whom Gwynne encountered. Where he referred to an address, the relevant *Post Office Directory* has sometimes made an identification possible. Several of the civilians mentioned – some obviously well known to Gwynne – have remained so far unidentified.

Identification of individuals has been structured into four groups. Where someone can be identified with a considerable degree of confidence, no comment is

---

[1]   TNA, WO 95/2023: war diary for 18 Div Chaplains (Church of England).

made. Where there might be a number of alternatives, but the evidence points to a particular individual, the entry has been noted as 'Probably' that individual. Where there are several possibilities and the evidence for a particular individual is weaker, then the entry has been marked as 'Possibly'. Those for whom no identification has been possible have been marked as 'Unidentified'. It is hoped that future research will help in the identification of these people. There is always the possibility that Gwynne's spelling in the diary entry was incorrect and that an entry in other parts of his papers might provide a clue to the identity of someone. Several military personnel who have so far been unidentified fall into a group of those individuals whom Gwynne had known in the Sudan. A limited number of identifications have been found with the use of *A biographical dictionary of the Anglo-Egyptian Sudan*,[2] but that work only contained entries for those who had died before 1948; Gwynne and many others are not included. It is possible that were Gwynne's diaries for his period in the Sudan before August 1914 to be annotated, some of these individuals might then be identified.

The location of places has proven less easy. Gwynne's spelling of place names was often idiosyncratic, as for example 'Looz' for Loos. Again, cross-reference to the known location of military units at the date on which they are mentioned has provided a useful method to clarify his meaning. Locations from July and August 1915 can be verified both from published trench maps of the period and also from the war diaries in the WO 95 series at TNA. The advent of computerized mapping has also permitted possible locations to be identified. Using maps of France and Belgium, together with entries in war diaries, a decision has been made on most of the places. In such cases, the spelling in the diary entry has been corrected without comment. In a few instances, where the identification has proved impossible, the original spelling has been retained.

Some words are consistently misspelled. The most frequent was the use of 'batallion' for battalion. Another example was the use of 'Haigh' for the name of the new commander in chief of the BEF on the first few occasions in which his name appeared in the diaries. The names of two regular chaplains, the Reverends H. Blackburne and J. G. W. Tuckey are spelled in several different ways. Attention has not been drawn to individual variations in spelling. They have been left in their original form. The variation in spelling has meant that the search for an individual has been widened to use several different spellings. In some cases, that decision, as for example where 'Jeffcoat' has been considered in place of 'Jeffcote', has produced the name of an individual who would appear to fit with Gwynne's location. Where a word is indecipherable, a possible interpretation is included in brackets, or an ellipsis is used if no word appears to fit the context. Gwynne's language was of his generation and words in common use then have not always survived into the contemporary vocabulary.

The background to Gwynne's experience with the BEF can be found in the volumes of the *Official history of the war*.[3] Detailed maps of the ground where Gwynne exercised his ministry prior to his appointment as DCG can be found in

[2] R. Hill, *A biographical dictionary of the Anglo-Egyptian Sudan* (Oxford, 1951).

[3] *History of the Great War based on official documents by direction of the Committee of Imperial Defence* (various authors and dates.) The volumes entitled, *Military operations France and Belgium* that covered 1915 and 1916 provide background to what was taking place during the period covered by the diary entries.

the trench maps of the area around Bethune. The National Library of Scotland has sheets from 1914 to 1918 available on their website.[4] Official maps of the areas and towns behind the lines are more difficult to find. There is no extant town map for St Omer. The most complete map showing British units is a three-sheet map of the French port of Le Havre.[5]

As the entries for early July 1915 showed, Gwynne was already conducting services of confirmation for the troops before he became DCG. The pace increased after he was given oversight of all Anglican matters in France and Flanders. During the next year, the BEF was visited by a number of British and colonial bishops, including, in May 1916, the archbishop of Canterbury. The note of these visits frequently included a mention of a confirmation. From the diary entries, it has been noted that Gwynne conducted eighty-four confirmations in the period from 1 August 1915 to 31 July 1916. Of these, he recorded the number of people confirmed on forty-one of the occasions. The number ranged from a single individual in a private service in the chapel established in his personal mess to 170 men at one service in April 1916 just prior to Easter and 270 at a service in September 1915. The diaries recorded that a total of 1,269 candidates had been confirmed in that year. Whilst for the first six months it was more likely that a figure was given, in the second six months, with the exception of May 1916 where a figure was given for both services, the total number confirmed was rarely given. Some chaplains appear to have used Gwynne's availability as an opportunity to hold preparation classes for confirmation and then, despite the demands of the battlefield, to take their candidates to a confirmation service. The figures reflected an interest in religion and a willingness to make a public declaration of faith that has not always been acknowledged by those writing about the spiritual experience of troops on the Western Front. Nevertheless, Gwynne rarely reflected on the reasons behind the decisions to seek confirmation.

After his promotion, and having taken time to create an office, Gwynne adopted a life-style largely made up of office work and visits. He installed two chaplains to assist him in the office. The Reverend W. Drury, who had already been assisting the Reverend Dr J. Simms, the principal chaplain, oversaw what Gwynne described as the army side. The 'episcopal' work was the responsibility first of the Reverend E. H. Thorold, a regular army chaplain who was eventually to become CG, and then of the Reverend B. G. O'Rorke. As a young man, he had been prepared for confirmation in Nottingham when Gwynne was vicar of Emmanuel Church. He had subsequently become a regular chaplain in the army. Gwynne's office was established in St Omer. This was some distance from the headquarters of the BEF, based at Montreuil. It was also not co-located with the office of the principal chaplain which was in Hesdin. Indeed, although there were several references to the Reverend Dr J. Simms, principal chaplain, it was striking that there were few other references to other non-Anglican chaplains.

The following conventions have been followed in respect of formations above the level of individual units. The hierarchy is:

Brigade (Bde) commanded by brigadier general. Usually identified in Arabic numerals, thus 23 Bde.

---

4   The trench maps can be accessed at: https://maps.nls.uk/ww1/trenches/.
5   TNA, WO 297/108.

Division (Div) commanded by a major general. Usually identified in Arabic numerals, thus 2 Div.

Corps (Corps) commanded by a lieutenant general. Usually identified in Roman numerals, thus XII Corps.

Army (Army) commanded by a general. Usually identified with word in full, thus First Army.

Units are identified by abbreviations. Where relevant these have been given in footnotes.

Gwynne had to learn the structure of the army. As a unit chaplain, he had little interest beyond the level of a brigade. Once he was appointed DCG, he had not only to understand the working of the army but also then to develop a structure for Anglican chaplains that would fit with the wider organization of the army. The army of 1915 was organized into three 'silos', concerned with operations (G), personnel (A) and material (Q). At brigade level, the G side was controlled by the brigade major assisted by staff captains, and AQ matters by the deputy assistant adjutant and quartermaster general (QMG). At each higher-level formation, the separation would be maintained or even expanded. At a divisional level or above there would be general staff officers (GSO) who ranked from GSO1 (lieutenant colonel) to GSO3 (captain). In addition, departments and services would be represented by specialist staff advisors. In some cases, as with the RAMC, such positions also included authority over the way that service was delivered. At divisional level, there would be a deputy assistant director of medical services with a deputy director of medical service at corps, and director of medical services at army level, with the director general (DG) at the headquarters of the BEF. Behind the armies were the lines of communication under the command of an inspector general. He oversaw the efficiency of the bases and depots. Gwynne worked with the chain of command, and there are frequent references to various office holders in the diary entries. There was also a series of entries in which he attempted to develop a command structure for chaplains. The diaries reflected his intention to create posts of 'senior chaplain' for each army. Suitably resourced, they would be responsible for the chaplains in that army. Below them would be a senior chaplain at each corps with another senior chaplain below that at the divisional headquarters. The mix between priestly function and administrative responsibility would vary at each level. Gwynne had no direct responsibility, in the *rôle* of chaplain, for anyone in the St Omer area or within the headquarters of the BEF. His status as a bishop gave him an ecclesiastical *rôle*, but one not required of him as a chaplain. It is also important to remember that the army was in a continuous period of change throughout the war and that Gwynne would have needed to have responded to those changes.

It is not altogether clear what Gwynne felt about the importance of his diaries. Whilst at times it appeared to be a journal of record, entries in other notebooks contained information that was not included in the diaries. Those notebooks also contained comments about his feelings that were not then transferred to the diaries. Indeed, the diaries are notable for the limited amount of personal reflexion that they contained. Although there are some references to his spiritual condition, such entries were few and did not contain much detail. Although there were references to texts for sermons which he heard, or delivered in England, there is little information recorded about most of the sermons that he preached to the troops. That was especially true of the sermons at services of confirmation. The diary entries included in this volume include those for the first month of the battle of the Somme. Gwynne was aware of the significance and magnitude of the battle. He made special journeys to the area to meet with chaplains, the wounded and military leaders. He was clearly aware of the scale of the casualties. His visit to the 1st Battalion of the Newfoundland Regiment, which had been almost entirely destroyed in the opening minutes of the battle on the morning of 1 July, would have given him a clear picture of the fighting. Yet one does not sense that he saw the fighting in the way in which it has come to be regarded.

THE DIARIES

July 1915

At the beginning of July 1915 Gwynne was acting as chaplain to the 5 Bde. It was responsible for a section of the line around the town of Bethune. The trenches that made up the opposing sides had come into existence in November 1914 when the period of mobile warfare came to an end. They would remain in essentially the same place until the final battles of 1918 almost exactly four years later. As with other chaplains, Gwynne was attached to the FA that provided medical cover for the brigade. From that base, he visited the units in the trenches and in the rear areas.

On 17 July, he received a summons to the WO. On reporting to Bishop Taylor Smith, the CG, he discovered that he was to be appointed as a DCG. He was thus promoted overnight from being a chaplain to the forces class 4, with the relative rank of captain, to a position with the relative rank of major general. He spent the remainder of the month in London preparing for his new rôle.

1 July[1]

All my flock are now in the trenches[2] at Givenchy or lying back in Reserve near Gorre or Le Preolan. Once more I am too far from my Brigade[3] and am trying all I know to get nearer to them. I visited the Worcesters[4] in their Billets and had tea with their Officers who are billeted in a good chateau with a fine garden. I had a few shots at target with a rifle, but did little good.[5] I also paid a visit to the Brigade Head Quarters to find out whether I could get hold of a billet nearer the troops and how long the Brigade were to hold the line at Givenchy. Everything seems quiet along our line and there is comparative calm in the fighting. Now and then you hear a crash out of a hedge and the Germans always reply. One of the Oxfords[6] was killed today by a sniper. He got out of a trench and with a couple of sandbags to protect him, tried to shoot a sniper who was causing a lot of trouble. He had fired about 16 shots when he himself was shot dead, the man's name was Lemount.[7]

---

[1] At that time, Bishop Gwynne was attached to 5 FA. The nominal roll for 30 June 1915 in WO 95/1337/2 listed him as 'Rt Revd Bishop L H Gwynne, CF, 21/12/14, CofE'. This showed the confusion about how to indicate the rank of a chaplain. It also indicated that Gwynne had joined the unit on 21 Dec. 1914.

[2] The area of the trenches was to the east of the town of Bethune in the Pas de Calais some 45 miles south-east of Calais.

[3] On this date, Gwynne was serving as a chaplain in 5 Bde, which was part of 2 Div. This was a regular army formation that had been part of the original BEF of Aug. 1914. Gwynne had been posted to it in Dec. 1915.

[4] 2nd Battalion of the Worcestershire Regiment (2 WORCS).

[5] Chaplains were unarmed, and such a practice would have been frowned upon by some.

[6] 2nd Battalion of the Oxford and Buckinghamshire Light Infantry (2 Ox & Bucks).

[7] He may be referring to Lance Corporal Henry Frederick Mount 2 Ox & Bucks killed in action 1 July 1915.

2 July

We had a meeting of the Divisional Chaplains[8] today at 11. and a few words from Harry Blackburne* who was very helpful. The tone with wh. he spoke to men much older than himself was a bit trying to me. I only hope the others did not notice it. Somehow I think that the regular chaplains are to think that they and they only know how to work amongst men, wh. must be rather disconcerting to men who have had quite as much experience only in Civil life not in the Service. I fasted today and walked to Beuvry spending some time in the church reading a pamphlet on the Unity of Xtendom.[9] I drove Colonel Wilding[10] of the Inniskillings[11] to the trenches at Givenchy where we had tea with Colville,[12] after wh. I went round the trenches and saw nearly all the men of the Oxfords. It was nearly 8 when I reached home.

3 July

It seems to be true that the man who has been observing in the Balloon near Bethune has been caught sending wireless messages to the Germans. My informant tells me that he was shot within an hour of being found out. The Baloon which had been in the air near here was shelled by the Enemy and had to be hauled down and removed further West and as it was the 1st time it has been shelled it was said that this was done as soon as their man was removed from the observing basket below the Baloon. I went down and arranged the services for the Worcesters and the Inniskillings and No 5 Co RE.[13]

In the afternoon I read the burial service over the grave of a 3rd Coldstream named Dyer who was killed handling a bomb – most likely practicising throwing.[14]

I prepared some of the Inniskillings for Holy Communion today. Four officers turned up wh. is rather unusual, and three of those present asked to be prepared for Confirmation.

4 July

My Sunday was not very profitable or eventful. I held a celebration after the morning service in the hope that the men would come as well as the officers. About 40 remained after the Church Parade[15] of the Worcesters and we held it in the garden of the chateau. The Inniskillings had over 250 on parade in a rather dirty theatre at Le Preolan and thirty stayed afterwards for a celebration. A sad thing happened last

---

8   2 Div.
9   Christendom. There is no indication of the author of the pamphlet.
10 Lieutenant Colonel C. A. Wilding.
11 2nd Battalion of the Royal Inniskilling Fusiliers (2 INNISKILLINGS).
12 Major G. N. Colvile, senior major 2 Ox & Bucks.
13 Number 5 Company Royal Engineers which was attached to 2 Div.
14 Private John Dyer 3rd Battalion of the Coldstream Guards (3 COLDSTREAMS) died 3 July 1915.
15 *Kings Regulations for the Army* required troops to parade on Sundays to a service of their denomination.

night the Worcesters sent out with the working party a young officer named Willmott to arrange some digging in front of the trenches. Instead of waiting till dark one of the Glasgow Highlanders[16] and young Willmott jumped up out of the trench about 8.45 to mark out the work for their men, at that moment a German sniper shot Willmott just above the heart.[17] He was sitting in the room while I talked to the Colonel the same afternoon. I buried him in the Beuvry Cemetery at 2.30 this afternoon. The funeral threw my visit to the trenches so that late that I should only have arrived when the men were thinking of leaving.

5 July

I made another move today to Le Preolan in order to be nearer my Brigade. However before doing so I wrote up my correspondence and had lunch with my old friends of 3rd Coldstreams where I saw Campbell[18] and Arthur Smith.[19] I asked God's blessing and guidance on my new move and after tea walked down with Mr Pride* the Presbyterian as far as the 1st Canal Bridge after wh. I proceeded the rest of the way myself stopping at every knot of soldiers to have a talk with them. I stopped at the H.L.I.[20] headquarters. Saw Wolf Murray[21] – chaffed some of my flock and arranged the service for Wednesday morning at 11. am before they go into the Trenches.

I meant to slip in and have a little dinner of tea and bread and butter, but was waylaid by Cross[22] the Adjutant and taken to a first-class dinner with the Oxford & Bucks.

There is a rumour that we make no push forward for the present but wait for reinforcements. Also I hear it is probable that the whole division moves out after this spell of trench work.

6 July

What a splendid chance every chaplain has who is attached to a Batallion. For some unaccountable reason the Principal Chaplain has laid down a rule that no Church of England chaplain can be attached to a Batallion,[23] but an R.C. or Presbyterian can be. When I live amongst them as I am doing now I get know them so well. I went into the Trenches and buried one of the Inniskillings who was killed by a sniper this morning.[24] Some of his company were allowed to come down from the front trenches to the little trench cemetery at the end of the Communication Trench. It

16 1/9th Battalion of the Highland Light Infantry (1/9 HLI).
17 Lieutenant John Dyott Willmot Worcestershire Regiment died 3 July 1915.
18 Major J. V. Campbell.
19 Captain A. F. Smith.
20 HLI.
21 Lieutenant Colonel A. A. Wolfe-Murray, CO 1/2 HLI.
22 Captain R. B. G. Crosse, adjutant 2 Ox & Bucks.
23 This ruling refers to the discrepancy between the Anglican and Catholic establishments that did not allow enough Anglicans to provide a chaplain for each fighting unit. Gwynne was to argue strongly in favour of increasing the establishment figure for chaplains to make this possible.
24 Private Robert Branagh 1 INNISKILLINGS died 6 July 1915. The grave was subsequently destroyed in later fighting and he is commemorated on the Le Touret memorial.

was a very impressive experience, the crack of the rifle shot or the noise of the guns accompanying the words of the burial service. From the trench held by the Inniskillings I walked along to the Worcester trenches where I distributed some literature and cigarettes and chaffed the men. Wagman[25] [*sic*] gave me tea in his dugout, and right glad was I to have it for I had nothing to eat since breakfast. The enemy was firing continually and now and then a heavy shell came over and shook the ground while we sat in a dug out. One cannot help being a bit concerned when it drops near for no dug out can (*possibly is scored through*) keep out a heavy shell. An officer in the Irish Guards had a narrow squeak some time ago. He was in his dug out when a shell burst outside and he stepped outside to have a look when another came plump into the dug out.

7 July

Two services I took today one for the HLI and another voluntary one of A.B Company of the Oxfords.[26] Both were taken in the open air in a boisterous wind wh. rustled the trees so vigorously that it took me all my time to be heard. I had a celebration of Holy Communion after the morning service. It is very encouraging to find that nearly all the officers of the two companies were present at the Holy Communion. At both the services I preached on the subject of the War. Why war came – and how to stop the war and hazarded the opinion that for us English people this war laid bear the awful wound of our nation. When we pray for peace we ask the Great Physician to close the wound, and, it may be the open wound has still some proud flesh and bad matter and the Great Physician knows it must not be closed until the bad humours are out of the wound. I lunched with the HLI, and in the afternoon visited C & D Companies of the Oxfords in their Billets telling them of the service I propose holding in the Dancing Hall at 10.30 tomorrow. Last night a German shell killed two men,[27] injured and seven or eight at the mouth of a mine our men are digging in the front Trenches.   Every time a working party marches towards the Trenches you wonder what toll Death is going to take out of the brave lads.

8 July

We had a very large attendance at the Service in the Dancing Hall, and 14 stayed behind for Holy Communion. I spoke again on the reasons of decay and how to end the war to about 150 men. I lunch with 1st Coldstreams of the 1st Division and met my old friend John Ponsonby[28] who is now temporarily commanding the 1st Brigade. After lunch I confirmed two of the Coldstream – one a Sergeant Major and the other a man who has joined since the beginning of the war. The Confirmation took

---

[25] Possibly Captain P. S. G. Wainman, 2 WORCS.
[26] Soldiers were required to parade to a service of their declared denomination. This was normally a service held during the morning. Chaplains often organized voluntary services on a Sunday evening. Some believed that attendance at all services should be voluntary. Compulsory church parade was not abolished formally until 1946.
[27] The Commonwealth War Graves Commission (CWGC) website lists one soldier, Private J. King from 2 Ox & Bucks, as having died on 6 July 1915.
[28] Brigadier General John Ponsonby, an officer in the Coldstream Guards, was the commander of 1 COLDSTREAMS.

place in an Orchard near Head Quarters in the presence of the officers and about 30 men. Popham* the Chaplain is a first class fellow and very keen. He has just won his D.C.M. for excellent work in the field.[29] I had quite a good day, talking about spiritual things for after an hours talk with Popham I called on Henry Bentinck[30] on the way home and had a long talk and walk together. He told me how one of his bombers running up a sap to throw a bomb into the crater wh. they thought was being occupied by the enemy when he must have struck his hand on the side of the sap and dropped the bomb wh. exploded and injured him seriously.

9 July

After attending the weekly meeting of chaplains I called on my old friend Potter[31] of the Kings and brought him back to my little cottage to Lunch. He told me some very interesting stories of his first experiences at Givenchy trenches which was very near the Germans. The Germans here seem to be rather overbearing and Potter organised snipers and bombers. In one place our sap head is in the same trench with about 8 paces between their sap head. One of our bombers was ordered to go up the sap and when he reached the end he saw a periscope which showed him the Germans in their own trench. He immediately threw bombs and heard cries and groans. At night they dare not come to the end of their sap but they came up both sides of our sap in the long grass. However they were seen and immediately bombed with the result that some were killed and the others ran back. A German trick was tried in vain on Potter. A German sniper stood up head and shoulders … the trench and aimed a shot before disappearing. It was a bit too evident there was some trick or until he put up his periscope wh was immediately smashed to bits with a bullet.

The German was trying to decoy someone to show his head while his accomplices hidden in another part of the line were waiting for any part of our men to appear.

10 July

As usual I spent some of my time on this eve of Sunday arranging the services; the rest of the afternoon I spent in the Trenches with the Oxfords. A sad thing happened last night while the chaplain of the Glasgow Highlanders was burying seven of his Batallion killed by heavy shells during the day.[32] A shell came over and killed four and wounded eight including the chaplain. The chaplain tho' not badly hurt was injured enough to be removed to a clearing hospital. The trenches are so close to one another at Givenchy and Cuinchy that things are getting pretty desperate. We are mining and so are they. They throw over heavy minnenwerfers[33] [sic] and we throw back bombs.[34] At Cuinchy the Guards spotted one of these trench mortars and

---

[29] Gwynne was obviously misinformed as the Distinguished Conduct Medal was not awarded to officers and thus would not have been given to a chaplain.

[30] Probably Captain H. D. Bentinck.

[31] Captain E. A. Potter.

[32] The chaplain was the Rev. R. H. Pryde*. The soldiers are buried in the Guards Cemetery, Windy Corner, Cuinchy.

[33] A form of weapon designed to act as a mortar.

[34] Bombs in this context referred to early forms of hand grenades.

informed the artillery who knocked the whole thing in the air. Our men are very
keen. On my way back through the trenches to-night I met one of men who was
genuinely disappointed the Germans have not come and attacked as they expect
every night. There is a feeling along the line that the Germans will have one more
try before they check the whole thing. There is good news in the paper today. A
submarine success in the Baltic and the Russians holding of the Germans.[35]

11 July

In the main room of my little cottage I had a celebration of the Holy Communion
this morning at 8 a.m. Weyman,[36] Rolleston[37] and Strong[38] came. The Batallions in
Brigade reserves generally provide working parties for work in the Trenches so I
had about 300 men on parade this morning in a field near the Head Quarters. I am
still hammering away saying that God is waiting to be gracious if our people will
turn to him for healing. The Inniskillings are stationed in the next village, so I was
not long in getting hold of them and we held a service in the grounds of the H.Q.
chateau. The afternoon I spent visiting the billets and inviting men to come to the
voluntary services which I held in two orchards for two companies. I had tea with
Strong in his billet and had a very long talk on the eternal question of the war.
Whether the Germans were really going to try to push through and whether they
had any more machines of destruction up their sleeve. The voluntary services were
well attended considering the large number of our men working in the mines. One
of the minnenwerfers [*sic*] killed one of our men this morning and must have put
out a good many more for five were reported missing.

12 July

Two interesting (to me) experiences I had today were – the lunching with my old
friends Carter[39] and Potter[40] and the concert for the Worcesters which I arranged in
an orchard in this village.[41] Carter and Potter are about as valuable soldiers as we
have in this fighting area. I had a long talk with them at lunch today. They both think
the Germans will certainly have to break through our lines in the next few weeks,
but on the face of things they are almost certain to fail for one cannot imagine their
keeping anything up their sleeve in the desperate attempts to stop the French at
Souches[42] were every inch of ground lost is of the utmost importance.

---

35 A naval battle had taken place in the Baltic on 2 July 1915. The German cruiser *Prinz Adalber*
    was torpedoed and badly damaged by British submarine HMS *E-9* north of Danzig.
36 Possibly Captain P. S. G. Wainman, 2 WORCS.
37 Captain C. H. Ralston, adjutant 2 WORCS.
38 Unidentified.
39 Unidentified.
40 Captain E. A. Potter.
41 The activities that were appropriate for a chaplain to organize were a source of debate throughout
    the war. Chaplains who saw the pastoral needs of soldiers as including sports and recreations
    were willing to spend time organizing events such as this concert party. Others saw their *rôle*
    as restricted to more obviously religious activities.
42 Possibly the village of Souchez in Pas de Calais.

By the words 'up their sleeves' I mean not already launched against us. I think Ipres[43] is not going to be taken by the Germans now. They have played their best cards. What is rather disconcerting is that the Batallion officers feel that there is very little chance of promotion by merit in the field now and certainly the promotion to Brigades of Brooke[44] and Seely[45] seem to bear them out.

13 July

Most of the day I spent in the trenches at Givenchy I drove from Le Preolan about 11. And went straight into the Oxfords part. The Germans had shelled the brewery at Ponte[46] an hour before. They threw over heavy eight inch shells and at the second shot broke down the chimney stack. Fragments of the shell came back nearly 100 yards. I walked along the trenches and talked to the men. They are all very communicative and not at all shy of me as they know I am always on the look out to chaff them, they sometimes pull my leg, a thing wh pleases me very much, for no man ever took the trouble to chaff or pull the leg of an enemy or anybody else whom he disliked. At one point I saw a man on the look out. 'I just had two bullets just here putting his hand on part of the trench near him. I think the man is in that house there,' showing me a ruined house in our own lines. This is typical of the little he knows of our whereabouts. Two men were killed by snipers today, one was sniped by a sniper just putting his head above for a second while he was having a shot at the enemy. I walked back from Givenchy along the canal about 5 miles and met the 7th Kings Liverpools[47] and the South Staffords[48] on their way to take the place of our Brigade[49] coming out tonight.

14 July

I am back in Bethune once again. I came back last night to find my Ambulance had moved out the same day; so I settled down in my billet and sent on my groom and servant to join the Unit. Most of my time now must be spent in amusing the soldiers by concerts and polo competitions. I went round this morning and arranged with the Brigade Head Quarters and the Oxford & Bucks for some of the concerts and visited the HLI and the Glasgow Highlanders reminding them of the concert tonight. I walked out to Vendin about 2 miles from Bethune where the Worcesters and 5th Field Ambulance are stationed and saw there an old Egyptian friend named Evans[50] who came from Sir Arthur Sloggett[51] about the kitchen car which it is now decided to hand over to me for the use of the troops of the 5th Brigade, and have promised

---

43 The spelling of the town that was usually known as Ypres (or Wipers) by the British.
44 Brigadier General the Lord L. G. F. M. Brooke.
45 Brigadier General the Rt Hon. J. E. B. Seely.
46 Ponte Fixe.
47 7th Battalion of the King's (Liverpool Regiment) were in 2 Div at the time.
48 2nd Battalion of the South Staffordshire Regiment were in 2 Div at the time.
49 The units of 6 Bde were replacing those of 5 Bde in the front line.
50 Unidentified.
51 Lieutenant General Sir Arthur Sloggett was both head of army medical services and the chief commissioner for the British Red Cross and St John Ambulance in the BEF. The canteen car would have come under the latter part of his remit.

to get soldiers from our Brigade – one to drive and the other to superintend the distribution of the Coffee and Cocoa.[52] I heard very heavy firing from the Souchez district as I drove Vaudry[53] of the Worcesters to the concert at Bethune from Vendin. As this is a great day in France – the anniversary of the Republic there was a great uproar in the Restaurant where very excitable Frenchmen sang the Marseillaise and drank several toasts.[54]

15 July

When the Brigade is resting the duty of the chaplain is evidently to do all he can for keeping the troops amused and employed during the many hours they have to themselves. So far this morning I have organised a grand Water Gala and swimming competition. Almost at once men were practicing in the Baths and there was an air of keenness amongst almost every man who swims to do his best for his Batallion. Every night there is a concert in the Theatre and crowds of soldiers throng the place from hall to ceiling. One is truly grateful to see them all so cheerful; none of the songs are vulgar or evil, and some of them really good songs. So far there is good news of the fighting in this area, our artillery seems better supplied with ammunition and our people are really desirous for the boasted German advance.[55] One may in the trenches being honestly disappointed that the Doitcher[56] did not come on as they expected at 2. am the same morning.

16 July

At our clerical meeting today Blackburne* one of our chaplains gave us as news that Sir Douglas Haig[57] had expressed his opinion that the war would be over before the Winter. Please God that may be true, for the awful cost in precious lives is terrible. I feel now that God has the matter in Hand and the utter exhaustion of the nations will be God's opportunity to heal the wounds of the world when the proud flesh and the poisonous matter are cleansed out. I visited one of the Oxford & Bucks officers named Hawkins[58] – quite a lad who comes from the old Devonshire Hawkins in a clearing hospital at Chocques.[59] He was wounded in the head by a German shell. Thank God he is getting better. I promised to go and see him again tomorrow. He is a fine young lad and full of pluck. I could see it hurt him to think. Our new Brigadier

---

[52] Whilst the provision of refreshments by voluntary organizations such as the YMCA and the Church Army (CA) was acceptable, there were those who felt that it was not an activity that a chaplain should organize. Those opposed to the practice sometimes referred to chaplains such as Gwynne as 'holy Grocers'.
[53] The reference is probably to 2nd Lieutenant D. L. Vawdrey
[54] 14 July is celebrated annually in France as Bastille Day, marking the fall, in 1789, of the royal prison to the Paris mob.
[55] There had been a shortage of artillery shells in the BEF during much of the early part of 1915.
[56] Presumably he meant 'Deutcher' as a term for the Germans.
[57] Commander First Army.
[58] 2nd Lieutenant S. M. Minifie-Hawkins. The war diary of 2 Ox & Bucks described him as 'seriously' wounded.
[59] No. 1 Casualty Clearing Station (CCS) was established in Jan. 1915 at Chocques, a village located 3 miles west of Bethune.

is General Corkran[60] of the Grenadiers. He knows Howell and I know a brother of his who is Equerry to Princess Henry.[61] I took him and the two young Battenburghs[62] out shooting at Khartoum years ago.

17 July

Last night my groom Bond[63] drove in from Vendin – our Field Ambulance and woke me at 12.30[64] with a telegram from the Adjutant General[65] at Head Quarters ordering me to go at once to St Omer,[66] report myself to him there and proceed as soon as possible to London. I was up early making all the arrangements I possibly could to hand over the Fleming* the Divisional Chaplain who was unfortunately away. I hastened round to Head Quarters of the Division, my Brigade and did all I possibly could to get the things done which I had started and drove off in a motor soon after 11. I saw Father Waggett* on the way he told me he knew what I was going home for. On reaching the office of the AG at St Omer I was told the General was ill in bed but would like to see me. He told me I was to be appointed Deputy Chaplain General in the field and that there were difficulties in the way wh would take careful handling. He was more than kind and nice to me. I was very much impressed by his thoroughness and real keenness. He told me that the Chaplains' Department had given him a good deal of mischief and that one Church of England chaplain gave him such trouble that he was at the point of asking for his recall. I caught a boat at Boulogne at 4.30 a rough passage – and sat opposite Gordon Escher[67] a Sapper[68] in the train, wh arrived in London at 9.30 Stopped the night at the Grosvenor.

18 July

After trying S. Peter's Eaton Sq., I found that there was a celebration of Holy Communion at S. Michael's Chester Square at 8 am when I had a blessed time and where God gave me true repentance for my sins and weaknesses. After breakfast at the hotel I went to the 10 am Service at Westminster Abbey where God in his condescension drew near to me and spoke lovingly with me and made tears fall from my eyes by reason of His nearness to me. He spoke to me in the exhortation, 'ask those things that are requisite and necessary both for the body and soul.'[69] In the Psalms it seemed all for sure, in the beautiful anthem and in the sermon wh. was

---

[60] Brigadier General Charles Edward Corkran.
[61] Princess Henry of Battenberg (1857–1944) was born to Princess Beatrice, the youngest child of Queen Victoria and Prince Albert. Her husband died of malaria in 1896 whilst taking part in the Anglo-Ashante War. It was events surrounding his death that brought Bishop Taylor Smith to the notice of the queen and helped explain his appointment, in 1901, as chaplain general to HM Land Forces. He was to remain in office until 1925.
[62] Probably referring to Prince Alexander (1886–1960) and Lord Leopold (1889–1922).
[63] 308 Private E. Bond, 3 Kings Own Hussars, was attached to 5 FA on mobilization in Aug. 1914, most likely to serve as batman and groom to one of the attached chaplains.
[64] 12.30 am.
[65] General Sir Cecil Frederick Nevil Macready.
[66] Location of the headquarters of the BEF.
[67] Unidentified.
[68] Member of the Corps of Royal Engineers.
[69] Words from the call to worship in Morning and Evening Prayer in the Book of Common Prayer.

preached by a man I knew in the old days at Nottingham. Salmon[70] – who spoke on the, 'one Body of wh. we are the members.'[71] The Past linked to us – we are forging the links for the next generation, knit together by the same spirit, knit together with the dear and blessed dead.

I fasted and wrote of my diary in the club until 2.30 when I rode on a bus to Hampstead and found the MacInnes'[72] where I had a long chat with MacInn about the work in the Sudan and where I also decided to … MacI to ask some Bishop to carry on if I take on the job. I called on the Chaplain General this morning after the service but found him out. However I did the next best thing, saw Sir Reginald Braid[73] who was most kind and told me that 'K' had decided I was to be Deputy Chap. Gen. and I had to take it whether I liked it or not.

I heard William Temple[74] preach on 'Job'[75] in his church, a masterful exposition of Job – he is going to be a great power in our church.

19 July

Today was a memorable day in my life for I called on the War Office and reported myself to Taylor Smith* who told me that Lord Kitchener had appointed me Deputy Chaplain General in the Field. Honestly I would rather return to my job in Egypt and the Sudan, but it my acceptance of this Post solves a great difficulty I feel bound to take it on.[76]

After a long talk with Taylor Smith* which lasted over three hours I wrote a bit in the Club and called on Hawkes,[77] my tailor, and Elliott and Fry[78] the Photographers in order to supersede my former physiognomy with a moue head with another without it. I then called on Howell and gave him the a surprise as he had no idea of my coming back and was delighted to have my news and his pleasure was so evident that it made me more glad than ever that I have been called to this job for it showed me how wrapped up we all are as a family in each other's joys and sorrows. I promised to dine with the family if Harry[79] comes tomorrow. I was quite glad to hear of dear old Dick's[80] great success at Little Easton and how God had used him.

I spent the night at Northwood with Taylor Smith* and talked over his interview with the Bishops at Lambeth where he had laid down clearly his position.[81]

---

70 The Rev. W. Bryant Salmon, rector of Stoke Newington.
71 Possibly 1 Corinthians chapter 12 verse 27.
72 The Rt Rev. Rennie MacInnes, bishop of Jerusalem.
73 Sir Reginald Brade, permanent under-secretary of state for war.
74 The Rev. William Temple at that time Rector of St James's Piccadilly.
75 The Book of Job in The Bible.
76 An entry made on 9 Aug. 1915, in WO 95/1337/2, the war diary for 5 FA noted, 'Bishop L. H. Gwynne struck off strength 17/9/15.' This was almost certainly a mistake for 17 July.
77 Hawkes & Co. were a firm of military tailors.
78 Elliott & Fry were well-known photographers at 53 Baker Street.
79 His brother, Captain Henry Vaughan Gwynne.
80 His brother, the Rev. Richard Lloyd Gwynne.
81 The meeting at Lambeth at which Gwynne's appointment was announced.

20 July

Came back with the C.G. by the 9 am train and had a talk with him in the office. Called on Fitzgerald,[82] 'K's' Secretary. MacInnes came to the Club at 12 and talked over Sudan affairs until 1.20 when the C.G. came and carried me off to lunch to the Archbishop's. After lunch attended service at Westminster, found Charlie[83] at the Club and walked out to send telegrams and find out about Harry. 'Cinamaed' in the Strand and found Howell[84] waiting at the club. Dined together. Charlie stayed at the Charing Cross H.[85]

21 July

Went with T. Smith* to the War Office at 9.30. Had a talk with him about my status and standing in regard to the other chaplains. After lunch with Charlie, did some shopping and tried on my clothes with Hawkes and called on Howell about 4.30.

Saw the Moncks[86] about 6 and went with them to call on Mrs Monck, his mother,[87] and had a long talk. Stopped to dinner with the Moncks and met there Col. and Mrs Sutton[88] and young officer on his way back to the front, Cadogan[89] by name.

22 July

Worked on my, 'Notes on the use of R.C. Churches'[90] and wrote letters. Saw the C.G. about 12.30. Lunched with Bland Sutton[91] at 1 and met Harry[92] for the first time in 16 years. He looks very thin and run down. Bland Sutton looked at his leg and thought it would be quite well in a fortnight after being scraped. Went to the service in the Abbey. Called on the Bishop Barry[93] and talked over with him the question of assistance for Episcopal work in the field. Had another talk with the C.G. at the War Office. Went without dinner tonight and ate a little fruit instead. Called in at the Regent Street Cinematograph.

23 July

The C.G. called me to the War office at 9.30 to talk over the limitation of my work in the field to the C of E troops. MacInnes came at 12.30 and talked over the affairs of Egypt and the Sudan and decided to ask Robins[94] to stay on until next year.

---

[82]   Lieutenant Colonel O. A. Fitzgerald, personal military secretary to the secretary of state for war.
[83]   His brother, the Rev. Charles Brooke Gwynne.
[84]   His brother, Howell Gwynne, editor of the *Morning Post*.
[85]   This a reference to the Charing Cross Hotel that formed part of the station of the same name.
[86]   Possible Brigadier General (Retired) C. S. O. Monck.
[87]   Possibly Mrs F. Monck, 109 Eaton Square.
[88]   Unidentified.
[89]   Unidentified.
[90]   There was a hope that the Catholic bishops in France would give permission for Anglican services to be held in churches in the area where the BEF was fighting.
[91]   Sir John Bland Sutton, surgeon at Middlesex Hospital.
[92]   His brother, Captain H. Gwynne.
[93]   This could refer to Bishop Barry, bishop of the Catholic diocese of Chatham, New Brunswick, Canada.
[94]   Unidentified.

After lunch went to see Taylor Smith* and caught the 5.15 to Buntingford with Howell and met all the family at Mawbyns[95] where we dined together and had a really good time.

24 July

Up early and had a quiet time before breakfast, caught the 10.40 train at Bishops Stortford and called in at the War Office and saw Taylor Smith*. After wh. I had lunch with the Balfours[96] at 47 Cadogan Square and had a long talk with Lord Balfour who promised to do his best to allay the fears of the Scotch people on their Principal Chaplain being superseded by me in the field. I removed from his mind the mistake he made in thinking I was to be placed over Presbyterians. I just caught the 3.55 train to Bishops Stortford where I was met by the car. After tea at Dick's Rectory, Charlie and I went for a short walk in the Park.

25 July

Spent the day at Little Easton until 2 pm. Charlie celebrated Holy Communion at 8 am. At 11 I preached on Isaiah LV.5.[97] All lunched at Mawbyns Howell drove me to Loughton where I caught a train to Liverpool Street. I missed the train to Northwood at 4.45 but caught the next at 5.40. Stayed the night with T. Smith* and talked over my work in the field.

26 July

Came up about 9.30. Received a good many letters. Interviewed … Shaw[98] who offered for his congregation a good deal of money for any useful work in the field wh. I had to refuse on the ground that the army supplied nearly all necessities. After calling on the War Office to see Taylor Smith* I went off to Kings Cross to see Mr & Mrs Player who took me to lunch at the Haymarket.[99] We walked in the park until about 3.30 went they left for King's Cross while I called at the *Morning Post* office to tell Howell I was dining with 'K.' Dick Shepperd[100] to whom I had written saying I was going to tea with him today, was out. I visited a Cinamatograph at 5 pm. At 8.30 I dined with K and told him all my stories about the troops. We talked about the service for Aug. 4 for wh. he was choosing the hymns. He talked about Taylor Smith's* Advisory Committee, Howell's help, and talked at length about the war, dodges to kill the Germans and the futile results of these small attacks on the German lines.

---

95 Mawbyns was Howell Gwynne's country house at Little Easton in Essex.
96 Alexander Bruce, 6th Lord Balfour of Burleigh, a noted Presbyterian layman.
97 'Behold, thou shalt call a nation that thou knowest not, and nations that knew not thee shall run unto thee because of the Lord thy God, and for the Holy One of Israel; for he hath glorified thee.' Isaiah chapter 55 verse 5, The Bible (Authorized Version).
98 Unidentified.
99 Unidentified.
100 The Rev. H. R. L. Sheppard, vicar of St Martin-in-the-Fields.

27 July

At 8.30 I attended service at Lambeth and stayed to breakfast afterwards. From about 9.30 to 11.30 I was hard at it talking to the Archbishop and hearing his point of view. We talked over the work the Church of England needed, the visiting, the encouraging of the chaplains, the finding out of the proper proportion one chaplain could undertake, the War Office and Church, the mistakes some of our leaders make – York, London, Littleton.

Edward Woods* met me afterwards and walked with me to the War Office where I had an interview with Sir Reginald Brade[101] and talked over the staff required by me in doing my job. He thought it a very good idea to bring MacPherson* home and agreed to the suggestion that I should go out and visit all the chaplains before settling down at S. Omer. At one all out family met at the Norfolk Hotel and had lunch after wh. I saw Charlie, Harry and Nellie off at Paddington. Gwen I brought down to the Club and gave her and the CG tea in the Club. I saw her off at Liverpool Street, dined quietly at the Club and did a good deal of writing.

28 July

I drew up roughly my requirements for my new work (1) Staff Officer and clerk – separate office at S Omer. (2) Motor and Chauffaire. [*sic*] and took it before the CG at the War Office.

Caught the 12.40 to Woolwich Arsenal and lunched with Edward* and Clemence Woods and saw my godchild Frank.

Train so inconvenient that I had to motor all the way to London wh. was all in vain as I mistook the day of an appointment. After tea in the club I went to the War Office for ½ hour and talked over a few things with the C.G.

For exercise I walked to dine with Bland Sutton[102] where Howell was also dining and we heard from the latter the result of his visit to Portsmouth where Admiral Lambton[103] told him how splendidly the navy were doing and of the sinking of many submarines.

29 July

Spent some of the time writing letters and interviews. The Bishop of London[104] came to lunch with me at the club and talked over the affairs of the of the work of the chaplains in France. He told me I was his man for the job, the task of wh. I had my

---

[101] Sir Reginald Brade, permanent under-secretary of state for war.
[102] Sir John Bland-Sutton surgeon at the Middlesex Hospital.
[103] Admiral of the Fleet Henry (Lambton) Meux, commander in chief, Portsmouth. He had changed his name from Lambton to Meux in 1910.
[104] The Rt Rev. A. Winnington-Ingram.

doubts. Mike Bernard[105] came to the Club and had tea after wh. I went down with Taylor Smith* to stay the night at Northwood where I spent a quiet restful evening.

30 July

I walked with Taylor Smith* before breakfast in the first haze of an early morning. From the Great Central[106] I strolled through the Parks to Whitehall. Interviewed Lloyd of the Church Army who told me about the Church Army work in France. Storey has a long talk with me about the work in the Sudan and finance and I lunched with Mrs Duberley at 7A Eaton Square.[107] I had another long interview with Barry[108] from 3.15 – 4.30 and saw Howell at the station. I dined quietly in the Strand.

31 July

Attended the War Office at 10.00 after a long talk with Cheyne Garforth.[109] Did all my business with Taylor Smith* and Mitchell[110] and shopped all the morning, accomplishing all I set out to do at the Stores. McGrigor, Army Agents,[111] Whippels[112] and … out. Had a light lunch and did some letter writing. Took the CG to the Abbey service at 3 – the anthem 'O Taste and See'[113] brought back my boyhood in the old Swansea Grammar School and the little chapel services in which I sang. I caught the train to Dunmow where I was met by Edie[114] in the small car.

---

105   Unidentified.
106   Marylebone Station was the London terminus of the Grand Central Railway.
107   7a Eaton Square was a residence of the marquess of Abergavenny.
108   Possibly Bishop Barry.
109   Unidentified.
110   The Rev. P. R. Mitchell*.
111   Officers were paid through firms of army agents appointed by regiments. The agent for the AChD was Sir Charles McGrigor Bt.
112   Presumably Wippells the firm of church outfitters and clothiers.
113   The words are from Psalm 34 verse 8 of The Bible (Authorized Version). The setting might have been that by Sullivan.
114   Wife of Howell Gwynne.

August 1915

Gwynne spent the first week of August in London beginning to come to terms with his new appointment. He then returned to France to set up his office. The principal chaplain, the Reverend Dr J. Simms, had his office in Hesdin whilst Gwynne's office was to be in St Omer, about forty kilometres away. He then began the round of visits to chaplains and to military headquarters that was to occupy much of his time. He also noted the visits he received. Anglican chaplains paid regular calls on him. He also recorded visits by bishops and other leaders of the Church of England. At the end of the month, he returned to London for a meeting at the WO about the new Anglican Consultative Committee on Chaplains. There are a number of references to the war at sea.

1 August

Had a quiet Sunday with Dick, including a blessed time at the Holy Communion. Dick[1] preached very helpful sermon on, 'Who shall show us any good? Lift then thy countenance upon us.'[2] After lunch Dick and I strolled down to Mawbyns and saw the Cassons, Henry Wilson and Percy.[3] I preached in the Evening on, 'The Burden of the Lord',[4] and how religion had become a burden to so many, a burden of love. After supper Dick and I had a delightful stroll in the Park.

2 August

Said my prayers in the Park before breakfast and had a blessed time. Howell came in his small car and took me to Dunmow. By the 10.17 train. Saw C.G. and MacPherson* at the War Office and took the latter to the Club and gave him lunch after getting all the information I wanted for the work in France. Helped the C.G. to write his letter to Brade[5] about the proposed staff. Walked through S. James' Park for exercise and wrote a few letters before dinner with the C.G. at 7.30.

Took a turn in the Park before dinner in the rain. Had a talk with Allen Edwards[6] and the Bishop of Newcastle[7] in the Club and after prayer went to my room.

---

[1]   His brother, the Rev. R. L. Gwynne.
[2]   'Who will shew us any good? Lord, lift thou up the light of thy countenance upon us.' Psalm 4 verse 6, The Bible (Authorized Version.)
[3]   There are several possibilities for each of these people.
[4]   'And when this people, or the prophet, or a priest, shall ask thee, saying, What is the burden of the Lord?' Possibly Jeremiah chapter 23 verse 33, The Bible (Authorized Version).
[5]   Sir Reginald Brade, permanent under-secretary of state for war.
[6]   Possibly Allen Edwards the Liberal MP for East Glamorgan.
[7]   The Rt Rev. Norman Straton.

Howell told me this morning that National Service[8] was in the air and that Carson[9] was dining with 'K' tonight to talk it over. May God guide them in their Councils.

3 August

This is a terrible time for me, hanging round haggling over the settling of my position in the field. I had every intention of departing this afternoon, but a letter from Sir J. French[10] about the rank of the Principal Chaplain had to be considered and Brade who came into the C.G's. room and pressed the C.G. to let the Principal Chaplain be gazetted to the same rank on the same day wh. would give him seniority over me. It does seem so humiliating to haggle about Rank, but we have to fight on principle and we can have no idea what is behind it all and what further difficulties there are in the way. We must make our foundations sure.

After lunch I walked up to Victoria Street in the City with the C.G. after wh. I went into S. Paul's and looked round and said a prayer.

I then called on Howell and had a chat with him, before seeing the C.G. again.

After tea I called on Dick Shepperd[11] whom I missed. Dined quietly at the Club, called in at a Cinematograph, and wrote down my views on the position of D.C.M.[12] in the field.

4 August

I woke this morning with vague fears of what was going to happen, and God in His mercy and love quietened my fears when I said my prayers and left everything to Him.

I had written down my arguments in favour of having the C of E representative in the Field Senior to the Principal Chaplain and talked them all over before the great service in S. Paul's which the C.G. and I attended.[13] As a spectacular and musical effect it was inspiring – but whether I did not prepare for it or the unusual surroundings hindered, I was unable to fix my attention on worship, humility and praise. For

---

8   At this point all recruitment was still on a voluntary basis. The continued demand for more men meant that alternative methods were under consideration. This would eventually lead to conscription.

9   Sir Edward Carson MP had been appointed attorney-general on 25 May 1915.

10 Field Marshal Sir John French, commander in chief of the BEF. The letter strenuously opposed Gwynne's appointment. The text is reproduced in Howson, *Muddling through*, p. 89. It showed that Gwynne's appointment had not been discussed with anyone in the BEF. It also showed that Gwynne was given a higher rank than the Rev. Dr J. Simms*, the principal chaplain.

11 The Rev. H. R. L. Sheppard.

12 It is not clear to what 'D.C.M.' refers. It might be that it should read 'DCG', in which case it would refer to Gwynne's position in the BEF. It would normally refer to the Distinguished Conduct Medal and there might have been some discussion about what awards could be made to chaplains as they were neither commissioned 'Officers' nor 'Soldiers'. Given that they had 'officer status', it was usual for them to be awarded the same medals as officers.

13 The service to commemorate the first anniversary of the start of the war.

myself I prefer the 23rd Psalm said on my knees instead of a Gregorian Setting. The Hymn, 'Praise my Soul the King of Heaven', was sung to an unaccustomed tune.[14] The Archbishop said the right thing. It was 1.30 before we reached the Club and I almost loafed until 3.30 when I returned to the War Office. 'K' had not yet seen the C.G. so I walked out again. When I returned at 6 nothing happened, but immediately afterwards Brade came in and said 'K' would not hear of further promotion for the present Principal Chaplain. That settled the whole question without having to appear to fight for rank and money, for wh. I promised God. Sir John Kennaway[15] dined at the same table.

5 August

[Entries for 5 and 6 August are in pencil]

This morning caught the 6.43 train to Northwood where I breakfasted with the CG[16] and Mr A. Mercer[17] The CG and I had our photos taken by the local photographer and caught the 10 train to London. After shopping[18] and arranging my place on the train I wrote letters and had Howell to lunch with me at the Club.

Taylor Smith* came and had a chat with me afterwards in the Smoking Room. I came off by the 5.40 train. Edward Talbot* travelling with me. I also met Owen[19] of Ox & Bucks[20] on the boat. Some of the chaplains met me on my arrival. I stopped the night at the Dervaux Hotel.[21]

6 May [sic][22]

At 9.15 I attended a meeting at the Boulogne Base which the Wesleyans[23] and Presbyterians[24] also attended. I saw chaplains from 9.45 – 1, and heard all their views and any grievances. I walked up to the cemetery and saw the graves of those I had buried in the old days and came away at 3 reaching St Omer at 4.15 and reported to

---

[14] The full title of the service was *A service of humble prayer to Almighty God on behalf of the nation and empire at twelve noon on Wednesday, August 4th, 1915, after one year of the war.* The unaccustomed tune was 'St Helen', by Martin.

[15] A Conservative politician and long serving MP. He had been a member of the 1904 Royal Commission on Ecclesiastical Discipline.

[16] The chaplain general, with whom he was staying.

[17] Unidentified.

[18] SAD 28/5/4. Gwynne recorded that he needed a bath, shaving soap, a tin basin and a hold all. He also listed copies of 'Kipling' and 'Noyes'. His last need was what he referred to as 'putty stockings', presumably puttees.

[19] Captain R. M. Owen.

[20] Ox & Bucks.

[21] Hotel in Boulogne.

[22] This is obviously an error which was not noticed and corrected. This part of the diary seems to have been written in haste.

[23] The Wesleyan Methodist Church had begun its work among soldiers in 1858 at Aldershot. It only allowed its chaplains to accept commissions into the AChD on the outbreak of war in Aug. 1914.

[24] Presbyterian chaplains were appointed from churches in Scotland, Ireland and England.

the AG Office where I had a long talk with Childs[25] about the future of our work. He seemed to be very anxious about our working together. I saw Dr Simms* afterwards – he was exceedingly nice and kind. Saw Thorold* and Drury* who found me an excellent billet where please God I can pray hard and work hard for Him who has called us.[26]

7 August

Childs[27] took me to report myself to French[28] this morning. It wasn't long before I was in and out. There was something dull and heavy about him. He thought or said whether he thought it or no, that I had just come out from Egypt. He also repeated what he had often said before that the Chaplains in the army were doing good work, but he said it in a jerky, formal kind of way as if it was the only thing he could say to a man in my job. I worked in the office all the morning and motored in the afternoon to La Gorgue near Estaires to take a confirmation which was unfortunately mixed up badly and put off, without my knowing. I called on General Anderson[29] of the Meerut Division[30] and Blackburne* our chaplain of the 1st Army, before returning to St Omer I left a card on Tuckey*.

8 August

There was quite a good number at the 7.15 Holy Communion. I preached on Isaiah 'Seek ye the Lord,'[31] at 10.30 Sat in the Office and interviewed Smith,[32] Kegmour[33] and Page* on their way to their several jobs. Instead of lunch I had some coffee and bread & butter and had tea at the Stationary Hospital where Stewart* – one of our chaplains – a missionary from China is attached. I preached again at the 6 pm service on, 'From whence come wars and fightings amongst you,'[34] – after a walk I dined at the Restaurant with Dallas* and Thorold* and talked out many matters. I told Dallas* all that I knew about the 6th Brigade. It is extraordinary the number of men I have seen here whom I knew before. Turner,[35] James,[36] Morgan

---

[25] Lieutenant Colonel Borlase Elward Wyndham Childs assistant AG HQ BEF.
[26] SAD 28/5/8. Gwynne recorded a prayer:
  O my Lord and Master
    1. Give me love to Thee and the Chaplains.
    2. Go forth with me and prevent me, make me cling to Thee.
    3. In Tuas Manus O Domine.
[27] Lieutenant Colonel Borlase Elward Wyndham Childs assistant AG HQ BEF.
[28] Field Marshal Sir John French, commander in chief of the BEF.
[29] Major General C. A. Anderson, commander of the Meerut Division.
[30] Part of the Indian Corps which served with the BEF in 1914 and 1915.
[31] Isaiah chapter 55 verse 6, The Bible (Authorized Version).
[32] Unidentified.
[33] Unidentified.
[34] 'From whence come wars and fightings among you?' James, chapter 4 verse 1, The Bible (Authorized Version).
[35] Possibly Colonel E. V. Turner.
[36] Unidentified.

(doctor)[37] Levett[38] the old Coldstreamer and now one of the officers of the Flying Corps[39] – Jeffcote[40] – Grylls[41] the gunner who years ago went up the Nile with me. Bunberry[42] now Provo Marshal.

9 August

There was fighting at Hooge last night but only the slenderest reports come through to us here. The unvarnished truth seems to be that we have taken back the trenches we lost through fire jets[43] a few days ago – at Turner's[44] RE Mess where I dined tonight – the HQs of the Telegraph[45] I heard this, and that the Germans had bombarded right along the line out of pure hate or to show us that they were well supplied with ammunition in case we did go across to take their trenches. We started intercession at 9. am in our little Church in the town. From 9 – 2 (with the interruption of viewing a small hotel we propose taking as a mess) I worked in the office and interviewed chaplains on their way to their work, and on the whole a very good stamp they are. Thorold* and I walked out along the canal bank to Arques for a couple of hours and a half from 3 – 5.30 after wh I worked in the office until 7.45. Drury* did some work with me from 9.30 – 10.30.

10 August

I am gradually breaking the back of the work and by the help of God reducing the difficulties. Drury* who is what might be described as Permanent Secretary of the Chaplains' Dep. in the field is most usefull and Thorold* whom I found here as an additional chaplain attached to the office with other work in the town has been invaluable in helping me with the correspondence. Dr Simms* took me out in his car to some woods where we had a delightful walk and talk and very useful and valuable information about my work. The Bishop of Birmingham[46] and the Lord Mayor of Birmingham[47] [London is crossed out] came up from Boulogne tonight. Thorold* and I paid respects to them after our frugal supper in the office this Evening and found them both charming. I have saved a lot of time I usually spend reading the

---

[37] Unidentified.
[38] Unidentified.
[39] Royal Flying Corps (RFC) was created in May 1912 and merged into the Royal Air Force on 1 Apr. 1918.
[40] Possibly Captain Algermont Cautley Jeffcoat.
[41] Possibly Major Glynn Grylls Royal Artillery who was seconded to be a temporary ordnance officer.
[42] Brigadier General C. V. Bunbury had been appointed the provost marshal for the BEF on 13 Feb. 1915.
[43] The first use of flame-throwers by the Germans was at Hooge in the fighting that began on 31 July 1915.
[44] Possibly Colonel F. V. Turner.
[45] The Corps of Royal Engineers were responsible for the army's telegraph network.
[46] The Rt Rev. Henry Wakefield, bishop of Birmingham 1911–1924. He wrote *Fourteen days at the front* as an account of his visit to the BEF in 1915.
[47] Neville Chamberlain.

paper – reading an excellent book, 'God and the World,'[48] by the Dean of Wells [crossed out and word substituted is unclear].

11 August

After office work this morning (until 1.30) I had a short work and a cup of coffee bread and butter with an egg. I am going very easy with my food these days and do much better than our heavy meals for I have a lot of thinking out to do.

At 3 o'clock I started with Thorold* for Calais where I had to get at the difficulty between the Y.M.C.A. and our young chaplain Horwood.[49] All the trouble is the YMCA collect money in England for social and recreation rooms for the men in the field. They are not allowed to send out men of a serviceable age – so they send out mainly clergy as workers who interfere with the work of the chaplains.[50] It is rather a thorny question wh will take a lot of managing.[51] I feel I am gradually getting a grip of things.

12 August

The usual office was rather disturbed by interviews with chaplains on their way to their work or brought in on special duty. Early in the afternoon Thorold* and I motored out to a place beyond Poperinghe where the 46th or North Midland Division[52] had its head quarters. General Stuart Wortley[53] the Divisional General was the same Stuart Wortley who did so well on the expedition for the relief of Gordon and in 98 on the recovery of the Sudan when he commanded the motley crew of mixed native tribes and helped in the bombardment of Omdurman from Halfezel.[54] He very kindly brought in Conor* and Hunt* to see me. Stuart Wortley seemed to

---

48 The dean of Wells between 1911 and 1933 was the Rev. Armitage Robinson. He was the author of several books although not this one. The reference may be to *God and the world: a survey of thought*, published in 1913 by SPCK and the work of the Rev. Arthur W. Robinson. He was vicar of All Hallows-by-the-Tower between 1895 and 1917. The Rev. P. T. B. (Tubby) Clayton*, founder of TocH, was a subsequent incumbent.

49 Possibly the Rev. R. C. Harwood*, minister at Holy Trinity, Boulogne.

50 SAD 28/5/8. Gwynne noted that 'Horwood' thought that he had a right to use the YMCA room.

51 SAD 28/5/13ff. Gwynne noted some of the problems with the YMCA. At the centre of the difficulty was his belief that whereas the YMCA had been allowed out to France to provide social amenities for the troops, they now claimed that the *rôle* included religious work. Gwynne believed that such a position was unfair to the churches at home, the chaplains and the army. He based this understanding on an instruction to chaplains that had been issued on 24 July, and which he quoted in his notebook. It read,

Voluntary Workers

Chaplains are responsible for all religious ministrations within the bounds of their charges. Representatives of voluntary agencies which minister to the religious or social needs of the troops must obtain the sanction of a chaplain before undertaking religious services.

52 46 (North Midland) Div was a Territorial Force formation that deployed to France in Feb. 1915.

53 Major General Edward James Montagu-Stuart-Wortley was General Officer in Command (GOC) of 46 Div between 14 June and 16 July.

54 The then Major Stuart Wortley carried out attacks on the east bank of the Nile before the battle of Omdurman. The site mentioned has not been identified. He also participated in the earlier failed attempt to relieve General Gordon.

take an interest in the work of the chaplains and was anxious that the chaplains from the territorial area at home from whence the men are drawn should be appointed to these units: Stather Hunt* looked very well and fit and was anxious to stay on at his work with this Division. The Bishop of Birmingham and the Lord Mayor did not turn up for dinner at the Hotel de France.[55]

13 August

I had a number of interviews with men this morning wh. took nearly all my time. At one we lunched in our new house[56] for the first time and had simple meal. At 5 pm I started in the motor for Bethune where I attended a concert run by the Oxfords – after which I dined with the 5th Brigade officers who celebrated their arrival in this country. Their old Brigadier Haking[57] and Davies[58] were there and I had an enjoyable evening. The newly formed band of the 2nd Division played during dinner. It was a real pleasure to see the old friends of my Brigade.

14 August

I had a fairly strenuous day. It began at 8 am with a celebration of Holy Communion. I then had breakfast with the chaplains at the Hotel de France – after which I spoke to them and told them of my appointment and explained that state of affairs and my duties.

I motored over to La Gorgue in the afternoon and had lunch with Gordon* and saw Daubney[59] after the Confirmation Service. Confirmed about 26. After sce I saw a large of the clergy and spoke to them as I did in the morning to the clergy at Bethune and saw a good many individually. I returned to Bethune and dine with the General who kindly put me up.

15 August

I spent the Sunday at Bethune. Had a celebration at 8 in the Theatre Chapel and preached to a large audience of Oxfords in the Theatre at 9.30. I motored to Beuvry and preached to a large number of Worcesters in a field near the Cemetery. Unfortunately rain came down soon after I began my sermon, and my congregation was soon dispersed. I had a walk with Lambton[60] and Wyman[61] before I lunched with the Worcesters and I walked back to Bethune at 2.30.

---

[55] Hotel in St Omer.
[56] In St Omer.
[57] General Richard Haking had commanded 5 Bde at the outbreak of war and, from Dec. 1914, 1 Div.
[58] Possibly Major General F. J. Davies who had recently given up command of 8 Div.
[59] Possibly Colonel E. K. Daubney.
[60] Lieutenant Colonel G. C. Lambton, CO 2 WORCS.
[61] Unidentified.

I confirmed about 1 men of the 1st Division. Harry Blackburne* and Wilson[62] presenting the candidates. We gave the candidates tea in the Hotel de France.[63] I called on the No. 5th Ambulance at 6 and preached at the evening service in the Theatre.

16 August

The Bishop of Birmingham after seeing the Mayor of Hazebrouck,[64] who is also a priest of the Church excommunicated by the Pope, took a long time coming to me and therefore wasted my time and spoiled my programme for the day.

General Horne[65] kindly gave both of us lunch and gave permission to take the Bishop into the Trenches which the Worcesters are holding at Festubert. We visited Vermelles and saw Harry Blackburne's* wonderful institute under the Brewery Cellar. After which we made an effort to get to the Worcesters through the slush and the rain. We only succeeded in reaching one Company and the colonel's dug out where we had tea and just managed to get a quarter of an hour in the dug out before we returned.

17 August

The Bishop of Birmingham went off today after lunch to visit the bases in the car kindly lent him by Sir William Robertson, the Chief of Staff.[66] Drury* and I went out into the woods for a walk first motoring out of town to avoid the stones and the streets. Clair Marais is the name of the forest and is about two miles south of the town.[67] I am now trying my best to decentralize the work and get clear of the work others can do while the routine. At present I go back to the office after tea and walk again in the Evening after dinner.

18 August

One might be in Central Africa for the opportunity one has to hear the news of the war. Here we are at the Head Quarters of the Exped. Force and the only news we have of the war is for the London papers which reach us about 3 pm in the afternoon. My day's work after my own private devotions begin at 9 am with intercession in the little chapel here. At 9.30 I start work in the office which means dictating letters, talking over moves, interviewing chaplains, etc., etc., and thinking over the big questions as Promotions – Rewards – Establishments. I finish about 1.45 except when I have people to lunch. At 3 I usually motor out with one of the chaplains to some picturesque place and have a walk for an hour or so after wh. he motor picks us up and brings us back for tea.

---

[62] There were several chaplains with this surname.
[63] Hotel in Bethune.
[64] Abbé Jules-Augustin Lemire, parish priest of Hazebrouck, had become its mayor in 1914.
[65] General Henry Horne, GOC 2 Div.
[66] General Sir William Robertson, chief of staff, BEF.
[67] Clairmarais is an area of woodland to the east of St Omer.

19 August

After tea I usually try to do 1½ hours work before dinner at 7.30 and on some days I go back with the chaplains to the office for an hour or so to clear up any work. I have a passion for being up to date in one's work and mean if necessary to bring other clergy in to assist and make the work run smoothly and without haste. I had Tuckey* one of the Senior Chaplains into lunch today and I took him out for a walk into the country and talked out all the main points in the administration of our department. After tea I did about an hour work in the office and dined with Waugh[68] on his barge where he had a dinner party of seven people including two nurses.

20 August

For two days we have had bad news. Yesterday came the news of the sinking of the Transport in the Aegean[69] and today the sinking of the '*Arabic*' the White Star line by a submarine off the south of Ireland.[70] I worked in the office from 9.30 to nearly 2 pm and went without lunch reading Armitage Robinson's interesting book.[71] We found a new part to the country in wh. to have our walk and we found ourselves on light ground walking through heather.

Harry Blackburne* one of the Senior Chaplains came in from Aire to talk over his views of administration. I have brought a young fellow named Mitchell[72] to look after the troops attached to Head Quarters troops and to assist Thorold* in his Secretarial duties as well as in Domestic affairs.

21 August

The actual work of the office is easing off considerably thanks to the good work of Thorold* and Drury*, the assistant Deputy, who knows all the inner working of the office. There is a great deal to learn about the army administration and I am gradually getting a grip of things.

I meant to stop only a couple of hours in the office this morning but was kept so long that I did not get back into my house until nearly 1 pm. I worked at my sermons until 3 then drove out in a motor to Clair Marais woods and walked a couple of hours with Drury* before returning at 6. We had a very nice missionary chaplain, Stewart* of China, to dinner tonight after which I had a long council meeting with Thorold* and Drury*.

---

68 Possible Captain P. Waugh.

69 The transport *Royal Edward* was torpedoed on 13 Aug. 1915 by the German submarine *UB-24* whilst on passage to Gallipoli. 935 men were killed.

70 The White Star liner SS *Arabic* was torpedoed, south of Ireland, on 19 Aug. 1915 by the German submarine *U-24*. As was the case when RMS *Lusitania* had been torpedoed on 7 May 1915, United States citizens were among those killed. This sinking was again the subject of a diplomatic complaint by the American government.

71 The reference may be to *God and the world: a survey of thought*, published in 1913 by SPCK and the work of the Rev. Arthur W. Robinson.

72 Possibly the Rev. C. W. Mitchell*.

22 August

I celebrate the Holy communion at what we call the Upper Chapel at 7.45 where quite 35 were gathered together in His Name. At 9.30 the Artists[73] held their service and I preached to them on being fellow workers with God. They listened very attentively and I felt the Power of the living god reinforcing even a man like me. Thorold* and I had a most interesting walk together (after looking through letters) when we walked through the gardens into the woods. The sun shone brilliantly, casting shadows in the woods and turning into gold the harvest fields dotted with heaps of corn. We saw green woodpeckers flash like emeralds as they flew from tree to tree. One of the chaplains, Burrows*, took me to see some patients in the Hospital and I spoke to them on John XIV [verse] 1[74] and prayed with and for them. We entertained to dinner Malcolm Wingate[75] and Turner,[76] my old friends from the Sudan.

23 August

Thorold* and I started soon after 8.30 am for Boulogne in order to interview with the Bishop of Birmingham the Bishop of Arras[77] who is now looking after the diocese of Lille as well as his own. The interview was requested by me in order to get permission for him to use the naves of his village Churches when our troops are fighting in those parts. He received me gladly and evidently thinking we had come to make use of the Churches for the RC soldiers, but when we said we were asking for the use of these for the CofE troops, his chief priest, a very Jesuitical looking fellow, made a horrible face and said, 'tres difficile', and their former kindness seemed very much altered. I told them through the Bp. of Birmingham who speaks French perfectly that Lord K had attempted to settle the whole thing through Joffre[78] but I thought it wiser to approach the French Church. They asked for time to think it over and I will write at once and put down in black and white our request.

24 August

I had a good game of tennis with my friend Turner, once Chief of the Posts and Telegraphs in the Sudan and now in the office of the Chief at Head Quarters here. I found I was much stouter when I began to play and though it took me some time to get with it my hand had not altogether forgotten her cunning.

---

73 The Artists' Rifles, 28th (County of London) Battalion of the London Regiment, served as infantry providing local defence troops for GHQ.
74 'Let not your heart be troubled: ye believe in God, believe also in me.' John chapter 14 verse 1, The Bible (Authorized Version).
75 Possibly Lieutenant Malcolm Wingate Royal Engineers who served with 26 Field Company which was in 1 Div.
76 Possibly Colonel E. V. Turner.
77 Bishop Émile-Louis Cornil Lobbedey was bishop of Arras 1911–16.
78 General Joseph Joffre, commander in chief of the French army.

Good news through the *Morning Post* today of the Russian naval victory in Riga Bay.[79] God grant that the Russians may soon be in a position to take the offensive. It will cheer the people at home to know that one of our submarines has sunk a German super dreadnought[80] and that Italy has declared war on Turkey.[81] It is very little information one can pick up here, but I did hear the other day that the flames of the fire the Germans used at Hooge were so terrifying that our men were terrified out of their trenches and when they turned back were shot down in hundreds.

25 August

I miss seeing Tommy Atkins every day and chaffing him in his billet or on the way to the Trenches. Now I merely see him in the streets as they pass by saluting. From 9.30 – 1.45 I worked in the office, but took out in the afternoon for a walk a very nice chaplain named Burrows* who talked over with me the hopes and fears of the future after this great war.

I brought him back to tea. After which I went again into the office to go over a few letters before dinner. A young chaplain named Horwood[82] came in from Calais to dine and sleep. I had a long talk with him afterwards about his work. I think I know him better now.

26 August

This afternoon I visited the General Commanding the 1st Army, General Plumer.[83] He met us at the door of the chateau Head Quarters and introduced us to his staff. He asked a few questions about the administration of the Chaplains' Department and I explained to him that contrary to all other Departments in the Army the Chaplains' Department had only one recognized official wh. was the Deputy CG.[84] He took me up to his room afterwards and we talked privately about Tuckey's* CMG,[85] [and] the cemeteries in the 2nd Army Area. Rewards only to be given on the recommendation of the GOC Divisions. I had no exercise today having spent a great deal of my time in an office or in a motor.

---

79 The battle of the Gulf of Riga had started on 8 Aug. 1915 with a German naval attack on Russian ships in the Baltic.

80 This possibly refers to the *Barbaros Hayreddin*, Ottoman, Brandenburg class Pre-Dreadnought Battleship which was torpedoed by the British submarine *E11* in the Sea of Marmara on 8 Aug. 1915.

81 Italy declared war on the Ottoman Empire on 21 Aug. 1915.

82 SAD 28/9/16 noted that 'Horwood' was an Indian chaplain stationed at Calais. It further noted that 'He employs one of the CofE chaplains attached to the YMCA.' This would have been one of the causes of Gwynne's unhappiness with the relationship between the AChD and the YMCA.

83 General Herbert Plumer, commander Second Army.

84 Gwynne was arguing that there was no defined chain of command within the AChD in the BEF. He cannot have meant that the situation was the same as it had been before he was created DCG, or that he had authority over the principal chaplain.

85 Presumably the possible conferring of the Order of St Michael and St George on the Rev. J. G. W. Tuckey*.

27 August

After an interview with Mr. McCowen[86] of the YMCA at 9.30 this morning we started (Thorold* and I) for Nieppe where the XII Division Head Quarters is situated. As soon as we arrived I was taken to bless the small Grave Yards near the firing line. We saw the famous Plug Street Wood quite close. Gunner's Farm had two cemeteries and I motored again after lunching with the General and his staff. I held a Confirmation of nearly a hundred men straight from the Trenches and spoke on the Kingdom of Heaven suffering violence. I had tea with the mean afterwards – held a meeting for the chaplains and saw each one in the Division.

28 August

Had a good morning in the office today until 11.30 when I visited Childs[87] at the AG's office and talked over the questions of chaplains' contract wh. does not count until they actually arrive in this country.[88] At 1.30 Thorold* and I started for the 47th Division and motored through Bethune to the Head Quarters near Fouqueres[89] and afterwards motored to Allouagne where I held a confirmation and had tea with the officers of 142 Brigade. After which I addressed Wood's* Brigade late in the evening. There must have been about 4000 on Parade and General Barter[90] the Div. Deputy General was in command. I spoke to them of reform and regeneration of how God may be waiting to heal the wounds of the world until the poison and evil matter was cleansed away.

29 August

I had a blessed Sunday. Starting with a celebration at 7 a, (at wh. Humphry Snow[91] was present) I went on to a small parade in a Field Ambulance where Beck and Snow attended and then on to a large parade of Gunners not far from Allouagne after wh. I preached to the 142 Brigade (Gen Lewis,[92] Maj Trevor[93]) nearly 3000 being present. I lunched at the chateau – the Brigade HQ and went to a clearing hospital where I had tea with Div. Column HQ and returned to Bethune about 6 o'clock in the evening. Having had no exercise Thorold* and I walked through the Gardens for an hour before dinner. Jeffcote[94] and Major Thresher[95] dining with me.

---

[86] Oliver McCowen, described by M. Snape (ed.) *The back parts of war: the YMCA memoirs and letters of Barclay Baron 1915–1919* (Woodbridge, 2009) p. 29, 'As the organizing genius on the Western Front.' Presumably of the YMCA.

[87] Lieutenant Colonel Borlase Elward Wyndham Childs assistant AG HQ BEF.

[88] Temporary chaplains were employed on a contract lasting a year. The contract started when the chaplain reached the BEF.

[89] Possibly Fouquières-lès-Lens, France

[90] Major General Sir Charles St Leger Barter, GOC 47 Div.

[91] Possibly Captain H. W. Snow who was appointed deputy assistant adjutant and QMG on 7 Apr. 1915.

[92] Brigadier General F. G. Lewis, commander 142 Bde.

[93] Major H. E. Trevor.

[94] Probably Captain Algermont Cautley Jeffcoat.

[95] Possibly Lieutenant Colonel J. H. Thresher, camp commandant at GHQ.

30 August[96]

A letter wh. I opened on Sunday night called me back to England to give certain information to the Advisory Committee[97] to the Chaplain General. I crossed over in the afternoon after a very strenuous morning in the office. Col. Wilding[98] and Fr McCabe* came over in the same boat with me. I travelled up to London with M'Cormic[99] and Barclay* who persisted in paying for our dinner on the train. Arriving in London about 9.30 I went at once and saw Howell, having a chat with him about the state of affairs and getting sound advice from him. I managed to get a room at the club and only missed seeing Taylor Smith* who called a few minutes before I came.

31 August

Visited the War Office about 10 and saw the CG and worked at the information required at the afternoon's meeting. I lunched with Howell at the Bath Club[100] and heard all the news of home etc., after which we walked through the Park to Charing Cross. Another hour spent working on my answers to the questions asked by the Advisory Committee wh. I attended at 4.30. Lord Salisbury,[101] Bishop of Winchester[102] and Sir R Brade.[103] I began by asking the authority of the meeting and expressed my opinion that it would be an act of courtesy to inform the CG before asking me to appear as I was Deputy CG.[104] All my questions being answered satisfactorily I spread my papers on the table and gave them all the information required.[105]

---

[96] SAD 28/1/2 showed that Gwynne, possibly resulting from his talk with General Plumer on 26 Aug. 1915, instructed Drury* to write to the senior chaplains of the armies about cemeteries. The chaplains were to discuss the matter of cemeteries with the Graves Commission. They were also to raise the question with divisional chaplains as to whether there was a likelihood of obtaining a deed of conveyance of the land from the French government. They were also to liaise with Gwynne about the consecration of the cemeteries.

[97] A Church of England Advisory Committee to the WO had been established in Aug. 1915, another change to the oversight of Anglican chaplaincy.

[98] Lieutenant Colonel C. A. Wilding.

[99] This is the Rev. W. P. G. McCormick*.

[100] The Bath Club was founded at 34 Dover Street, W1, in 1894.

[101] James Gascoyne-Cecil, 4th marquess of Salisbury. A leading high church Anglican.

[102] The Rt Rev. Edward Talbot. Two of his sons were serving as chaplains in the BEF.

[103] Sir Reginald Brade.

[104] SAD 28/5/23. Gwynne listed a series of questions in his notebook.

    1. What is this committee
    2. Why have they the power to call on me.
    3. How much am I to tell them.
    4. Go through all the points with T. Smith.

[105] The relationship between the Church of England and the Anglican oversight within the AChD remained complicated.

September 1915

Gwynne returned to France at the beginning of the month. Much of his time was then spent in continuing to meet chaplains. He did this, in part, to ensure that they were able to meet the demands of their posting. During this month, the British were preparing for the battle of Loos. This was to be the first major offensive mounted by the BEF. Initially, it showed signs of success but counter-attacks meant the gains could not be held.

1 September

Last night I travelled down with the intention of arriving at Northwood with the CG. Unfortunately he led me into the wrong train and before I knew where we were we found ourselves on another line to another part of the county. We had to walk about four miles across country and reached home at 8.30 instead of 7.30.

I kept the CG back from his office until 11. I then did some shopping and got a ticket for the saloon to Folkestone. I worked in the office until 1.30 and caught the train at 2 from Victoria. The Prince of Wales travelled across to Boulogne, but I did not recognise him until we reached the other side. Motor met me at Boulogne and I was home again at S. Omer by 8 pm.

2 September

I did a good mornings work in the office this morning and did not return home until nearly 2 o'clock. In the afternoon, as my motor had broken down I walked out as for as the church near the Clairmarais woods and back again. Father Waggett* arrived with a Mr. Bevan[1] from his clearing hospital about 5. After tea I had a go at my letters again with Thorold* and after dinner had a long talk with Waggett* about his work and his desires. Poor fellow he was much cut up when I told him plainly of his failure with the 4th Brigade, but he took it like a man and asked for another chance at the front. I did not get to bed until 12.30

3 September

Waggett* came with us to intercession at our small church here. There was a good number of clergy present and we prayed for our soldiers at the front as well as the sailors on the sea. We started our new office today and opened it with prayer that God would bless the place to His Service and use us to co-operate with Him in this work. It poured with rain the whole day without ceasing. Stuart[2] who is going to my old Brigade came to tea, and walked out afterwards for a short time but were driven

---

[1] Unidentified.
[2] Possibly the Rev. R. W. H. Stuart of the IEE who was on furlough in 1915.

in by the rain. Kidderminster[3] and Campbell* came to dinner. The first named is a Harrow master the latter is a regular chaplain from whom I took off marks as he ran down the Chaplain General.

4 September

After an hour in the office Thorold* and I started off in a motor to visit the 4th Division which has taken over some of the Trench line south of Arras. We passed through Troyes and S. Pol in the pouring rain and came into a country much more hilly and pretty than our part of the line. As soon as I reached the Division I found myself amongst friends. The General was General Wilson[4] an old Khartoum friend. Ensor, the DADMS[5] was another of my flock and Martin[6] one of the Staff Officers was with his regiment. I knew him well in the old days. They gave me a warm welcome. In the afternoon I rode to Sartor[7] to see what could be done to send another chaplain.

5 September

It was good to see three of my flock at Holy Communion today. Gen. Wilson, Ensor and Martin. Nearly all the Staff turned up. I addressed no fewer than four lots of troops in the morning and gave them the same message that I feel God has given me, viz. that God will heal the wounds of the world when the flesh and bad matter has come away. When our people are regenerated. I had lunch with the Rifle Brigade wh. Prescott Westear[8] an old friend of mine had arranged for me. I addressed the Batallion directly at the back of the chateaux the Major General attended. I saw a very fine young officer named Campbell[9] whom I knew at Khartoum dreadfully mutilated by an old bullet wound in the mouth. He had done his bit for his country and was now doing a bit more. I held a Confirmation at 3.30 and confirmed about 10 of my old flock, the Inniskillings.[10]

6 September

Up soon after six I had a quiet time until 8.35, when I had a short walk in the Gardens before intercessions. I had a long talk with the AG[11] this morning who wanted to know all my communications with Sir R. Brade.[12] I laid all my cards on the table and told him how I meant to play the game with him and also how I had

---

3   This is the Rev. D. B. Kittermaster*.
4   Major General Henry Fuller Maitland Wilson, commander 4 Div.
5   Probably Lieutenant Colonel H. Ensor, Distinguished Service Order MB. The deputy assistant director of medical services at army headquarters, in this case First Army.
6   Unidentified.
7   The name of the location is unclear.
8   Possibly Captain W. V. L. Prescott-Westear.
9   Unidentified.
10 A battalion of the Royal Inniskilling Fusiliers.
11 The AG of the BEF who had oversight of all chaplaincy matters.
12 Sir Reginald Brade, permanent under-secretary of state for war.

to play the game to my church.[13] About the transport for the 3 Senior Army Chaplains I was advised to use our Committee at home for that purpose. I worked hard in the office until 2 pm when I had an hours read and coffee and fruit in my room. I interviewed Marshall* who goes to the 23rd Division as S. Chaplain and drove out in a motor to see the 1st Coldstreams and found Egerton[14] there and other officers. I came back and interviewed three chaplains, Griffiths,* Hogarth* and Marsden*. Prescott Roberts[15] came to dinner – Green Wilkinson[16] stayed the night.

7 September

I much fear there is going to be another attack. This I heard from one of my Sudan flock in the XVth Division wh. I visited today. The General commanding the Division and one of the chief officers are old friends of mine.[17] I motored down to Bethune and beyond it to Vaudricourt where the HQ of the 2nd Division are billeted in time for lunch. After lunch I saw Eddowes*, Broughton*, Forbes* and Moir* our C of E chaplains with the Division the rest are all Scotch. I heard all their troubles and had prayer with them after which I went up to tea with Snow[18] at Head Quarters and talked about the old days in Khartoum. From what I can gather the French are very keen on making a dash through the Germans and are willing to use as many as 80,000 if necessary. They say that 50 Divisions are massing round the point of attack. If our cavalry get through they say that the Guards Division will go in behind them. I should much like to be somewhere near when the attack comes off. Perhaps I may be able to visit my own Brigade. I motored back very quickly from Bethune tonight.

8 September

'A long and weary day in the office', would sum up my day's work. I had long interviews with people and got through a great deal of work. With the exception of an hour and a half walk in the afternoon I was hardly out of the office. In the evening I had two of the chaplains to dinner. Griffiths*, who has been with his Division since November, is rather too old a man to be there and I have brought him in to send him down to the Base. After dinner I again went back and finished with my private letters. The War Office is a peculiar institution. It is the store house of red tape which ties up every source of supply from an eighty ton gun to a paper clip and from a Field Marshall to a drummer boy. The principle is never let anything go without

13   SAD 28/5/27. Gwynne noted that following things for discussion with the AG:
     1. Promotions.
     2. Rewards and Decorations.
     3. Transport of Chaplains [sic]
     4. Reinforcement Camps.
     5. Establishment.
     6. Indian Chaplains
     7. Territorials.
14   Lieutenant Colonel A. G. E. Egerton, Coldstream Guards.
15   Possibly Major P. A. Prescott-Roberts ASC who was on the staff at BEF Headquarters.
16   Possibly Lieutenant Colonel L. F. Green-Wilkinson.
17   Major General Colin John Mackenzie.
18   Possibly Captain H. W. Snow.

a fight. So one has to spit, scream, claw and bite like a tiger before it unlooses its grip. This is not congenial for me.

9 September

Worked very hard in the office all day except when I had a walk with Anderson* one of our chaplains whom I am bringing to take charge of the work in and around GHQ.

Ryall*, a man from the Indian Cavalry Division, came in reported that a Wesleyan was taking some of our parade services. We had Johnson (the brother of Leslie Johnson of the Oxfords)[19] in to dinner tonight.

10 September

At 7.30 we began our journey to Rouen and stopped at Abbeville to see the IGC[20] with Dr Simms*. I soon found out my ignorance about work in the field – the number of reinforcements etc. They were very kind to me and helped me to understand.

Dale[21] of Khartoum had lunch with me.

In the evening we arrived at Rouen about 7 pm and after a wash and change had dinner in the hotel where I was staying.

11 September

The chaplains met me at the Archbishop's Palace this morning at 8 am where we had a celebration of Holy Communion at which I gave and address on our work. I asked for their confidence and their prayers. We also had intercessions for the war.

At 9.15 we breakfasted in the Church Army Home in the town where I got to know some of the chaplains. An opportunity was given to every chaplain to have a talk with me and tell me all their desires and any other matters of wh. they wanted advice. I held a Confirmation in one of the hospitals where one of the nurses was confirmed with some of the patients. Two of the doctors I knew before, one O'Connor[22] was at Khartoum with me while the other O. C.[23] Riddick[24] was with me at No. 11 General. I attended two tea parties given by the Matrons of different hospitals and I confirmed two in the small chapel. There was quite a crowd in the YMCA tent at 8.30 at a devotional meeting which I addressed.

---

[19] 2nd Lieutenant John Leslie Johnston Ox & Bucks LI was killed on 12 May aged thirty. He was dean of Magdalen College, Oxford, and son of the Rev. Canon J. O. Johnston, chancellor of Lincoln Cathedral.
[20] Inspector general of the lines of communications.
[21] Unidentified.
[22] Unidentified.
[23] Officer commanding.
[24] Possibly Lieutenant Colonel G. B. Riddick, RAMC.

12 September

Today was not so crowded as an ordinary Sunday thanks to the skilful arranging of Thorold* the chaplain.

I celebrated the Holy Communion at 7.45 and spoke at the same place, the Archbishop's Chapel. Preached to a large congregation at 10 am after which I motored out to speak to about 3,000 men in the reinforcement camps. I had to settle a trouble after the service. Owing to lack of chaplains and some mismanagement some of the base depots have been ministered to by some excellent Presbyterian ministers, one of them so good that he was a real blessing to the permanent staff and persuaded some of them to go to their Communion. Now that we have more chaplains and can look after our own soldiers, the present chaplain, Campbell[25] and the senior officer are very unwilling to divide the service and wish to continue what they term a combined service. I called on my friends the Mourclans[26] who first put me up at Rouen in August 1915 [should this be 1914?]. Took a Confirmation of a boy in Hospital (47 wards) another at the YMCA and Hadow[27] came to dine.

13 September

Outside Rouen there is a hill called Bousecourt from wh. there is magnificent view of the city [and] of the River Seine. We passed this about 9.30 this morning and spent about a quarter of an hour admiring the scenery. We dashed over the ground at a great pace showing down as we drove through towns and villages. Instead of tall poplars or chestnuts or other trees wh. line the roads we motored through rows of apple trees for miles. The trees were laden sometimes with red apples wh. gave the mother tree and autumn glow. I ate some of these apples. Found them rather woody to the palette with not much juice wh. was the only thing one could swallow.

We reached Versailles around 2.30 and was shown round the huge hospital once used as a hotel. A young chaplain named Hope* is now working at the hospital. He took us over the grounds of the Palace wh. was the most magnificent I ever saw.

14 September

Last night after visiting the Versailles grounds we motored into Paris and stayed at the King Edward VII Hotel. I had a sumptuous room with bath room attached and dined wisely and well. Bennett*, the curate to Blunt[28] the Embassy Chaplain came in after dinner. At 9.30 we motored out to see the Motor Works where 800 ASC[29] men are employed and committed Bennett* to Major Organ[30] the Officer in Charge as my chaplain in Paris.

---

[25] Unidentified but he would appear to have been a Presbyterian chaplain.
[26] The name is unclear.
[27] Possibly Lieutenant Colonel A. Hadow.
[28] The Rev. A. S. V. Blunt*, chaplain to the British embassy in Paris 1912 to 1921.
[29] ASC.
[30] Probably Major C. A. Organ, ASC.

On the way back to GHQ we stopped at Beauvais for lunch and to view to the two great buildings – both chancels to would be cathedrals. One very old with beautiful glass, the other showed signs of being built piecemeal. Ruskin wrote *The Seven Lamps of Architecture* on this building. At Abbeville I had some business with Colonel Bunden.[31] Had a cup of tea and shoved along to S. Omer wh. we reached rather late owing to a punctured tyre.

15 September

A heap of letter enough to turn one's hair met me on arrival at the office today. But I didn't choose this job, but God my Father in spite of my failings and weaknesses chose me. So I looked up and faced it and found that it was not so formidable after all and tho' I had to spend most of the day in the office I cleared away the greater part of it before 11 at night. Fleming* stayed the night with us. He is S. Chaplain of the Guards Division and was with me near Bethune through the winter, and is one of the most capable of the regular chaplains. We talked till past midnight about the organisation of chaplains and talked over the number of chaplains required to each Division.

16 September

Two great mercies vouchsafed to me today. A good understanding with Dr Simms* the Principal Chaplain who agreed with me to send in our requisition for more chaplains separately. Otherwise there could be continual jarring, gangling and quarrelling; the other was the settling of a great difficulty at Boulogne where one of our chaplains came across one of the British officers in command of the Depot in wh. he worked. Thanks be to God the thing was settled very amicably and ended up by both sides shaking hands. I also confirmed four men in the hospital and visited another of my flock who happened to be lying ill in Lady Norman's Hospital.[32] I brought back from the Base a chaplain bound for the Guards Brigade reaching home about 8 pm.

17 September

In the first time for over a week I walked in the woods after a heavy morning in the office. Quite a lot of chaplains turned up. Gibbs* and Neville Talbot* and my friend Harry Blackburne* for the night. We are expecting Lord Grenfell[33] and Salisbury[34] from our Advisory Committee. I am very glad they are coming for it is time our dear old Church made a move for she has been terribly neglected – partly I think because we have not made use of our huge force to get our rights as the R.C.'s and

---

[31] The spelling of the name is uncertain, and he has not been identified.
[32] No. 4 (Red Cross) Hospital was run by Lady Norman but appears to have been also known as 'Sir Henry Norman's Hospital'. It was at Wimereux between Nov. 1914 and Dec. 1915.
[33] Field Marshal Francis Wallace Grenfell, 1st Baron Grenfell. He was an Anglican layman.
[34] James Gascoyne-Cecil, 4th marquess of Salisbury. He was an Anglican layman.

the Presbyterians have done.[35] Another late night. Blackburne* gave me valuable information about the work of chaplains. He is I think the best man in the field.

18 September

Lords Grenfell and Salisbury were in my office when I arrived after the 9 am intercessions. But they did not stay long as they had to go to meet Plumer[36] the 2nd Army General. I saw them afterwards at the C.Chief H.Quarters[37] and I told them all I knew about reinforcements and formations. I had to fly away in the afternoon, after a walk with Thorold* in the Gardens, to Etaples where I was due to take services etc., on the Sunday. The motor broke down thro' a punctured tyre near Boulogne and just before I reached H. Quarters Etaples. I dined with dear old Nason[38] at his mess – he is now commanding the reinforcement camps at Etaples.

19 September

I stayed at Le Touquet about 8 miles from Etaples at the Hotel Anglais.[39] I motored into Etaples and took the Celebration at 7.30 in the Church Army Hut. After breakfast I preached to a large number of nurses, wounded, doctors, etc., in the YMCA. I lunched with Mrs Stoneham[40] whose husband owns almost all of Le Touquet. I held a Confirmation at 3.30 and another at 5.30 in a hospital and ended up preaching to a large crowd of Doctors, Nurses, Orderlies, Patients, etc., in the open air after which I dined with the Hospital staff to wh. Mr. Thompson[41] belonged. I met a doctor who was in charge of young Battenberg in Khartoum many years ago.

20 September

Dorothy Anson[42] came to breakfast at 8.45 to my hotel, but I had already taken a service before she came, at the American Hospital Etaples.[43] At 11 I held a devotional meeting at the Church Army Hut for all the chaplains and spent a long time afterwards seeing chaplains individually until 1.40 when I took Day* to lunch at

---

[35] SAD 28/5/32. Gwynne wrote in his notebook that he needed to consult Drury* and Thorold* on the following matters that were likely to be raised with the committee members:

> 1. Decentralising (3 Senior Chaplains) [presumably for each army].
> 2. Transport (motors for these).
> 3. Establishment. One Battalion.
> 4. Reinforcements (pressing).
> 5. DCG's Funds for furniture for churches, harmoniums, equipment for Institutes and cars for chaplains.

It is of note that even at this stage Gwynne was thinking about an establishment of a chaplain to each battalion. Such a move would require a considerable increase in the number of chaplains.

[36] General Herbert Plumer, commander Second Army.

[37] Presumably the commander in chief's headquarters, i.e. GHQ.

[38] Colonel Fortesque J. Nason.

[39] The hotel was close to the casino.

[40] Allen Stoneham had bought much of the land in Le Touquet in 1902.

[41] Possibly Major Douglas Stokes Brownlie Thompson.

[42] Probably Dorothy S. Anson, Voluntary Aid Detachment, British Red Cross.

[43] No. 22 General Hospital at Camiers, north of Etaples, was, from June 1915, staffed by Americans from Harvard Medical School.

the Anglais and had a long talk afterwards. I motored into Boulogne in the afternoon and interviewed Harwood* about the proposed payment of chaplains and Mrs Northcote[44] for her husband who was out.

21 September

After office work today I motored to Ramnelhelst not far from Ypres where I held a devotional meeting for the clergy of XVII Division.[45] Saw a bombardment from a hill with General Pilcher[46] and held a Confirmation of about 15 men, which was very impressive.

22 September[47]

[No entry.]

23 September

Worked in the office until one o'clock and motored out to Stizeel where I confirmed five excellent fellows belonging to the Army Service Corpse. Matthews* and Tuckey* also attended. I reached home at 8.

24 September

After my routine work in the office I motored to Sailly le Bac the Head Quarters of the VIII Division. Unfortunately I had two burst tyres on the way and in consequence I was more than an hour late. I was very glad I was just in time to stop the men marching off into the Trenches. I confirmed 270 men, very fine men they were too, all dead in earnest and keen as they make them. I heard they were going to attack in full strength all along the line so I motored to Bethune to get alongside my old Brigade. Dined with No. 5 F.A.[48] and slept in the car.

25 September

About 5 am we drove our motor to Beuvry having some trouble with the guard on the Bridge on the Beuvry road. But I magnified my office and passed through. At the Dressing Station at Le Preolan I left the car and walked along the canal bank across Westminster Bridge past Home Farm to Windy Corner where I saw some of the 5th F.A. I reached the Worcester through the communication Trench. The bombardment

44 Possibly the wife of the Rev. P. M. Northcote* who was appointed a temporary chaplain on 14 July 1915.

45 SAD 28/5/34 includes a reference to VII Div. From a reference to the commander being General Sir Thomas Capper, this would appear to be correct and the diary entry wrong. Gwynne also noted that Milner White*, who was serving in 7 Div wished to be transferred to a CCS.

46 Major General Thomas David Pilcher.

47 SAD 8/5/34 contains a note of prayers at 6.15 followed by planning before preparation for a confirmation service at 12.30.

48 No. 5 FA

from 4 am had been terrific and the Oxfords and HLI had taken 3 and 3 of the German lines respectively. The Gas (our own) had come back from Givenchy and stopped the advance of the Glasgow Highlanders. I tried to cheer the Worcesters and saw the Adjutant, Ralston,[49] who is now reported missing and Wainman[50] who I heard since has been killed. One of the Worcesters I saw in the Hospital at Lillers said he was shot in the thigh and through his chest and taking his book from his pocket he crossed his arms and died. I had to come away at 8.30, but managed to bring six of the slightly wounded back in the car to Bethune. After a meal and a wash at H. Quarters I motored to Abbeville saw Burden[51] about reinforcements and after tea went on to Le Treport where I led a most striking confirming at wh. God Himself was present to Bless.

26 September

Le Treport is one of the prettiest of many watering places on the coast. Three hospitals are on the top of the cliff, two under canvas and thither in a large hotel.

I celebrated the Holy Communion at 7.45 and confirmed more candidates in the Hospital, after wh. I preached in the YMCA hut. The wounded began to come in about 12 and continued to do so the whole afternoon. There were four men of my old Brigade in the Hospital. Wilson[52] of the Glasgow Highlanders, McBeath of 2nd HLI,[53] Shepherd of the Worcesters[54] and Tulden Davies[55] who comes from Charlie's parish.[56] In consequence of the inrush of wounded a proposed 2 pm service was put off and I visited Lady Gladstone's Hospital[57] instead. I motored through Abbeville as I had to report the CO's of the Canadian Hospital for tyrannising over one of our chaplains.[58]

---

[49] Captain C. H. Ralston, adjutant 2 WORCS. He took part in the battle and returned from it.
[50] Captain P. S. G. Wainman attached 2 WORCS. died on 25 Sept. 1915 and is buried at Vermelles Cemetery.
[51] Unidentified.
[52] 2nd Lieutenant J. Wilson, who had injured a knee during the fighting.
[53] There were several men with the surname McBeath in the HLI.
[54] Unidentified.
[55] Unidentified.
[56] The Rev. C. Gwynne was vicar of Neston.
[57] He may have confused the name of No. 10 'Lady Murray's' Hospital which was at Le Treport.
[58] SAD 28/5/35 contained a record of a complaint from a chaplain named Abbott* about conditions at no. 2 Canadian Hospital. It was alleged that,

> CO 2 Canadian Hospital does not seem to understand his position in regard to his Church of England chaplain.
> 1. Ordered his moustache to be grown.
> 2. Ordered him to turn out on parade and was ordered to appear in the Orderly Room on failing to do so on one occasion.
> 3. Interferes with the services by objecting to the use of the Prayer Book at services.
> 4. Orders the chaplain to give a weekly report of nominal roll of patients visited during the week and when this was done the report was sent back desiring him to add whether he had prayed with them, given Communion or other spiritual consolation.

This appeared to have been an extreme case of the relationship between a military commander trying to impose his control on a chaplain who would be working independently.

27 September

After a few hours in the office I made my way to Bethune stopping on the way to see the Clearing Hospital at Lillers where I saw some three or four of the Worcesters. I also visited Clerques and found in the Clearing Hospital there Griffiths,[59] one of the officers of the Worcesters who had been shot through the lung and the side. I then motored to Le Preolan and had tea with the 5th Brigade Head Quarters. I heard that we had lost some of the ground we had gained but that the Guards were attacking tonight. After tea I went back through Clerques and Lillers and found the streets and roads covered with rolling wagons, Red Cross ambulances, etc., etc., who kept us late on the road. I managed to get back to S. Omer about 8.

28 September

The great fight is still waging. The French have broken through at Souchez and the ground we gained has been made good, for the Guards took Hill 70[60] at a loss of 500 wh. does not seem very many these days.

After a few hours in the office I motored to Merville and visited our two hospitals and the chaplains, Goddard* and Fitzgerald*. I found 'Laddie' Gordon[61] who commanded the Leicesters through most of the war and was once the Governor of Babr el Glazelle.[62] He was shot in the arm in a terrible fight when his Batallion had to retire with others after having taken two lines of Trenches. I reached Bethune but found the Oxfords still in the Trenches and the Worcesters too far away so I returned to Clerques and saw Griffiths[63] after wh. I visited the No. 6 C.C. Station at [Lillers].

29 September

S. Michael's Day. I celebrated Holy Communion at the little church room at wh. six were present. Drury* came back off leave last night. I did a couple of hours work with him before going out towards the front to see what I could do in this great fight. I stopped and saw Broadbent*, chaplain at No. 6 Clearing Hospital [Lillers] and Capt. Griffiths of the Worcesters who seemed much better. I stopped at Clerques and saw Selwyn* who had a cup of tea in my car. I did not reach Bethune until late in the afternoon but managed to see the Oxfords before they went to Essars.

I tried to find the Guards at Nouex la Mines and Sailly la Bac but failed. I hear they were attacking again tonight and they got the Germans on the run.

---

59 TNA, WO 95/1351/1, the war diary of 2 WORCS, lists a Lieutenant Giffey as having been wounded.
60 This position was fought for during the battle of Loos. It was between Loos and Lens.
61 Lieutenant Colonel Herbert 'Laddie' Gordon had commanded the 2nd Batallion of the Leicestershire Regiment (2 Leicesters) from Jan. 1915.
62 Bahr-el-Ghazal.
63 Possibly the Rev. J. W. Griffiths*.

30 September

Most of the morning I spent looking at the Casualty Clearing Stations behind the line and visited Lapugnoy and Lozinghem where are two chaplains are working there. There had been a great rush but things were easier when I arrived though many more were expected. I met one of my friends, George Armitage,[64] who had been commanding 1 KRR's[65] in the fight. He told me how the Batallion operating on his right gave way before the German who were chasing them down a Trench when a young officer named Hall[66] of his Battalion let fly with Bombs found in the German Trenches wh. were much superior to ours and arrested their triumph by plumping bombs amongst them whilst another young officer led about 20 KRR's across the open and beat them back with their bayonets. I motored to Doullens, but found Waldegrave* out and motored back hoping to find news of the Guards. Very sad news. Major Egerton[67] killed and Laurence[68] and Guy Durrell[69] wounded. The Welsh Guards took Hill 70[70] in great style and over running it we[re] badly cut up by the enemy.

---

[64] Probably Lieutenant Colonel George Armytage.

[65] 1st Battalion of the King's Royal Rifle Corps.

[66] Unidentified.

[67] Lieutenant Colonel A. G. E. Egerton, Coldstream Guards, was killed in action on 29 Sept. 1915 and is buried in Vermelles Cemetery.

[68] Possibly Captain L. E. H. M. Darell, although his first name was Lionel.

[69] Probably Captain G. M. Darell.

[70] The Welsh Guards had been formed in Mar. 1915 and arrived in France in Sept. 1915. The battle of Loos was the first battle in which the regiment was engaged.

October 1915

There are a number of references to the situation in the Balkans. Bulgaria declared war on Serbia on 12 October. The British and French decided to send a force to assist the Serbians. The line of approach was to be through Greece, at that time neutral. Pressure to allow the Allies passage through Greece resulted in a crisis, of which Gwynne makes mention. The BEF continued to be engaged in the battle of Loos until it was ended on 8 October. In the middle of the month, he paid another visit to London to meet with the CG.

1 October

Reached home about 8.15 pm last night. Worked in the office from 9.30 – 1.15 and interviewed Foster*, Bowden* and Masters*, the latter is applying for a commission in our Department. At 2.15 I motored to Poperinghe to try and find the Robin Hoods[1] but could not get along side of their Division and had to come away without seeing them. The Chauffeur made some tea in … village about 5 miles N. West of Poperinghe and I reached S. Omer soon after 7.30. A Major Jacob RAMC[2] came to dinner with us tonight and after he went all four of us, Anderson*, Drury*, Thorold* and I thrashed out the question of promotion.

2 October

The visitors today were Leslie Johnson[3] the brother of the Dean of Magdalen who was I fear lost at Richebourg on May 14 also a chaplain returned from sick leave. I worked at my office until 12 then started with Thorold* for the 37th Division. Stopped on the way and had a short walk and some tea. We reached the chateau of the H. Quarters about 5.40 and after leaving my kit proceeded to S. Venant where I held a Confirmation for about 30 men.

On my return to Head Quarters I found Gleichen[4] the Div. General was an old friend of mine in the Sudan and Airey[5] of the ASC made himself known at once. Savage,[6]

---

[1] The 7th (Robin Hood) Battalion of the Sherwood Foresters (Nottinghamshire & Derbyshire Regiment) were popularly known as the 'Robin Hoods'.
[2] Possibly Major A. H. Jacob RAMC.
[3] 2nd Lieutenant John Leslie Johnston Ox & Bucks LI was killed on 12 May 1915 aged thirty. He was dean of Magdalen College, Oxford, and son of the Rev. Canon J. O. Johnston, chancellor of Lincoln Cathedral.
[4] Major General Lord Albert Edward Wilfred Gleichen, commander 37 Div.
[5] Possibly Lieutenant Colonel R. B. Airey, ASC.
[6] Possibly Captain M. B. Savage.

Bainbridge[7] and Charlton[8] are all in the Division as well as Toke[9] of the Welsh. So I am amongst my friends.

3 October

Gleichen[10] came with his ADC[11] to the service at 7.30. I was glad to see him as our Senior Chaplain said he never came to Holy Communion. I preached to some gunners at their wagon lines at 10 am. They did not seem to be as stalwart looking as the regulars. I went out by motor to a service for one the Brigades and felt much happier in speaking for the men were allowed to sit down. The Brigadier said promotion was rapid on one condition only – and that was that you should keep alive. Only do that and you must get promotion. At the next service for gunners and infantry Charlton,[12] one of my old Sudan flock was present and God helped me to speak to them man to man. This Division, the 37th is one of 'K's' and will very soon be put into the fight. So thinking of the recent fighting and our awful losses, I spoke to them of the noble cause for wh. they were out here to fight. I lunched with another old friend of mine, Bainbridge,[13] who is Brigadier of the 110 and saw Savage[14] there. After lunch in came MacIntosh[15] another intimate member of my flock and we talked of the old days in the Sudan. Carlton[16] and MacIntosh[17] took me to see some guns wh. had to be dug in because of being placed in rather an Oxford place.[18] Yet another old friend, 'Bob' Cochrane[19] who played cricket and golf with me at home turned up here. I had tea with him. I hung around or candidates for Confirmation from the Trenches. I did them in two batches of four. Thorold* and I stayed the night at Doullens.

4 October

Today I heard from Charlie of Nellie Miller's[20] death. This will be a greater blow to our Nellie than to any one for they were such friends. Poor Nellie Miller did not have the happiest life but I do believe she had the happiest time when she was with us in Father and Mother's time. Thorold* and I started back from Doullens about 10 reaching S. Omer soon after one.

I visited No. 10 Stationary Hospital at 5.30 doing some work in the office from 3 pm. I attended a concert this Evening and said a few words to the men congratulating

---

7   Probably Brigadier General E. G. J. Bainbridge, commander 110 Bde.
8   Unidentified.
9   Major R. T. Toke.
10   Major General Lord Albert Edward Wilfred Gleichen, commander 37 Div.
11   Unidentified.
12   Unidentified.
13   Brigadier General Edmund Guy Julloch Bainbridge.
14   Unidentified.
15   Unidentified.
16   Unidentified.
17   Unidentified.
18   The meaning of the phrase is unknown.
19   Possibly Captain R. W. Cochrane.
20   Sister-in-law of the Rev. C. B. Gwynne.

the performers and promising that our chaplains were going to do great things for them in the Winter. I also distributed two prizes to prize winners in a draughts competition. There seems to be a lull in the fighting but one hears very little news at H. Quarters. It is however possible that the French and us are getting ready for another break through somewhere.

5 October

Most of the day I spent at the office except part of the afternoon when I visited three of the Worcesters in Hospital and another, Griffiths,[21] in the Officers Hospital. Four very nice chaplains came along to H. Quarters and were promptly sent to their posts, one Ainsworth* to a Cavalry Regiment[22] and the other three to hospitals. There was a good deal of heavy gun firing in the East this morning and the afternoon. Bulgaria hangs in the Balance if she sides with Austria and Germany there is no doubt that she goes against the wishes of the majority of her people – betrayed by the German Ferdinand.[23] Tuckey* one of our Senior Chaplains came and spent the night, but he kept me up till the early hours of the morning talking over things wh. could be settled in half an hour. However these are trials of the new job.

6 October

Another busy day at Head Quarters. Two important jobs I had in hand.

1. The answering of the important questions asked by the Advisory Committee.
2. The shuffling and sifting of the names of the chaplains for rewards, etc.[24]

I don't suppose I had ½ hours exercise during the whole day. I dined at night with Sloggett,[25] a friend of Howell's and director of the RAMC in France. An old friend of mine, Bobbie Black[26] is his ADC.

The news of the enforced resignation of Venezelas[27] arrived tonight. We still hope Bulgaria will be too frightened to move.

---

[21] Possibly Lieutenant Giffey.
[22] SAD 28/1/6 indicated that Ainsworth* was posted to 2 Indian Cav Div on a temporary basis. It made no mention of chaplains posted to medical units.
[23] Bulgaria joined the other Central Powers in Sept. 1915.
[24] SAD 28/5/39 noted that Gwynne intended to raise the questions of promotions. He believed that some mistakes had been made and that there had been dissatisfaction in the resulting appointments as senior chaplains at divisional level. He planned to argue that, as deputy chaplain general, he should see the lists for promotions.
[25] Lieutenant General Sir Arthur Thomas Sloggett, director general of medical services BEF.
[26] Possibly Captain George Balfour Black who was the commander of Haig's mounted escort between Apr. 1915 and Jan. 18.
[27] Eleftherios Venizelos, prime minister of Greece resigned on 7 Oct. 1915 over disagreement about the entry of Greece into the war on the side of the Allies.

7 October

Chaplains are coming out in great numbers. 10 have arrived and will be posted to their work before tomorrow night. I posted four this morning[28] before I motored to Vlamertinge – between Ypres and Poperinghe to take a Confirmation there. I lunched with Major Gen Cashman[29] who was most kind and there was Ironsides[30] whom I used to know at Boulogne. There were about 31 confirmed and amongst them policemen from Ypres. I came back in the car and slept part of the way reaching home about 8. I went after dinner to the office and worked until twelve.

8 October

Saw six chaplains today before starting for Havre.[31] I had a very full morning writing letters and interviewing people amongst whom was a chaplain to a Cavalry Brigade of the Indian Corps who seemed indignant at being removed to the infantry. Started at 12 for Havre and came through Abbeville and Dieppe. Had a break down and ran out of petrol just before we reached Havre. Col Welsh[32] and Mr Longstaff[33] with whom I stayed came to dinner at the hotel after which I motored to Mr. Longstaff's house who received me very kindly.

9 October

We had our celebration, devotional meeting and intercession for the war all in one today at 8 am in the English Church at Havre.[34] All the chaplains were there as well as the Scripture Readers[35] and Mr. Pilkington[36] of the YMCA.

We had breakfast together after wh. I saw each one separately.

I lunched with the … [37] – English people with whom Parry Evans* lives. There I met Col. Scholfield[38] and Col. Welsh[39] as well as the other residents.

---

[28] SAD 28/1/6 indicated that the following were posted on 7 Oct., Browne (not identified) temporarily to B Echelon Cavalry FA in 2 Div, Adderley (the Rev. C. Adderley*) to No. 8 CCS at Bailleul, Lee (possibly the Rev. T. A. Lee* who was available from 5 Oct.) and Robinson (possibly the Rev. P. F. Robinson*) to Etaples.

[29] Possible Colonel Sir W. B. Leishman, late RAMC.

[30] Possibly Captain A. E. Ironside, RAMC.

[31] SAD 28/1/6 indicated that the following chaplains, Harper* (not identified), Milner (the Rev. G. R. Milner*) and Johnston (probably the Rev. G. F. Johnstone*) were posted to Le Havre, Aldred (the Rev. C. C. Aldred*) and Davies (possibly the Rev. G. A. Davies*) to Boulogne and Cook (the Rev. A. M. Cook*) to North Midlands CCS.

[32] Unidentified.

[33] Possibly William Langstaff after whom the Rugby stadium in Le Havre was named.

[34] The English church at Le Havre was Holy Trinity and the chaplain the Rev. E. D. Burridge.

[35] Members of the Army Scripture Readers (ASR) organization.

[36] Mr L. G. Pilkington worked at Le Havre for the YMCA.

[37] The name is unclear.

[38] Possibly Lieutenant Colonel G. P. Scholfield.

[39] Unidentified.

I spent the afternoon looking around the docks and spent some time with my old friend Douglas[40] who showed us over the supplies stores in a dock shed wh. is supposed to be the largest in the world.

I dined at the Langstaffs[41] and met some young officers.

10 October

On Sunday morning I started the day with a celebration at the English Church where 32 persons celebrated.

The cinema at the Reinforcement Camp was crowded (1500 men) at 10.30 when I spoke to the men about the war.

One man, Thomas Evans,[42] a Welshman was confirmed by me at 12.

At lunch with Kitson Clarke[43] I met an old friend, Major Greenwood[44] who commanded 5th RE Field Company when I first went to the 5th Brigade. Winnie[45] was out when I called on him at the Camp of Instruction and I had tea at the large Casino Hotel now turned into a hospital where I met, amongst other, Miss Steere[46] and Miss Wood Martin[47] a sister of an old friend of mine who was killed in the war.

11 October

My own car having broken down Parry Evans* lent me his – wh. was much slower than mine – Girdlestone* came with us to take the car back again. It took us from 10.00 am to 11.15 pm to get back to GHQ. At Dieppe I stopped and lunched with Alfred Acland[48] who commands a Remount Depot. He seemed fairly sick at the unbusiness way things are carried out by the Army. We stopped again at Abbeville to send a telegram to Montreuil where I was expected to take a confirmation and once to put the light in good running order.[49]

I arrived at 11.15 and had a large supper before going to bed about 12.

---

[40] Unidentified.
[41] Possibly the home of William Langstaff.
[42] Unidentified.
[43] Probably Lieutenant Colonel E. Kitson Clark, officer commanding 49 Div depot.
[44] Probably Major H. S. Greenwood.
[45] Major G. S. Whinney.
[46] There were at least four nurses with the surname Steer.
[47] Possibly the sister of Captain F. Wood-Martin, killed 17 Feb. 1915.
[48] Colonel Alfred Dyke Acland who commanded the Remount depot. Remounts were replacement horses.
[49] Presumably one of the head lights of the car.

12 October

Another long day writing with the exception of an hours walk in the afternoon. The two important matters I had to settle today was [*sic*] the question of the question of the Canadian chaplains[50] and the posting of a man at the Duchess of Westminster's hospital,[51] Le Touquet in place of the present resident chaplain who is said to have bored the officers to tears in their hospital.

Canon Scott* of the Canadian Division is very anxious to get his full complement of chaplains for the Canadians who are very short. There is no discipline or method in the selection or management in the Canadian Contingent who seem to be a law unto themselves.

Gen. Lowther,[52] a great friend of Howell's came to dinner with me in the Evening.

13 October

Our house is very comfortable – situated in a long street (165 Rue Dunkirk.) The name of the house is the Hotel de Ventes an auctioneers house and passage.[53] We are fitting up out one of the Rooms as a Chapel where we can have prayers read every evening and a celebration whenever we are so inclined. My work in the office is very strenuous when I am at it, these days. An old missionary Finnimore* of Ceylon was posted to a very pretty place, La Treport. I motored to take confirmations to a Casualty Clearing Hospital near Poperinghe and another at a Hospital on the top of a hill, Castre Oatre which is a monastery of the Jesuits now turned into use for the wounded.[54] Here I saw Thwaites of Jerusalem[55] and had a chat with him. There was a fierce bombardment going on near the line. Probably our Bombardment to employ enemy while we attack elsewhere.

14 October

After very strenuous work in the office I motored out about one to Sailly la Bac to the VIII Division where I confirmed about 100 men mostly of the Worcesters and Rifle Brigade. Ted Talbot*, Hargreaves*, Goudge*, Tyrwhit*, Conran* and Marshall[56] were present at the Confirmation. This division has produced more candidates for confirmation than any other in France. After the Confirmation I had tea

---

50 The Canadian chaplaincy arrangements in the early years of the war were unsatisfactory
51 No. 1 (British Red Cross) Hospital at Le Touquet was known as 'The Duchess of Westminster's'. SAD 28/1/7 indicated that Harvey (possibly the Rev. J. G. Harvey) was posted to Etaples to serve at the Duchess of Westminster's Hospital.
52 Brigadier General Cecil Lowther had commanded 1 (Guards) Bde.
53 Ventes is the French for 'sales'.
54 It is possible that the reference is to the abbey on the Mont de Cats. It is not certain that there was a medical facility there in 1915.
55 Unidentified.
56 There were two regular chaplains with this surname. It is unclear which is meant.

with the Artillery General and Oxley,[57] an old Sudan friend who is now a Brigadier in this Division.

I then motored to Merville and confirmed 8 candidates, one a man in his bed. Father Fitzgerald* who is of the Mirfield Brotherhood,[58] he is a remarkable man and has powers of healing. He told me of the case of a lad whose nerves were completely upset by the shock of his wound and was calmed to sleep by prayer and soothing.

15 October

I held a short devotional meeting today with the VII Division.

I had an unfortunate duty to perform to remove a man who was evidently drinking too much. We must remove him from his post and probably out of the country.[59]

I had a blessed time and a good talk with each of the chaplains of the Division.

Trench* and Milner White* are the two outstanding men of this Division.

I motored back through Bethune which had been badly shelled during the counter attack on Loos by the German on wh. occasion they lost so heavily coming on in dense masses and being mowed down in thousands. It is said they lost 20,000 in the attack.

16 October

The whole of the day I spent in the 1st Canadian Division where Canon Scott* has recently been made Senior Chaplain.

I called on General Currie,[60] a straight forward Canadian with whom I discussed the questions of chaplains. I then met one or two of them, but Canon Scott* who is a poet of no mean order and a bit of a dreamer is not much of an organiser. I found things in a deplorable state. Our C. of E. chaplains have very little conception of their work. Methodists take our Communion Service and read our Prayer Book prayers absolution, etc., as if they were ordained members of our Church.

I took Mitchell,[61] a Canadian, with me.

---

57 Brigadier General R. S. Oxley.
58 The Mirfield Brotherhood was a reference to members of the Anglican Community of the Resurrection. Founded in Oxford in 1892, the mother house moved to Mirfield in Yorkshire in 1898.
59 SAD 28/5/40 noted that a chaplain had had a charge made against him both by an FA and the divisional staff. The issue was that of drinking excessively. The intention was to post the chaplain to a base location. SAD 28/1/7 indicated that on 14 Oct. a decision had been made to post Williams to England. This might be the same person.
60 Major General Arthur Currie.
61 Unidentified.

17 October 20th Sunday after Trinity

A blessed Sunday. I celebrated H.C. at the Upper Church when Christ was truly present and impacted Himself into my Soul. My trouble is that I do not do more in His strength. At the 9.30 Service in the large Hall of the lower club I preached on 'life' and felt the Power in my heart as I spoke. A real thick of love and affection came into my heart s I looked at the throng of eager faces of the Artists Corps who filled the Hall. I had to work for a couple of hours in the office after wh. I motored to Montreuil to confirm 4 young English girls, the children of an Artist who lives there.

I preached to a crowded Church in Boulogne,[62] where our chaplains are doing excellent work. I saw Harwood* and Blucoe*. Supped with Harwoods* and caught the boat at 10 to Folkestone.

18 October

Stayed the night at the Pavilion Hotel[63] and had a quiet morning until 11, writing, reading and making plans for work in London.[64]

I strolled over the hill on the right of the town, walked past the Flying Park and returned down the cliff along the shore reaching the hotel about 3.30 when I had tea.

I travelled to Charing X[65] by the 5.13 and saw Howell in his office.

19 October

Saw the C.G. at the War Office at 10 am and immediately proceeded with the C.G. to the Club to talk over matters.[66] After lunch I was to see Stevens[67] then I dined with Howell at the Bath Club and worked until 5 after wh. I accompanied the C.G. to his cure for Neuritis in the oven baths, where he kept his elbow baked for ½ hour. We then caught the train to Northwood at 6.13.

---

[62] Holy Trinity, Boulogne.

[63] Opened in 1843 and a leading hotel in the town until it was mostly demolished in 1982.

[64] SAD 28/5/41 indicated that Gwynne spent the day at Dover. This would appear to be a mistake. Wherever he spent the day, he commented in his notebook that he had had a truly blessed time. He felt that 'God walked and talked with me and even if the Devil could break into the conversation I would not listen.'

[65] Charing Cross station.

[66] SAD 28/5/42 contained a list of points that Gwynne wish to raise with the chaplain general. These were Promotions, the Indian Corps, Canadians, Advisory Committee, assistant, visits by the CG, a new establishment for the lines of communication, position regarding marriages within the British lines and that there would be no permanent appointments to commissions in the AChD during the war. He also noted that the subjects of uniform for ASRs and payment for the use of civilian church buildings needed to be discussed.

[67] Possibly the Rt Rev. Thomas Stevens, bishop of Barking.

20 October

Another morning at the War Office. Saw Ch. Army at the Club and lunched at the Club. Spent the night at Northwood.

21 October

I had an interview with Carlile[68] of the Church Army at the Club and went through the proposed building schemes for the Expeditionary Force and Salisbury[69] at the War Office and went through the proposed Report of the Advisory Committee. I had lunch with Dick and Harry at the Norfolk Hotel and heard all the family news. I gave Harry Tea and sent him off at Charing Cross after wh. I visited Kemp[70] in Hospital at the Military Hospital Grosvenor Road. Caught the 6.53 to Northwood where Mitchell[71] was also travelling.

22 October

We came up by the 8.57 train from Northwood and I had a long interview with Lord Salisbury and Brade.[72] MacInnes[73] called just before we started for Lambeth where we met the two Archbishops and talked over the various matters among chaplains. I liked the Arch. of York[74] better than ever before. He was most sympathetic about the attack on the Chaplains' Dep. in *The Scotsman*, but I have no objection to it at all.[75]

Howell and Dick came to tea and I walked back with Howell to the office.

The Bulgarian traitorous break with her old friends the Russians causes a lot of bother and worry to H. who condemns our lamentable lack of policy. Stayed at Northwood.

23 October

Came up to town about 9.30. Wrote down in the club all things we have tried to do and for wh. we ought to press. I also wrote a long letter to Lord Salisbury.

I started for France at 2, met McCracken[76] on board who told me how splendidly his Division had done. Thorold* met me at Boulogne. I motored up to GHQ by about 8.

---

68 The Rev. Prebendary W. Carlile, founder of the CA. They provided canteens to support the troops.
69 4th marquess of Salisbury.
70 Unidentified.
71 The Rev. P. R. Mitchell*.
72 Sir Reginald Brade, permanent under-secretary of state for war.
73 The Rt Rev. Rennie MacInnes, bishop of Jerusalem.
74 The archbishop of York, the Rt Rev. C. G. Lang.
75 Many in the Church of Scotland were angry about Gwynne being given a higher relative rank than Simms, the principal chaplain. This anger found expression in columns of *The Scotsman*.
76 Major General Frederick William Nicholas McCracken, commander 15 (Scottish) Div.

24 October

Stayed in bed all day to get rid of a slight chill in the stomach, but in the afternoon I went thro' all my letters with Thorold* and wrote my diary up to date. I had a trying time at home and feel that I have great need of the Guidance of God to help me through.

25 October

Quite fit again this morning, which began, continued and ended in rain. I spent all the morning in the office until 2. Going through heaps of letters etc. One result of the work so far has been procuring permission for the Scripture Readers[77] to wear uniform, wh. seems a small thing after so many weeks toil. I read and wrote and walked out for an hour this afternoon. I posted two men today,[78] one to GHQ troops – Turnbull*, and a voluble Irishman name Montmorency* to Etaples. Both these men came to dinner afterwards.

26 October

The anniversary of the opening of the Soldiers Institute Boulogne took place this Evening. I motored down in the afternoon and had a long talk with Archdeacon Southwell* (now made Senior Chaplain of the Boulogne Base) before the Concert.

The Col. Com. the Base, Wilberforce,[79] spoke thanking the ladies and so did I telling them how nobly and well our ladies worked to give them a good home. We thought of those who had passed through the Institute now passed to their rest saying what rewards had come to us through the death of our heroes. John MacMillan*, the Archbishop's chaplain who had come out as a Chaplain to the Forces accompanied me to GHQ.

27 October

The rain has brought down most of the leaves from the trees and carpeted the forest with blood red. There was something very really but inarticulately sad in the twilight this evening when MacMillan* and I walked in the forest. There still linger the autumn tints on the mass of trees in Claire Marais but they are daily vanishing into the grey of winter. I managed to get through a fair amount of work this afternoon

---

[77] ASR belonged to an organization that had been founded in 1818. They were former soldiers who carried out missionary work in the army. They continue to the present as members of the Soldiers' and Airmen's Scripture Readers' Association.

[78] SAD 28/1/8 listed twelve chaplains that were to be posted. The list did not include either Turnbull* or Montmorency*.

[79] Brigadier General Herbert William Wilberforce, commander Boulogne base.

and talked over matters with Col. Lambert[80] who has been appointed to look after the Church affairs. I met Sir William Robertson[81] by appointment this afternoon.[82]

28 October

MacMillan* left today for Etaples to take Clayton's* place at a hospital. I had a walk out in the afternoon and returned to work again in the Evening at 6. The office work is very heavy these days and I must try and learn to pray more to square with my work.[83]

29 October

Early Communion at 7.15 in the Temporary Church and back to the office until late. Cummings came to dine with Evans tonight and we talked long on the old days in the Sudan. The Balkan question is a good deal in the minds of people who almost entirely blame the Government for her unpreparedness. The King had an accident today reviewing his troops. He fell from his horse.[84]

The Abbe la Mayor came to lunch with Tuckey* today. He is a priest, the Mayor of Hazebrouck and member of the French Senate, for retaining the last name he was indicted by the Pope. Harry Blackburne* came today and had a walk with me in the gardens coming back to tea with me and stayed the night.

30 October

Harry Blackburne* went off this morning and at 12 after office work I went to Dieppe. I had a walk and tea in the woods of Hesdin and arrived at Dieppe about 5 pm in time for tea. Alfred Acland[85] put me up very comfortably in his house.

---

[80] Possibly Colonel E P. Lambert, Royal Artillery.
[81] QMG of the BEF.
[82] SAD 28/5/46 noted that Gwynne intended to raise the following with Robertson,

> 1. The Question of Decentralisation
>> a. Can I give temporary rank?
>> b. To give my best men a chance.
> 3. CA Huts for the front.
> 4. Is it wise to put them up now? If so ought I to do it through the AG or the Corps Generals?

[83] SAD 28/5/46 showed that Gwynne was preparing a paper for the AG. It was to cover

> 1. Promotion Scheme noting the Temporary Promotions that had caused great dissatisfaction.
> 2. Chaplains to the Red Cross and other voluntary organisations.
> 3. Establishment for the Lines of Communications.
> 4. Contracts of Chaplains.
> 5. Is it possible to make use of some of our best men by giving them temp. rank?
> 6. Huts for the front.

Under this was added in pencil, 'Motors for Senior Chaplains.' These were presumably the appointments at army headquarters.
[84] King George V was visiting the BEF when the accident occurred.
[85] Colonel Alfred Dyke Acland.

31 October

Worked fairly hard all day. Preached 5 times and talked to the men in the hut about the Sudan and the front in the afternoon. Interviewed Irwin* and Mr Merk* of the English church who is in charge of the S.P.G.[86] Church here. I preached in the Evening at the Church and saw a nurse, Sister Louise,[87] who comes from Charlie's parish.[88] In the afternoon I walked over the golf course wh. gave me a chance of exercise wh. as a rule I do not get these days. Acland[89] and I both agreed about some of the wasters in the army. They not only waste themselves but waste public money. In Dieppe it is said that £30,000 could have been saved if the work had been done by contract.

[86] Society for the Propagation of the Gospel.
[87] Unidentified. There were a large number of nurses with the Christian name 'Louise'.
[88] Neston, in the Wirral.
[89] Colonel Alfred Dyke Acland.

November 1915

With winter approaching, large-scale battles came to a halt on the Western Front. There were numerous raids and skirmishes. Casualties still resulted from artillery fire. During the month, Gwynne continued his series of visits. He often met men whom he had known whilst in the Sudan.

1 November All Saints Day

The R.C.'s.[1] played the low down today and tried to stop my attendance at a religious ceremony at Hazebrouck, where the Mayor who is also a member of the French Senate and priest under interdict from the Pope for refusing to leave the French Parliament. I went to the cemetery with, many of our chaplains in a long procession, our soldiers and their band in a long procession of the inhabitants, and listened to a long and dramatic speech of Abbe La Mayor, after which I spoke of All Saints Day and what our heroes have died for. It poured with rain during the Ceremony. Thorold* and I dined with Abbe La Mayor afterwards and talked long and keenly on the questions of the Day.

2 November

Another down pour of rain today. It hardly left off for a moment from morn till night. I could not go out even for a short walk but spent most of my time either in the office or at the house. In the Evening, Doctor Simms*, the Principal Chaplain came to dinner and stayed until late. I had a long talk about our differences and the bad blood shown in the *Scotsman*[2] to wh. he said he had nothing to say.

3 November

After office saw the A.G. with whom I talked over many things. He honestly thinks the nonconformists are increased in the army and the C. of E. decreased. I did not concur in an establishment for the Reinforcement Camp. Came home feeling we are rather 'drowned' by the Denomination. I walked with one, Stone*, in the afternoon and worked a bit in the office before dinner.

4 November

The chaplains are finding out now that one is glad to see them. Two turned up from the front, good fatherly figures who had a lot to say about their Divisions. I had

---

[1] He may have been implying that the senior catholic chaplain in the BEF was the one who tried to stop his attendance.

[2] *The Scotsman*, during the autumn of 1915, had printed several articles and letters that attacked Gwynne's seniority over the Presbyterian principal chaplain, the Rev. Dr J. Simms*.

a walk in the woods again for an hour this afternoon and had a blessed time looking at sights which are new to me – the last flash of autumn against a reddish sky all reflected in a flooded field along a tree lined road with a sweep towards light. I worked hard in the office until 8 and found the Talbots[3] had arrived. We had a long talk about Unity and the work in the Divisions, altogether a most profitable afternoon.

5 November

A Life Guardsman[4] was brought in by Pelling* today to be confirmed. He was a very fine fellow, earnest and most keen about religion. He was confirmed in our little chapel which we have made out of our drawing room down stairs. I almost envied him his enthusiasm and keenness wh. he showed.

6 November

After office I started for 27th Division wh. is a long way down the line near Amiens. It took about 5 hours with a break of about an hour for tea. Verney Asser[5] one of my old friends from the Sudan came to dinner at 8 pm also the brother of White Thompson[6] was there. Everybody most kind. General Milne[7] was away.

7 November

A small room in the chateaux which does duty for offices was our chapel this morning at 8 am. At 10 I preached to a large parade of 80th Brigade Troops. Verney Asser was there. At 11.15 I went to Sieux where I had a large parade on the side of the hill and the pulpit was a platform cut out of the side of a slope.

I confirmed about 120 in a small school room, for too small for the purpose. It was very hearty. After tea I motored with Stephenson[8] and Brook* to the Div. Ammunition Column where I preached to about 200 men. Amongst the officers was the brother of Col. Edge[9] of the 52nd.

8 November

At nine a.m. I left Bovelles stopping at S. Pol for lunch and at Amiens to see the Cathedral. I went through S. Omer where I did a couple of hours in the office before dinner.

---

3   The Rev. E. K.* and the Rev. N. S.* Talbot.
4   The Life Guards were the senior regiment of the Household Cavalry.
5   Major Verney Asser, Royal Artillery.
6   This might possibly be Major Douglas Stokes Brownlie Thompson, RAMC.
7   Major General George Milne, commander 27 Div.
8   There were two chaplains with this surname.
9   Unidentified.

9 November

In addition to the work of the office I motored to the 19th Division but found my visit was in vain as Walkey* the Senior Chaplain was away and I was not expected, but the General[10] gave me lunch and I spent the rest of the afternoon looking up George Armitage[11] and Potter,[12] who was out, and Lewis.[13]

10 November

Office work too up the greater part of the day but I managed a little recreation by taking out Drury* into some woods near where we saw a small deer and lots of pheasants. We saw a steam thresher with all the farm hands employed feeding and clearing full sacks and packing them on waggons.

11 November

My old Division, the 2nd, is still at Bethune. I dined with the Headquarters and saw some of my old friends there. I confirmed about a hundred in the chapel of the Theatre at 2.30. Had a short meeting with the clergy and tea at the Hotel de France[14] after wh. we had short intercession. I interviewed poor Cass[15] afterwards and Milner White*.

12 November

I was away from the office at 11.30 to lunch at the Head Q. of the IX Division. On my arrival after many vicissitudes (for I lost my way and the roads were bad) I found with General Furze[16] and General Chichester[17] who was my old Brigade General in the 2nd Division.

There was a pavement of stones in a sea of mud and a very narrow pavement at that if the car left the Pavement – we were done. I motored to Bailleul after lunch and met my old friend Gen. Sir Chas. Fergusson[18] who kindly out me up. He had kindly asked Griffiths,[19] one of our chaplains, to tea to meet me. I had a short walk in the evening.

---

[10]   Major General C. Fasken, commander 19 Div.
[11]   Lieutenant Colonel G. A. Armytage.
[12]   Lieutenant H. C. Potter.
[13]   Brigadier General F. G. Lewis.
[14]   Hotel in Bethune.
[15]   Possibly the Rev. A. W. Cassan*.
[16]   Major General William Thomas Furse, commander 9 (Scottish) Div.
[17]   Possibly Brigadier General Arlington Augustus Chichester, Distinguished Service Order.
[18]   Lieutenant General Sir Charles Fergusson, Bt, commander II Corps.
[19]   Possibly the Rev. J. W. Griffiths*.

14 November

I had a blessed Sunday. At 7.30 we had a celebration in a town hall at wh. about 30 or 40 were present. At 9.30 I preached in the same hall to a large number of officers and men. Motored out directly after to Canadian Ammunition Column at Meteren where I spoke about the Fatherhood of God. After lunch at the Casualty Clearing Station where I met Sir Armstrong Bowlby[20] I preached in a large hall of another hospital at 2.30 and at another at 4 pm.

I met a good number of people at tea in Griffiths'[21] rooms and preached at a voluntary service in the Evening. Sir Charles Fergusson who was very ill with a cold could not come out. I dined with the Corps Headquarters Mess in the Evening.

15 November

[No entry.][22]

16 November

Nothing out of the ordinary happened today except a very pleasant walk in the woods. I motored back from Ballieul about 9. There are a fair number of chaplains passing through now, and a very good lot they are. I was distressed to find quite by accident that I no right to have Senior Chaplains at Armies. Tonight General Carter[23] and Thresher[24] came to dinner.

17 November

Carey*, one of the best of our chaplains came today to talk over the question of going to Rouen. Lewis[25] also came to the office and dined. Two others from the Sudan also dined with me and gave me great pleasure. I confirmed about 15 candidates this afternoon and one in hospital. The candidates came to tea with me afterwards.

18 November

A fair number of chaplains are going through to their work.[26] Some of them very useful men and some of course [feeble and indifferent – crossed through] not so good but all are very keen and earnest about their work. As soon as office was over

---

[20] Colonel Sir A. A. Bowlby.
[21] Unidentified.
[22] SAD 28/1/10 indicated that four chaplains were posted on 15 Nov. 1915.
[23] Brigadier General George Tupper Campbell Carter-Campbell, commander 94 Bde.
[24] Possibly Major J. H. Thresher.
[25] Brigadier General F. G. Lewis.
[26] SAD 28/1/11 listed nine chaplains on 17 Nov. 1915 and seven on 18 Nov. 1915.

I motored with Carey* down to Doullens, interviewed Hamilton,[27] and attended a concert at Stone's* CC Station and gave dinner to Acland[28] – a friend of Sterry.[29]

19 November

Drove out in the car to Boulogne to see Allenby[30] the 3rd Army Commander who was very nice to me and promised to put up Day* with Army Head Quarters. I then found Hamilton[31] and looked over his CC Station and called on King[32] of the North Irish (Ulster Division). Returning to Doullens with Stone* I lunched at his unit and motored back to S. Omer in 2½ hours.

20 November

I was off again early this morning to visit the North Midland Division where a good many of my old boys from Derby and Notts. I spoke to a few of the Robin Hoods in a barn and lunched with the officers afterwards. I had a walk with Hales* in the afternoon and called at my old billet in Zelobes[33] dining with Hales Brigade HQ.

21 November

I had a blessed Sunday. We began with a celebration of H.C. in the small room of a brewery and spoke to the Derby boys in one of the larger rooms. I then preached in another Barn and spoke of the Cross of Christ to Derbyshire lads. Next I addressed Div. Head Q. where General S. Wortley[34] was present after which I spoke to gunners in a farmyard where Col. Blake[35] commanded. I then lunched with the Heavies and took Hales* and Connor* back to G.H.Q.

22 November

Hales* went away today after a very happy time together. I have known him now for 30 years. He is a simple earnest Xtian. Knows many of the people and incidents of my Nottingham days.

In the afternoon I went out to some new woods I had never seen before and had a quiet walk and prayer after which I worked in the office.

[27] Possibly the Rev. L. Hamilton*.
[28] Colonel A. D. Acland.
[29] Unidentified.
[30] General Edmund Henry Hynman Allenby, commander Third Army.
[31] Unidentified.
[32] Probably the Rev. S. W. King*.
[33] Zelobes Indian Cemetery is north-east of Bethune on a minor road, the D 945.
[34] Major General Montagu-Stuart-Wortley, commander 46 (North Midland) Div.
[35] Possibly Major William Henry Blake.

23 November

I worked until 1. Came in to coffee and fruit and motored out to Tuckey* to one of the Motor Am. Parks[36] where I addressed and confirmed confirmation candidates. Capt. Boyle[37] in charge of this column married one of the Smiths of Wilford[38] and is uncle to Allan Tritton.[39] I got get back until 7 pm at night.

24 November

After office I motored out to Abele to see General Fenshaw[40] commanding the 5th Corps and arranged with him about placing a man at Head Quarters of the Corps. He seemed very keen and earnest about out work. I had tea in the car on my way home near Cassells. Saw Blackburne* at Tea and did a couple of hours work in the office before Dinner. Bunbury[41] dined.

25 November

I had a long interview with MacCready[42] this morning and thrashed out a good many things. I had to do rather a hard thing. One Hill* – a Senior Chaplain at Rouen – a good and earnest man – with the heart and mind of a louse – no sympathy with wh. his school calls heretics. I had to move him. He kicked. I persisted. So he has to go home. Malcolm Wingate[43] called and had tea. Day* of Etaples spent the night.

26 November

After office, at 10.30 took Day* down to Etaples. Lunched in a small restaurant with Goudge* and Day*. Motored to Boulogne and walked out with Southwell* in the cemetery and had a long talk about the work. Promised to leave Balleine* and Masters* for the winter, and MacNutt*. Met the C.G. Found George Armitage[44] and Dent[45] stranded took them up in our car. The 'Chauffeur' took time to get out of the town so I went outside – very cold – reached G.H.Q. about 8.45. Fox* also dined.

27 November

Leaving the C.G to come on at G.H.Q I took George Armitage and Dent as far as Mazingarbe having missed Harry Blackburn* at Noeux-les-Mines. I had a

---

36 Probably 'Motor Ambulance Park'.
37 Possibly Captain M. Boyle, ASC.
38 Wilford was a village that has now been incorporated into Nottingham. The family are unidentified.
39 Possibly Captain A. G. Tritton.
40 Lieutenant General H. D. Fanshawe, commander V Corps.
41 Brigadier General C. V. Bunbury, provost marshal of BEF.
42 The AG of the BEF and thus responsible for the administration of the chaplains.
43 Possibly Lieutenant Malcolm Wingate Royal Engineers who served with 26 Field Company which was in 1 Div.
44 Brigadier General G. A. Armytage.
45 Unidentified.

confirmation in the Theatre at the latter place for about 70 men of the Kings Territorials and others. I dined at Harry Blackburne's* mess and had a long talk with
Harry Blackburne* in my room. It froze hard all day.

28 November

The frost was so hard last night that the oil froze in the pipes, and we had an anxious
time thawing the pipes ready for an early start at 7.30. We held a service of Holy
Communion at 8 am in the H.Q of the 1st Division. I preached to a large number of
troops in a huge warehouse. Saw Bircham[46] of the 1 KRR.[47] I called on different
people before lunch. At 1.45 I preached in a cellar at Philosphe.[48] Took a Confirmation in an office. Had tea with Bircham.[49] Preached at 6 pm service and motored
back to G.H.Q by 9 pm.

29 November

After office work at 1 motored to Lillers where the C.G. took a confirmation for
the 47th Division at 3.30 between 40 – 50 chaplains came in from the surrounding
country to a devotional meeting in the chapel Theatre after wh. I gave them Tea at
the Hotel de France. At 5.30 we motored back to G.H.Q worked in the office and
dined with the Q.M.G.

30 November

S. Andrews Day commenced with Holy Communion in the Upper Chapel and held
intercession at 9. After office, at 12 I motored with the C.G. to Cassells where we
lunched with Plumer[50] and met Jack Collins[51] at the Head Quarters of the Army.
I also saw Swift[52] at the Casino at Cassells. After lunch we motored to Merville
where we had another devotional service in the chapel of No. 7 CC Stationary H.
Major Macnalty[53] an old friend from the Sudan gave us tea in his mess afterwards.
We reached GHQ about 7.

---

[46] Possibly Major H. F. W. Bircham.
[47] The 1st Battalion of the King's Royal Rifle Corps.
[48] Now site of a CWGC cemetery.
[49] Possibly Major H. F. W. Bircham.
[50] General Herbert Plumer, commander Second Army.
[51] Unidentified.
[52] Possibly Major H. F. Swift.
[53] Possibly Major A. G. P. McNalty, ASC, assistant director of supplies and transport.

December 1915

Gwynne continued his work with the BEF until, on 30 December, he returned to England for a period of leave. He was to spend the New Year with his family.

1 December

The Corps Commander of the Canadian Contingent[1] received us at lunch at Bailleul where we met amongst others Canon Almond* who is now appointed the Corpse chaplain. At 3.30 we had a splendid gathering of the chaplains, 56 in number, 1st in the chapel of No. 2 Clearing Hospital where Griffiths[2] is attached and 2nd tea in the hospital place at our disposal by the Colonel.

2 December

After an early lunch with the C.G. motored into Rummelhelst[3] and confirmed 98 candidates in the YMCA hut. Amongst the candidates was a Sergeant who has served in Khartoum in the early days, with the Fusiliers. I saw quite a number of the chaplains at the Confirmation and had tea afterwards with the General of the 3rd Division, General Haldane.[4]

3 December

The C.G. left for Amiens about 8.30 am. I spent a great part of the day in the office – entertained Hales*, Col. Wraith.[5] I confirmed afterwards, and Crosse*. Guinness* came to report before going to E. Africa. I had a long talk and walk with him in the afternoon and worked for a couple of hours in the office before dinner. Dined alone with Drury*. Chief item of news tonight was Italy signing the compact not to make a separate peace.

4 December

Did a long morning in the office until 1. Wrote to Nellie[6] and read before I went to Montreuil by motor. A heavy rain storm met us on the way, but I managed to get out and walk a couple of miles. I reached Montreuil about 7.30 and put up for the night with Col. Bamfield[7] of the Indian Hospital.[8]

---

[1] Lieutenant General Edwin Alfred Hervey Alderson.
[2] There were several chaplains with this surname.
[3] The location is unclear.
[4] Major General James Aylmer Lowthorpe Haldane, commander 3 Div.
[5] Possibly Colonel E. A. Wraith.
[6] Member of Gwynne's family.
[7] Probably Lieutenant Colonel Harold John Kinahan Bamfield, Indian Medical Service.
[8] It is not clear to which Hospital he was referring.

5 December

We had a service for one of the Parks[9] at 9 and a celebration afterwards. I preached on the Fatherhood of God at nearly all the services. Kempe* motored with me to two more services before lunch after wh. we motored to Somme where I had a walk before motoring to a park close to G.H.Q. where I had another service. Simms* and two chaplains dined and Harry Lewis[10] came in and had a talk afterwards. To bed late.

6 December

Quite a good number of chaplains turned up to intercession this morning at 9. Some of them were new men from England.[11] It poured with rain nearly all day. I braved the elements by walking out for the greater part of the afternoon. I wrote some letters and finished my office work before 8. Bunbury[12] was coming to dinner, but wrote saying he was too ill. Turner[13] came and talked about the Sudan.

7 December

The C.G. went from Boulogne today. So I made an early start from G.H.Q. and saw him before the boat went at 10 am. I afterwards had a long talk with Archdeacon Southwell* about the work at Boulogne. On the way back I walked 3 Kilometres for exercise – about the average of what I do every day. It rained again in the afternoon and I had none. The AG talked to me about the use of French Churches.

8 December

Things are not going so well in the Near East. Owing to our bungling the Anglo French force is being threatened by the Bulgarians. After the work in the office I walked out through the woods and saw a couple of small deer and a long flight of birds.

Burrows[14] came in and stayed the night with me. We had a good long talk afterwards.

9 December

I took Burrows* back to his unit near Reninhelst this afternoon. We stopped the Car and walked. I called on the 5th Corps and found Gen. Hoskins[15] who was in the

9   Term for a depot where engineer or other materiel was stored.
10   Brigadier General F. G. Lewis, commander 142 Bde.
11   SAD 28/1/13 listed seven names, Buchanon (might be the Buchanan referred to in entry for 9 Dec.) who was to go to 3 Div, Lewis (the Rev. T. F. O. Lewis*) to Boulogne, Rider (the Rev. J. D. S. Rider*) to Le Havre, Mourilyan (the Rev. C. A. Mourilyan*) and Browne (possibly the Rev. P. F. Browne*) to Etaples, Walker (the Rev. J. M. S. Walker*) to 21 CCS and Hazeldine (the Rev. F. J. Hazeldine*) to 20 Div.
12   Brigadier General C. V. Bunbury, provost marshal.
13   Possibly Colonel E. V. Turner.
14   There were several chaplains with that name.
15   Brigadier General Arthur Reginald Hoskins, commander 8 Bde.

Egyptian Army. Also saw Gen. Haldane[16] and talked about the chaplain Buchanan*. The motor stuck in the mud on the way to the Chaplains' Mess. Did not get back until nearly 8. (The Boarderers[17] pulled my car out of the mud.)

10 December

I spent the whole day in the trenches near Looz.[18] It cleared up splendidly as soon as we reached Mazingarbe. I saw the 11th Kings, Sussex and some of the Welsh as cheery as could be in their trenches. I also saw the deep German trenches about 30 feet under the ground and beautifully built.

11 December

In addition to the work in the office today I visited the sick men in the Hospital and motored to the 1st Division Head Quarters at La Gorgue. I took a Confirmation in a loft lighted dimly with candles and lamps. There were about 20. I dined at the Div. Head Quarters afterwards where the Prince of Wales is attached.

Bad news from Salonika – the British badly attacked, one Brigade cut up.[19]

12 December

Holy Communion at 8 am only 3 present beside Fleming* and self. I preached to a large congregation at 9.30 with the band of the Grenadiers. At 10.30 I preached to some of the 3rd Coldstreams and took another Confirmation at 11 in the presence of about 200 men. I saw my old friends George Lane[20] and Skeffington Smith.[21] Said a few words to a company of the Welsh Guards before they went into the Trenches. Had tea with Harking,[22] commanding 11th Corps and brought Ponsonby[23] back with me to G.H.Q. Thorpe[24] and Heywood[25] also dined.

13 December

I worked hard at the office – morning and evening, and had a visit from Dr Simms* where we discussed the YMCA question.[26] A good walk in the Clairmarais woods in a beautiful twilight, the myriad twigs which formed a lovely haze. The softened

---

[16] General Sir James Aylmer Lowthorpe Haldane, commander 6 Corps.
[17] Probably the Border Regiment.
[18] Loos.
[19] The reference may be to the action, in late Nov., at Kasturino, which forced a British withdrawal.
[20] Unidentified.
[21] Possibly Lieutenant Colonel R. C. E. Skeffington-Smyth.
[22] General Sir Richard Cyril Byrne Haking, commander XI Corps.
[23] Brigadier General John Ponsonby, an officer in the Coldstream Guards, commander 1 Bde.
[24] There were several officers with this surname.
[25] Possibly Major Cecil P. Heywood, Coldstream Guards
[26] The continuing problem of the relationship between the YMCA and members of the AChD over the conduct of services.

crimson sunset touched with bluish green and the Moon shining forth in the cold crisp air before daylight died added great pleasure to the exercise. Better news tonight.

14 December

Worked hard in the morning, and afterwards went out to find Bowman*,[27] Geoffrey Fielding[28] and Eaddie Gordon,[29] who is now a Brigadier. I found the first and the last but the middle named had gone out of hospital cured. I brought Gordon[30] in to dinner and Bunbury[31] came after dinner and had a talk. Prebendary Carlisle[32] came to stay.

15 December

I had a long conversation with the A.G. this morning about the YMCA huts and the relation of our chaplains and their workers. After the interview, I motored to Strazeele where I left the Prebendary and his son. I lunched with General Fergusson[33] and took a confirmation for the Canadians – and interviewed the Chief Canadian Chaplain.

16 December

Wilson Carlisle went to Ypres today with Stanley.[34] I had a dull day, office until 3 and a walk out in the dusk along a mean suburb and back again to tea and office. The news seems fairly good. Germany must be pretty rotten inside and hopes to make a diversion all over the world.

17 December

The Church Hut was opened here today in the Presence of quite a number of British officer and others. General Wigham[35] in the absence of Sir W. Robertson[36] declared it open. I offered prayers and Wilson Carlisle made an excellent speech.

18 December

My departure for the V Division was delayed by a call from the A.G to a meeting

---

[27] Possibly the Rev. H. Bowman.
[28] Major General Sir Geoffrey Percy Thynne Feilding, commander 1 (Guards) Div.
[29] Brigadier General H. Gordon.
[30] Unidentified.
[31] Brigadier General C. V. Bunbury, provost marshal BEF.
[32] The Rev. Prebendary W. Carlile, founder of the CA.
[33] Lieutenant General Charles Fergusson, commander II Corps.
[34] Possibly the Rev. W. Stanley.
[35] Major General Robert Dundas Whigham was deputy to William Robertson as chief of staff BEF.
[36] General Sir William Robertson, chief of staff BEF, was about to be appointed Chief of the Imperial General Staff.

to talk over YMCA matters with Simms* and McCowan.[37] I did not start south until 6 nor arrive at Etenham until 11.30 when all had gone to bed. I met Stockwell's[38] brother at Heilly.

19 December

I had a blessed time today. The rooms were very small in wh. to hold the service, far too small to hold the people who wanted to come. I found some of the Iniskillings[39] of the 5th Brigade at the morning service at Siesanne.[40] After lunch with the Brigade I went up to Manancourt wh. was being shelled and saw the small church and the cemetery. I confirmed in the afternoon a large number of Cheshires[41] and R.F.A.[42] and in the evening confirmed at Bray and saw the wonderful underground chapel. Dined at Div. H. Quarters.

20 December

At 9.30 I went round the Trenches with the Div. General and from an observing post saw the German lines stretching miles beyond. The morning was unfortunately misty and the glorious view was mostly hidden. After lunch I motored back to GHQ by 7.10 and did a job of work in the office before dinner.

21 December

I held a confirmation for the Cavalry this afternoon at Head Quarters. About 49 were confirmed and sat down to tea in our new hall wh. was lighted up for the purpose. Andrew Balfour[43] came in after dinner and had a long talk about the Sudan.

22 December

Early before the service of intercession I started for the 3rd Army and lunched with Maxse[44] who commands the V Division. I had lunch with him and his staff. He knows Howell well and thought he was the finest that ever stepped. I confirmed about 40 in the afternoon and after tea with the clergy I called on Ruthven[45] at a Brigade H. Quarters and drove to Boulogne where I found Allenby[46] the Army CO and Day* the Senior Chaplain.

---

37 Unidentified.
38 Unidentified.
39 Presumably some members of the battalion whom Gwynne had known. 2 INNISKILLINGS had left 5 Bde in July 1915.
40 Location unidentified.
41 The Cheshire Regiment.
42 Royal Field Artillery.
43 Lieutenant Colonel Andrew Balfour, RAMC, who had worked in the Sudan between 1902 and 1913.
44 Major General Ivor Maxse was commander of 18 (Eastern) Div and not 5 Div.
45 There were a few officers with this surname.
46 General Edmund Allenby, commander Third Army.

23 December

I left Army HQ at 8.45 and went straight through to Nieppe and lunched with Doran[47] Div. Gen. of the XXV Division. I found I knew his brother in the Sudan. After lunch I confirmed about 30 men of this Division, after wh. I had a devotional meeting and tea with the chaplains of the Division. I motored back to the office by 7.20. I had a Sudanese dinner tonight and collected, Heywood,[48] Turner,[49] Ensor,[50] Cummins,[51] Jack Collins,[52] Edgeworth[53] and Malcolm Wingate[54] and bucked about the Sudan.[55]

24 December

Worked at the office all the morning and went out with Thorold* in the afternoon to the woods and worked before dinner.[56] At 7 all our staff came to dinner. At 7 pm the clerks and orderlies, Thorold* and I had our Xmas dinner – a really happy family. After dinner I sat down to prepare my sermon for Xmas Day.

25 December – Xmas Day

Xmas Day. I began with a celebration of the Holy Communion at wh. about 30 officers of GHQ were present. At 9.30 I preached to a crowded audience in the large new Church Institute amongst whom was the new C in C[57] and his staff and a large number of officers of GHQ. I worked at the office till one and after lunch motored to Noeux les Mines beyond Bethune and had tea with Harry[58] and his mess. I returned and preached at Bethune a 6. I saw Potter[59] – had a long talk and dined in the 2nd Division Mess.

26 December

Took a celebration at 8 and visited Harley Street[60] at 9.30. Saw some of the Oxfords and H.L.I. also saw Riley[61] and Scott[62] at the Corner.

---

47 Major General Beauchamp John Colclough Doran, commander 25 Div.
48 Lieutenant Colonel C. P. Heywood.
49 Possibly Colonel E. V. Turner.
50 Colonel H. Ensor.
51 Possibly Colonel S. L. Cummins.
52 Unidentified.
53 Major K. E. Edgeworth.
54 Lieutenant M. Wingate.
55 This group of individuals are mentioned regularly and were important to Gwynne.
56 SAD 28/1/15 listed 'Studdart Kennedy [sic]' as posted to Rouen.
57 General Douglas Haig had been appointed commander in chief of the BEF on 10 Dec. 1915.
58 Captain H. V. Gwynne.
59 Lieutenant Colonel H. C. Potter.
60 The name of a trench.
61 Unidentified.
62 Unidentified.

I addressed the men of the Irish Horse in a hut surrounded by mud. The piano was out of tune in one hymn and in the next we started too high. After lunch I preached in the Cinema Church – had tea with Potter[63] and reached S. Omer about 6.30

27 December

The Bishop of Oxford[64] came last night too late to preach as advertised. I took him today to Plug Street Trenches where we were shewn over by Lord Harris.[65] Soon we were only about 35 yards from the German in places. We also inspected the Trench Mortars, the rifle grenades and the new parapet. They are wonderful Trenches and one can approach them straight through the woods. After lunch with Gen. Doran[66] at the H.Q. of the 25th we returned to GHQ.

28 December

All day I spent in the office with the exception of a short walk in the afternoon. The Bishop of Ox. Visited the hospital at Argue this morning and went out with General Stopford[67] in the afternoon. In the evening Beattie[68] and Gort[69] came to dinner while the Bishop of Ox. went to dinner with the Q.M.G, Maxwell.[70] I am preparing as well as I can (for my visit home.)

29 December

Harry[71] turned up with his friend Wood in time for dinner. The Bishop of Ox. went to the Guards Division while I spent nearly the whole day in the office except for an hour in the afternoon when I went out with Thorold* for a walk. Timins* turned up this afternoon and told me all the doings of the 2nd Cavalry Dismounted Division. Drury* turned up from leave.

30 December

I took Harry by motor to Boulogne to catch the 10.30 boat, but found that the boat did not sail until 1.40 I spent the morning with Archdeacon Southwell* and found out all the news of the place. We not reach London until 6.30 too late to go down to Dunmow so I put Harry up at the Club, gave him dinner and went to a cinema.

---

[63] Lieutenant Colonel H. C. Potter.
[64] The Rt Rev. Charles Gore.
[65] Possibly the 4th Lord Harris, who had raised the 10th Battalion of the Queen's Own (Royal West Kent Regiment) as a 'Pals' battalion.
[66] Major General Beauchamp John Colclough Doran, commander 25 Div.
[67] Possibly Brigadier General Lionel Stopford.
[68] Possibly Lieutenant Colonel W. J. K. Beattie.
[69] Possibly Major John Standish Surtees Prendergast Vereker, 6th Viscount Gort, who had been brigade major of 4 (Guards) Bde and was serving at HQ BEF in Dec. 1915.
[70] Lieutenant General R. C. Maxwell.
[71] Captain H. V. Gwynne.

31 December

I had a blessed time at the Abbey service this morning – after shopping at the Stores.[72] I prepared for my holiday and made my requests in the private chapel. Harry and I caught the 12 train to Dunmow. Howell fetched us. Edie took me up in her small motor. After lunch I went to the Rectory, saw Dick, Nellie, Poppie and Gwent. I took young Donald Snow[73] out to the Park with a rifle in the hope of shooting something.[74]

[72] Probably the 'Army & Navy Stores', in Victoria Street, Westminster. It was originally a Co-operative Society set up, in 1871, by a group of Royal Navy and army officers. It is now part of the House of Frazer Group.
[73] Unidentified.
[74] The New Year was spent with the Rev. R. L. Gwynne and other members of the Gwynne family.

January 1916

January remained a month of relative quiet for the BEF. Gwynne was on leave in England until the 8th. During that time, he spent time with the CG at his home in Norwood. He joined with the Reverend Dr J. Simms, the principal chaplain, in a complaint to the AG about instructions being given to chaplains without the knowledge or permission of their respective offices. The question of who exercised authority over a chaplain was a matter of concern for the churches. The reference to the town of Kut was to the British force that had been besieged in the town since 7 December 1915.

1 January

Holy Communion at 8 am with Dick and the girls. It poured with rain, but Howell, Edie and I motored to see the Stackpoole's[1] for lunch. They have a very nice house and seemed very pleased to see us. In the afternoon on our return Howell and I went for a long walk in the Park and visited the game keeper to see about ferreting for rabbits.

2 January

I had a blessed Sunday. Early in the morning I went to the Holy Communion and preached in Dick's Church on S. Paul's epistle to the Romans. The whole creation groaning etc.[2] In the afternoon I spent quietly in the Rectory and had a walk out before tea. I preached again at the Evening Service on Ps LXXI, 'If ye had hearkened not my voice. I should soon have put thine enemies to confusion.'[3] I had supper with the Mawbyns[4] and good talk with Howell and Harry afterwards.

3 January

Dick and I walked in the Park all morning and met Nellie and the girls taking the air.

And in the afternoon while Howell and Donald Snow[5] beat the bounds in the glebe, Harry and I had a shot at the birds – none of us were clever enough to bring one down.

---

1 Unidentified.
2 Romans
3 The text is unclear. It does not appear to be from Psalm 71 but might be from Psalm 81 verses 14 and 15 in the Book of Common Prayer. 'O that my people would have hearkened unto me: for if Israel had walked in my ways, I should soon have put down their enemies: and turned my hand against their adversaries.'
4 Country home of Howell Gwynne.
5 Unidentified.

4 January

Charlie arrived yesterday afternoon. I walked towards Dunmow in the Evening. This morning we had some ferreting with dogs – a poor miserable sport wh. soon sickened me – so Charlie and I went out for a long walk and talk all over the park. In the afternoon we had another shoot over the glebe without much result. Harry left tonight.

5 January

Dick, Charlie and I walked out in the morning over the Park and returned to lunch at Edie's. While Charlie and I had a long walk over to Great Easton, saw the Church and walked back to the Rectory to tea. In the Evening we all dined at the Mawbyns.[6]

6 January

Poppy, Donald and I journeyed to London. After seeing Poppy off at Euston I went to the W.O. Lunched with the C.G. at the Army & Navy Senior.[7] Worked at the War Office. Saw Col. Cleeve[8] about the Scripture Readers[9] and spent the night at Northwood with the C.G.

7 January

Maurice Buxton[10] spent the night with C.G. and self. In London at the W.O. all day. Lunched with Canon Pearce[11] at Westminster and in the Evening went down again to Northwood. Saw Shaw[12] at Westminster Abbey and took him out to tea afterwards.

8 January

Crossed over to France. Rather rough. Met on board Gower Rees*. Archdeacon Southwell* met me and took me to the Dervaux.[13] Visited Bate* and Wiley[14] in the hospital and dined with Archdeacon Southwell* and Lister[15] and Cunningham[16] at night.[17]

---

[6] Unidentified.
[7] The Club was then based in Pall Mall in a building now housing the Institute of Directors.
[8] Colonel Stewart D. Cleeve.
[9] Former soldiers who were employed as ASRs. There was an issue about their wearing uniform.
[10] Unidentified.
[11] The Rev. Ernest Pearce, canon of Westminster.
[12] Possibly the same Shaw who was mentioned in the entry for 26 July 1915.
[13] Hotel at Boulogne.
[14] Possibly Captain H. O. Wiley.
[15] Possibly Lieutenant Colonel A. H. Lister.
[16] There were several officers with this surname.
[17] It is noteworthy that there is no reference to the death in action of the Rev. James Robert Stewart* who was killed on 2 Jan. 1916. See entry for 8 Aug. 1915.

9 January

Took the celebration at 8 am.

Preached at S. Johns at 11. Archdeacon Southwell* lunched with me at the Dervaux,[18] visited Wiley[19] in the afternoon and motored to GHQ in the Evening where I dined alone.

10 January

Got into my stride very quickly today as men are coming out apace to full up our new Establishment. Went out to the flying Corps[20] with the Bishop of Birmingham[21] and shewn over the Aerodrome by Laurence,[22] a Corpse [Corps] leader.

11 January

The Bp. of B. started for Abbeville today. Posted a large number of men to their new places. Fleming* turned up this Evening and kept me up late at night.

12 January

Worked hard at the office. Walked out in the afternoon round the aerodrome and the cemetery and called on Maxwell the Q.M.G.[23] and had tea with him afterwards.

13 January

Worked in the office until 11. Motored to Etaples. Held a devotional meeting to which all the Non. Com and others were invited and gave them lunch afterwards.

Confirmed in the American Hospital at 3 and motored back to GHQ by 8. Dined with Sir Douglas Haigh[24] and very much encouraged by his sympathy he shewed in the work of the chaplains. After dinner he walked into the room where a large number of officers were assembled and before them all he said, 'You know Bishop I am one of those who have great belief in prayer.' I cannot express the encouragement all this was to me. He asked me to come and see him whenever I wanted anything. Ben O'Rorke*[25] came and dined with me at my house and slept the night.

---

[18] Hotel at Boulogne.
[19] Possibly Captain H. O. Wiley.
[20] RFC.
[21] The Rt Rev. Henry Wakefield.
[22] Possibly Captain G. A. K. Lawrence.
[23] Lieutenant General R. C. Maxwell.
[24] General Sir Douglas Haig, who had recently replaced General John French in Command of the BEF.
[25] The Rev. B. G. O'Rorke.

14 January

Drury* walked out with me in the Clairmarais this afternoon though it was rather dirty under foot [Ben O'Rorke* came – these words are crossed out] and tried to avoid as far as possible the subject of the Department.

15 January

Started for Havre[26] soon after 10.30. Stopped at Abbeville for half an hour and travelled along without a break reaching Havre soon after 6.30. I saw Hills[27] dining with some of his friends. Parry Evans* dined with me.

16 January

Preached at a Voluntary Service at one of the Hangers at 7.30. At 9.30 spoke to the Printers,[28] and after that to a large service arranged by Hills[29] and Duffus[30] in their large Hanger at 12. Lunched with Parry Evans'* hosts and took a confirmation at 3.30. Opened a small room attached to the Henderson[31] – built by Garwood's[32] friends. At 6 spoke to remounts and I preached to the Mechanical Transport. Dined with the Horse Transport up at the Camp. To bed at 10.

17 January

At 8 am had a celebration of the Holy Communion at the English Church.[33] All of the chaplains and some of the Scripture Readers came. I gave an address on the bigness of our Mission to preach Christ as God, to try to be big hearted for His sake, to preach big things to inspire our flock to fight for the Kingdom of God.

I saw the chaplains one by one after Breakfast and then spoke to the Scripture Readers. At 12.30 I went to see Asser[34] in his office before lunching with him. It was a great pleasure to see him again. Parry Evans* motored me over to Etretat by 3 where I confirmed men from No. 1 Hospital – was shown over the hospital by the C.O. and the Matron. Had tea with the staff and motored back in time to have a walk along the Pier before going to dinner with Duffus[35] and Hills[36] in a small old fashioned restaurant in the lower part of the town where I met Asser,[37] a naval

---

[26] The port of Le Havre contained many units by late 1915. A fictional account of chaplaincy in the port can be found in R. Keable's, *Simon called Peter* (London, 1921).

[27] Possibly Major C. E. Hills, ASC.

[28] The ASC were responsible for military printing.

[29] Unidentified.

[30] Lieutenant Colonel F. F. Duffus, ASC.

[31] A Church of England hut for the use of troops.

[32] Possibly Captain H. P. Garwood, Royal Artillery.

[33] Holy Trinity was the English church in Le Havre.

[34] Brigadier General J. J. Asser.

[35] Lieutenant Colonel F. F. Duffus, ASC.

[36] Possibly Major C. E. Hills, ASC.

[37] Brigadier General J. J Asser.

Captain and Mrs Pitt,[38] a French naval officer's wife. We had a musical evening in the upper room where some of the Paris opera performed.

18 January

I breakfasted with Hills[39] at his hotel at 8.30 and was shewn over the Bakeries and labourers quarters of the A.S.C under his control. Saw some of the training of reinforcements under Whynnie[40] which included a bombing attack witnessed by J.J. Asser. I threw a few bombs myself before a large company. Asser and I had lunch at Whynnie's mess. I visited the convalescent camp and spoke to a goodly number in the YMCA hut and was shewn over No. 9 Stationary[41] a sad and distressing sight to me – there were 125 officers and over 3000 men. I had tea with Miss Steere's staff at the Dock Hospital[42] and dined at the mess of the London div. Reinf. Camp.[43] Attended a large Concert in the Cinema Hut and a reception afterwards. To bed about 11.

19 January

Took Parry Evans* to GHQ starting about 10. Stopped and lunched at Dieppe, arrived about 6.45. Did an hour's work in the office. Thorold* dined with us and did some writing for me afterwards.

20 January

In the office all day. Took Parry Evans* and Bill Drury* for a walk in the afternoon in the woods. Worked in the office until 8. Matthews* of the VII[44] stayed the night with me and told me all the news of his Division. Thorold* and I worked late at night on a letter to K.

21 January

Called on Boyce[45] of the Transport at 11. He was very nice to me but I am no forwarder with the cars of S.C.Fs. of Armies. Stone* arrived from Doullens and Major Partridge[46] had a conference on a new prayer book for the use of troops. Stone* came to lunch.

I motored over to bring Bentinck to GHQ, had tea with the 2nd COLDSTREAMS

---

38 Unidentified.
39 Unidentified.
40 Major G. S. Whinney.
41 No. 9 Stationary Hospital treated those with sexually transmitted diseases.
42 No. 2 General Hospital was located on the dockside.
43 Reinforcement camp for the London Div.
44 7 Div.
45 Possibly Lieutenant Colonel Harry A. Boyce who was serving in the supply organization.
46 There were several majors with this surname.

and called at Aire to pick up Parry Evans* on the way back. Worked in the office until 8 and worked at my sermon for Douglas Haigh.

22 January

Motored with Parry Evans* to Abbeville after 3. Had a walk on the way. Ensell* had arranged a confirmation at 6.30 for 23 candidates. Kittlewell,[47] a friend of Edward Woods* and Bowman* dined with me. One of the 'Inner.' Saw dear old Herbert[48] afterwards.[49]

23 January

A blessed and glorious day with the Holy Comm. At wh. there were over 40 present – some of them had been confirmed yesterday. I preached at a YMCA Hut at 10 and had an excellent service for the Motor Transport people at 12. I lunched with Holden[50] at 1. Confirmed 3 men is Hospital at 3 pm, had tea with the sisters after looking over the hospital. Walked into Abbeville, interviewed Stone[51] of the YMCA at 5, called in at the Soldiers Ch. Institute and preached to a large congregation in the Evening on the 55th Chapter of Isaiah and on the inner meaning of the war. Percy Dearmer*, Ensell*, Watney*, Cave[52] dined with me. I filled in this diary before going to bed.

24 January

Came up from Abbeville in 2½ hours arriving at G.H.Q about 12. Worked hard in the office until 1.30. Drury* lunched with me. At 3 I went out alone for a walked – was much tempted by the old enemy. To the office at 5 and worked until six – telling Drury* of my scheme for a Senior [Chaplain] of an 1st Army. Stanley,[53] his friend MacNutt* and King* of IVth Division dined.

25 January

Quite a good number came to intercession this morning. At the office I had a visit from Dr Simms* who intends to go with me to the A.G. and protest about not being consulted before instructions are issued to the chaplains.[54] Bate* of the 2nd Division also called about his work. I took King* and Woods* out to the woods at 3. Office at 6. O'Kell*[55] and Turnbull* and King* dined. I worked with Thorold* afterwards.

---

47 Probably the Rev. H. H. Kettlewell* interviewed on 24 Nov. 1915.
48 Unidentified.
49 These last entries for 22 Jan. are unclear. It is not certain to whom they refer.
50 Unidentified.
51 Unidentified.
52 Possibly the Rev. A. M. Cave*.
53 Unidentified.
54 The question of military officers issuing instructions to chaplains was a complex one. The Rev. Dr J. Simms* was the principal chaplain.
55 This refers to the Rev. F. J. Okell.

26 January

After posting 5 chaplains to the new units I motored with King* to Acheux the H. Quarters of IV Division where I lunched with Generals Lambton[56] and Cavan.[57] I confirmed about 40 in the afternoon, had tea with one of the Brigade Head Quarters, where I saw an old friend Col. Higginson[58] of the Dublin Fusiliers who was at Khartoum. Dined with IVth Division.

27 January

I was taken round to see the Institutes, Canteens and Ambulances in the Division until 12 when I left for Choques where I saw the Commander of the 1st Corpse [sic] and at Lillers where I saw the 1st Division H. Quarters but missed Harry Blackbourne*. I then motored to GHQ where I did a couple of hours before dinner and hour and a half afterwards. No news in papers tonight except the change in the news about Kut.[59]

[There is a sum in the margin 64 + 98 = 162 with the figure of 88 beside it.]

28 January

Did two hours before I came away from GHQ, also called on Kennedy Rumford[60] before I left for Rouen. I came to Abbeville in two hours and did the rest in 2½. So I was in very good time. Carey* was on the look out for me and obtained a room in the Hotel de France.[61] I had a walk before dinner with Carey* and saw Hull,[62] and old friend of the 18th General Hospital who is stationed here.

29 January

Saw Marable[63] the C.O. of Rouen and tried to put things right about Carey*. He seemed a cantankerous sort of man but I would not let him lose his temper by losing mine.

I took confirmations in a Hospital and walked out into the woods with Carey* before having tea with Jameson[64] the C.O. of the Hospital in wh. Grant[65] is chaplain.

---

56 Major General the Honourable William Lambton, commander 4 Div.
57 Lieutenant General Frederick Rudolph Lambart, 10th earl of Cavan, commander XIV Corps.
58 Lieutenant Colonel H. W. Higginson.
59 The town of Kut Al Amara had been besieged since Dec. 1915. A relieving force had just been defeated by an Ottoman army.
60 Possibly Lieutenant Robert Kennerley Rumford.
61 Hotel at Rouen.
62 Possibly Major A. J. Hull.
63 Brigadier General A. Marable.
64 There were several officers of the RAMC with this surname.
65 There were several chaplains with this surname.

30 January

I had a truly blessed Sunday. After Celebration at the Echelon Chapel I preached there on the 2nd Lesson, 'If any man will follow me.'[66] I preached the same sermon to the patients and doctors of No. 2 Red Cross[67] where Mrs De Winton is a Nurse.[68] I took a confirmation after preaching twice in the afternoon.

31 January

I want a round of visits to Hospitals and Reinforcement camps in the morning, visited the work at the Station for the Reinforcements and lunched with Hull.[69] I took confirmation, walked out with Carey*, and had tea with the Coopers.[70] In the Evening spoke to a large number of workers in one of the YMCA Huts.

---

[66] 'If any man will come after me, let him deny himself, and take up his cross, and follow me', Matthew chapter 16 verse 24, The Bible (Authorized Version).
[67] No. 2 British Red Cross Hospital.
[68] Possibly A. A. C. de Winton, British Red Cross.
[69] Possibly the Major A. J. Hull.
[70] Unidentified.

February 1916

A month full of routine visits and office work. The reference to the attack on the French colonial troops may have been part of the battle of Verdun that had begun on 21 February 1916.

1 February

All the chaplains came to a Celebration in the Echelon Chapel where I spoke to them on, 'Preaching Christ and Him crucified.'[1] I had breakfast with them all and saw each one individually all the morning. After lunch I went with Cooper[2] to try and obtain a large room in the Hotel de Ville for our work amongst men on Sunday nights. I had tea with Mrs de Winton,[3] called on the Gordons[4] and spoke to Corkey* about the Echelon Chapel.

2 February

MacNalty* who had been invalided at Rouen came up with me in my car to G.H.Q. in about 4½ where I found a good many things to worry one, – the 1st Army chaplain, the A.Gs.' difficulties. I stopped in the office all the afternoon and settled some of the worries.

3 February

Saw and Posted three new chaplains who arrived last night.[5] Also visited the A.G. and discussed our offices and working. He agreed with me about Blackburn*. In the afternoon I saw the Commander in Chief. He was very helpful, backed me up about Blackburn and told me how keen and interested he was in our work.

4 February

We sat some time on the Prayer Book.[6] Simms* and I made an attack on the Adjutant General's office about the instructions to chaplains.[7] Conran* and Southwell* came up and stayed the day. Southwell* and I drove out in the car to see Barclay's*

---

1 Possibly 'For I determined not to know anything among you, save Jesus Christ, and him crucified.' 2 Corinthians chapter 2 verse 2, The Bible (Authorized Version).
2 Unidentified.
3 Possibly A. A. C. de Winton, British Red Cross.
4 Unidentified.
5 SAD 28/1/17 showed that Spink (the Rev. H. O. Spink*, later killed in action on 9 Aug. 1916) was to go temporarily to 55 Div, Burnaby (the Rev. H. B. Burnaby*) to 33 CCS and Maddrell (the Rev. H. Maddrell*) to 23 CCS.
6 An abbreviated version of book of services for use with troops.
7 This is part of the continuing debate about how chaplains were to be administered in the army.

Head Quarters and visited General Beale Browne[8] and got back to the office about 7.

5 February

Worked hard in the office all the morning and tried to find the 35th Div. on the way to Poperinghe in the afternoon. I fetched up at Talbot House[9] in Poperinghe about 6.30 and found a very flourishing establishment used by soldiers as a club and by officers as a House of Rest for those coming and going on leave.

6 February

Sunday at Poperinghe. We had about 20 at the early service where I celebrated at the chapel in the roof.[10] Well filled by Talbot.[11] I preached in the Cinema to a Batallion of ......[R.B.'s. is crossed through] and visited the Church Army Hut in the wood. I lunched with the VIII Division where I saw Ironsides[12] and in the afternoon drove through Ypres to the Canal Bank where I saw the Chaplains' Dug-out. Later in the day I held a confirmation and preached to a large number of men in the club itself. Got home the same night.

7 February

Visited Etaples and confirmed in the afternoon.

8 February

A long morning in the office and in the afternoon drove out with Gordon[13] to see the Cavalry Corps Commander, General Bingham.[14] He was most kind but did not fall in with my wish that the Corps should have a Corps Chaplain. I also visited the 35th Division. Crick* stayed the night.

9 February

General Pinney[15] whom I knew in Cairo and now commands the 35th came to see me this morning at 10. About seven new chaplains also arrived just before I started for Wormhout to confirm in the XXth Division. At lunch I met Sweeny[16] and Annesley[17]

---

[8] Brigadier General Desmond John Edward Beale-Browne, commander 2 Cav Bde.
[9] The first reference to the establishment that was to become the foundation of the TocH organi-
     zation. It was named after Lieutenant G. W. L. Talbot, brother to the Rev. E. K.* and the Rev.
     N. S.* Talbot.
[10] The chapel remains in use.
[11] The Rev. N. S. Talbot*.
[12] Possible Major W. E. Ironside
[13] Unidentified.
[14] Major General C. E. Bingham.
[15] Major General Reginald John Pinney, commander 35 Div.
[16] Unidentified.
[17] Unidentified.

– both old friends of mine. I confirmed again in the afternoon near Poperinghe and returned back before seven.

10 February

Crick* left for his Division this morning and I worked in the office until 2. Harry Blackburne* came in at 2.30 and walked out with me until 5.30 when we threshed out the future of the work of the Senior Chaplain of an Army. Mitchell[18] turned up at GHQ in the afternoon and dined with Harry Blackburn* and myself at 8.

11 February

This afternoon I confirmed at GHQ in the little chapel adjoining the new Church Institute. One was a nurse from a neighbouring Casualty Clearing Station and two Flying Corps and two R.A.M.C. Gittens* came along for a walk afterwards and we visited Anderson* who was in hospital. MacNalty* came to dinner.

12 February

Mitchell[19] went with me in the afternoon to Lillers where I stopped to confirm while he went on to E Battery R.H.A.

At 5 I had a most inspiring time addressing about 60 officers after tea. I do believe God the Father gave me a message. I only wish I had more of the Spirit of Christ to prepare and to speak.

13 February

I always feel the Christ near me with the two or three wh. I love. Two of my old flock from the Sudan came to the Holy Communion. Harry Lewis[20] and Woolcombe Adams.[21] Unfortunately they both had to move off early and take up their gun positions when the Division goes in. I preached to the 25th, 39th and 26th Brigade of Artillery. They were all held under cover, the 1st in a Railway Station, the next in a Theatre and the 3rd in a Protestant building. I felt the Power twice thanks to Him who called me. After lunch I motored towards Bethune and sent the car off to Mitchell[22] while I walked in – about 3 miles. We had tea with the 2nd Division before starting for GHQ wh. we reached soon after 6.30. I wrote up my diary and one or two letters After going very strong all day – books sent by one of the chaplains for me to criticize and take action brought evil into my mind.

---

18   Probably the Rev. C. W. Mitchell*.
19   Probably the Rev. C. W. Mitchell*.
20   Brigadier General F. G. Lewis, commander 142 Bde.
21   Probably Major C. E. G. Woolcombe-Adams.
22   Probably the Rev. C. W. Mitchell*.

14 February

Mitchell[23] went off this morning and I spent a long morning in the office doing many things and keeping up to date. I saw Livey[24] from the Cavalry and Beresford* on his way to the 56th Division. I walked out in the afternoon and felt cleaner – prayed in the Church and realised something of the Presence of God. I had a talk with the Duke of Teck[25] about the promotion of Divisional Chaplains and pleaded for a C.M.G[26] for Tuckey*.

15 February

Another morning in the office which lasted until nearly 2. At 3 pm I walked out with Gordon* and thought over a cycle of prayer for the Expeditionary Force in France. Townsend* one of our chaplains came in from the Cavalry before being posted elsewhere. I worked in the Evening until 8 pm and entertained afterwards, Leakey,[27] Townsend* and Blakeston*.[28]

16 February

The office work had become such routine (posting me and administration with Drury*, Episcopal work with Thorold* and letter writing) that I might as well stay after office and chronicle the day from that time. Now and then a man comes in from the front with news. I took Blakeston[29] back to his unit, or most of the way, and called on the Canadians. Spent some time with the Corps Commander[30] and Canon Almond* – looked over the Institute and spoke to the men.

17 February

Worked nearly up to date in the office and had a quiet time in the middle of the day and had a quiet walk out along the canal bank and saw a glorious sunset – dark clouds made the East frown a dull dead red but above was a dazzling silver lining wh. gave me heart to believe that above the bloody hate of war – there is the self-sacrifice dazzling white.

[23] Probably the Rev. C. W. Mitchell*.
[24] Probably the Rev. A. A. Liney*.
[25] Adolphus Cambridge, 1st marquess of Cambridge, brigadier general the duke of Teck, military secretary BEF. As the position concerned with matters to do with careers and postings, he would have the person with whom Gwynne discussed such matters.
[26] Commander of the Order of St Michael and St George.
[27] Possibly the Rev. A .B. Leahy*.
[28] Unidentified.
[29] Unidentified.
[30] Lieutenant General Sir Edwin Alfred Hervey Alderson, commander I (Canadian) Corps.

18 February

I posted four men before I started for the 3rd Army, Palmer*, Bray*, Bamell[31] and Hughes Davies*, all new men.

It was 11 before I left, but I was held up by a Division on the march. I spent ½ an hour at Doullens having something to eat. I came thro' Albert and saw the sticky statue of the Virgin holding out her child in an almost impossible position which no engineer could attempt [there is a small marginal drawing of the statue at its oblique angle to the tower on which it sits.][32] I confirmed for the 7th Division in an old Church wh. I had used for the same purpose before. I stopped at Corbie to confirm an officer named Bramble[33] and came along to the Hotel Rhin[34] a bad arrangement for I might have stopped with Julian Steele[35] and gone up to the Trenches.

19 February

I had a most comfortable bed at Amiens and walked out after breakfast to see the Cathedral. I met Thomas[36] of the 48th Division at the station and had a talk and a stroll with him through the broad Boulevard. I afterwards lunched at the hotel before starting of Étinehem. The roads were so bad that at times I thought we should never get through. However I managed to persuade the Chauffeur to go on and we reached our destination about half an hour late. After the confirmation of about 30 candidates we had tea with the gunners.

20 February

General Shea[37] the Officer Commanding the 30th Division is a most religious and keen man very interested in the chaplains. He and his son came to the Early Comm. with about 15 others, I preached to few men about Head Quarters and address a Batallion of Guards in the open under a sunny sky I met an old friend of Susanne,[38] Stevenson[39] of the 1st Kings, and in the Evening preached at Bray. Canon Linton Smith* had a talk and walk with me in the afternoon.

21 February

There was a heavy bombardment early this morning further South where the French colonials were attacked. The attack was repulsed by them. A sniper must have

---

[31]   Possibly the Rev. E. R. Burnell*.
[32]   The story of the golden virgin of Albert was well known. It was believed that the war would end when the statue fell from the tower.
[33]   There were several officers with this surname.
[34]   Possibly the Hotel du Rhin in Amiens.
[35]   Brigadier General J. M. Steele.
[36]   There were a several chaplains with this surname.
[37]   The commander of 30 Div was Major General John Stuart Mackenzie Shea.
[38]   Unidentified.
[39]   Possibly Major C. A. Steavenson of the King's Liverpool Regiment.

slipped through on high ground when the Germans took Treize[40] last week for a younger office reported that he was sniped standing near his door and had to retire. I had a talk with the General this morning about the work of the chaplains before starting. Waggett* of the VII Division came with me to GHQ where I had piles of letters and 5 visitors awaiting me. George Armitage[41] and young friend of his turned up to dinner. Pat MaCormic* also came along.

22 February

A full morning with interviews and letter passed very quickly until 2.30. Sleet, snow and rain prevented me going out and brought Daubney[42] and Tyrwhit* to see me. After tea I again went to the office again and worked until 8. Haywood dined[43] with me and Tyrwhit* stayed the night. Wrote a few more letters with Thorold* afterwards

23 February

Worked in the office in the morning and took Tyrwhit* back to Laventie in the afternoon. I then called on the Oxfords near Robecq where I tried to get Crosse* to come and stay the night with me. I also called on Cockran,[44] the Brigadier of 5th and took a long time to get back to G.H.Q. where Daubney[45] was waiting to dine with me. We talked together of our old friends in the Sudan and Thorold* came and wrote letters afterwards.

24 February

After a couple of hours and a half in the office I made a journey to Aire and had lunch with Sir Charles Munro.[46] He kindly consented to do 3 very important things for me. 1. To give orders to the Corps., Div. Generals that H.W. Blackburne* should visit all Divisions and Corps to inspect and instruct all the chaplains. 2 To allow the Ch. Army to have huts in the 1st Army, and 3. To give transport to S.C.F. of his army to do his job. Brought Harry Blackburne* back. Held Confirmation in No. 6A Stat.[47]

25 February

After 10.30 started for the 3rd Army dropping Harry Blackburne* at Aire. The snow fell heavily as I passed through Lillers, S. Pol on the slope into Doullens. We met some of the French Division and so slippery was the road from snow and frost that more than once our car had to be guided into heavy snow. I had a cup of tea in

---

40   Location has not been identified.
41   Brigadier General G. A. Armytage.
42   Possibly Colonel E. K. Daubney.
43   Possibly Major Cecil P. Heywood, Coldstream Guards
44   Brigadier General C. E. Corkran.
45   Possibly Colonel E. K. Daubney.
46   General Sir Charles Munro.
47   No. 6A Stationary Hospital.

Doullens Hotel and found that the car had been held up by traffick. We started for Amiens at 6. Our car refused the first hill, the wheels having no grip. After 4 hours the Chauffeur thought of rope wh. was tied round the tyre and we mounted the first hill. Before Beauval we met an English Division which held us up so long that we determined to try a loop road on the left which brought us beyond the Division. A Frenchman piloted us in his car and we stuck once in the loop. On reaching the main road I heaved a sigh of relief and thought all was well. Alas! We stuck badly at the last hill, so badly that the Chauffeur counselled sleeping in the car. 'I am blowed if I will', said I and ordered him to try the spare rubber tyre instead of the studded steel one wh. slipped by that time. It was past 2 pm but with our new tyre we managed to get over the hill. Even then we should not have reached our destination had not the French soldiers given us a leg up on the way. We reached Hotel Rhea[48] about 3.20 m. I slept without any solid food from the night before.

26 February

After a poor breakfast, with a prayer in my lips but doubt in my heart, that I should fulfil my engagements, I started for Corbie where I found Campbell* full of sorrow that his lads could not be confirmed. I promised to return on Monday and made for the 37th HQ where I was due to lunch at one. I eventually landed up a 4 pm. Confirmed in a cold damp hut lately vacated by the French and had tea with ham (ravenous was I) We had a meeting of chaplains afterwards. I saw Gleichen[49] before facing the journey to Bus, HQ of the 48th wh I reached soon after 8.

27 February

I spent my Sunday speaking and preaching to Batallion and Artillery and confirmed twice was backed up in every way by Gen. Fenshaw[50] an old friend of mine.

One of the chaplains, MacReady*, told me of an experience worth repeating. A volunteer was asked for form one of the Warwicks, for a night venture on the German lines, to take prisoners and destroy machine guns. 300 answered the call, 120 were chosen. They were all very excited and blackened their faces in order to deceive the enemy. About an hour before they started some of the lads asked the chaplain to hold a service – which he did. 35 of them received Holy Communion afterwards. At the last minute owing to the thick fog the attempt was given up – but all the same it showed how many of our lads felt they could ask God's blessing on that work.

28 February

General Fenshaw took me up to see Done's[51] Brigade. Done was an old friend of mine at Wadi Medanie in the Sudan and has proved himself to be a first class

---

48 Possibly a hotel in Amiens.
49 Major General Lord Albert Edward Wilfred Gleichen, commander 37 Div.
50 Major General Sir Robert Fanshawe, commander 48 Div.
51 Brigadier General H. R. Done, commander 145 Bde.

fighting man. I visited the 51st on my way to Amiens and confirmed the men I failed
to do on Saturday, and made the peace. Spent the night in the Rhea Hotel.[52]

29 February

I had breakfast with the Duke of Argyle[53] in the Hotel this morning. He seemed a
very earnest and warm hearted man. His Batallion the Argyle and Sutherlands saw
him off at Corbie yesterday and I heard their shouts. At about 10 am I started back
to S. Omer, picked up Pym* on the way at Doullens and came along in time for tea.

---

[52] Possibly a hotel in Amiens.
[53] Niall Campbell, 10th duke of Argyll. He was honorary colonel of the 8th Battalion of the Argyll
       and Sutherland Highlanders.

March 1916

Another busy month of visits. Gwynne began to put into operate his scheme for a chain of command for chaplains with ACGs general at each army headquarters. Towards the end of the month, Gwynne paid a short visit to the CG. A series of actions took place between British and German forces around St Eloi.

1 March

Ensell* spent last night with me left today. Harry Dibben* who came in last night came in over strained in nerves and looked after by Pym* and put into hospital here at S. Omer. He was not really bad but on the verge of a break down. We all feel he will be well soon.

2 March

Saw Harry Dibben* off this morning from the Officers Hospital. After work in the office went to Lestrem to confirm with the 35th Division (Bantams.) Pinney[1] the General was very good to us and gave all the clergy tea and allowed me to see them afterwards in his private room. I motored back by about 6.30 and did some work.

3 March

After the mornings work in the office motored to Fleming* at Lillers to keep a confirmation in his Division, 47th. It was a cold snowy day. I saw Beattie[2] the Brigade Major in the same mess as young Woods.[3] I brought Fleming* as far as Aire to stay with Blackburne*.

4 March

Confirmed at Poperinghe in Talbot House this afternoon and saw John Ponsonby[4] afterwards. Rogers* and Neville Talbot* and Clayton* etc., were all there. I took Canon Scott* with me and motored to Ballieul to visit the Canadians. At 6.30 we had a most harmonious dinner. Canon Almond* entertained all his chaplains of all denominations and speeches were made afterwards. Presbyterians, Methodists and R.Cs. came and then after wh. I was to pray and give a blessing.

---

[1] Major General Reginald John Pinney, commander 35 Div.
[2] Possibly Major J. W. K. Beattie.
[3] Possibly the Rev. E. S. Woods*.
[4] Brigadier General John Ponsonby, commander 1 Bde.

5 March

I preached three times and visited every Brigadier in the Division as well as the Divisional Generals. I heard an amusing story from the Canadians. Two men who had drunk more than they ought as a punishment were sent out to fix wire in front of the trenches. While the others were working they crept into a shell hole and slept off the drunkenness. Before dawn they both woke feeling very cold and uncomfortable, but for the life of them could not agree wh. were their trenches or wh. were the Germans. They almost came to blows about it and one of them said, 'Well I don't care what you say I am going for their trenches' and he went but the other immediately set out for the other trenches. By the time the man who had reached our trenches had told the others and they watched with great interest the poor fellow who was making his way to the enemy. They saw him stop, parley with a German and then saw him running back with all his strength while the Germans were firing at him. It appears that when he arrived at the German trenches he asked where he was and held up his hands by order of a German who informed him to lay down his rifle to come and take him prisoner. The Canadian struck him a heavy blow on the jaw and ran back under fire from the Germans until he reached his own trenches.

6 March

Early this morning, 7 am, I started for Bethune and held a celebration at the beginning of a quiet day for our chaplains. It was a real time of blessing. In the afternoon Sir H. Gough[5] the Commander of the 1st Corpse read a paper on the work of chaplains from a soldier's point of view.

I asked Harry[6] to come and stay the night but could not so I came back alone with a very heavy cold.

7 March

This afternoon I held a confirmation at Ballieul for the 25th Division wh. was held in the Church Army Hut. I had a short service for the chaplains afterwards in the small chapel and came home with a heavy cold by 8.

8 March

I tried to defeat my cold by staying in bed. An old lad from the Sudan came in the afternoon. Otherwise the day uneventful.

Lord Salisbury[7] turned up this evening.

---

[5] Lieutenant General Hubert de la Poer Gough, commander I Corps.
[6] Lieutenant H. V. Gwynne.
[7] James Gascoyne-Cecil, 4th marquess of Salisbury

9 March

I got up after breakfast today and tried to do some work in office, but found it diffi-cult to do much with a heavy cold on me and though I had another try in the office I did no good. Lord S. and I dined with Sir Douglas Haig[8] tonight and had a talk with him about the work of the chaplains.

10 March

Still a very heavy cold but rose after breakfast and had a go in the office. I took Lord Salisbury out to SARCUS to see the Herts Territorials[9] while I confirmed about 35. Hornby* came back with me. Blackburne* dined with us.

11 March

Had to give in and stay in bed. Pascoe,[10] one of my old friends from the Sudan in GHQ, doctor, came to see me, ordering me to stay in bed and gave me medicine. Nothing of importance to relate, read 'Ordeal by battle'[11] etc.

12 March

Ditto – in bed all day. Lord Salisbury departed today. Only allowed up in my room and read more of 'Belief and Practice' by Spens[12] and found it very helpful. Drury* and Thorold* came to tea.

13 March

Worked in my house, not allowed out – feeling much better as my cold is departing. Read a good deal of Spens[13] book.

14 March

Indoors all day. Had the papers brought to me in my room and spent much of my time reading Spens, 'Ordeal of battle',[14] etc.

---

8   Commander in chief of the BEF.
9   The 4th marquess of Salisbury was a member of the Territorial Force and honorary colonel of several units with connexions to Hertfordshire. He was also a member of the Church of England Advisory Committee to the WO.
10   Possibly Major J. S. Pascoe.
11   F. S. Oliver, *Ordeal by battle* (London, 1915).
12   W. Spens, *Belief and practice* (London, 1915).
13   See n. 12.
14   See n. 11.

15 March

Indoors in the morning and did a certain amount of work and was allowed out in the afternoon. Walked along the canal North of S. Omer and dined quietly.

16 March

Went to the office today. Had a walk in the afternoon. Harry Blackburne* came to see me this afternoon about decentralising the S.C.F Armies. Worked in the office in the Evening.

17 March

Holy Comm. at 9.45 in the chapel of the house with three present. Thanked God for his goodness in restoring me to health and strength, and went to see Maj. Dick Payne[15] close to S. Omer, in the car and brought him back to stay the night and had a long talk of the Sudan.

18 March

After a long day in the office I motored to Fouquabourg[16] hoping to have a walk on the way, but it rained hard so I could only walk a short distance and to eke out the time motored by a detour to Fruges and returned to Fouquabourg[17] by 6. I had a long walk with Liney* before dinner and dinner with Charles Campbell,[18] the Brigadier, and met Godfrey Gilson[19] as well as Frank Stout[20] at dinner.

19 March

Had a blessed day. Holy Communion at 8 am after wh. I rode in the car to a service for the 12th Lancers – then to the 20th Hussars and returned to Fouquabourg[21] for a service in the school. Godfrey Gilson and the Brigadier were there and the band which had already played at the last service bumped along in gun carriages in time for the last. I preached on the call of the Master to his disciples, 'If any man will come after me.'[22]

[15]   Possibly Major Robert L. Payne, who had been appointed to the staff on 10 Jan. 1916.
[16]   The location may be Fauquembergues.
[17]   Possibly Fauquembergues.
[18]   Possibly Brigadier General C. L. K. Campbell, commander 5 (Cav) Bde.
[19]   Possibly Major F. G. Gilson.
[20]   Possibly Lieutenant G. F. Stout.
[21]   Possibly Fauquembergues.
[22]   Probably Matthew chapter 16 verse 24, The Bible (Authorized Version).

20 March

After working in the office until 12 I motored out to Cassel and had lunch with Gen. Plumer,[23] the Commander of the 2nd Army. I had a long talk with him afterwards about decentralisation and promised to take away his present Senior Chaplain of the Army. I then motored back to GHQ and had a confirmation of two candidates prepared by Gordon*. Worked in the Evening at the office.

21 March

Lunched with Gen. Monro[24] today at Aire where Harry Blackburne* was also lunching and had a long talk with the General about decentralising in his Army. Motored afterwards to Hazebrouck where I saw Tuckey* and broke the news to him. He seemed rather hurt but took it like a man. I saw Daubney[25] and Goschen[26] at tea and held a confirmation for one of Ellison's* public school boys.

22 March

Started at 11 with Linton Smith* who had stayed the night with me the night before, to lunch with Gen. Allenby[27] at S. Pol. I arrived there in an hour and a half and met Day*, the Army S.C.F. Allenby kindly had a talk with me afterwards and agreed to give me the help he could to decentralise. We motored to Querrieu in the afternoon and I dropped Linton Smith* at his chateau on the way.

Gen. Sutton[28] kindly put me up in the chateau and helped me all he could. I had a long talk with MacIntosh,[29] one of my flock from the Sudan. Rawlinson,[30] the Army Com. was at Amiens ill – but I could see what a splendid lot of men he had gathered round him.

23 March

I brought Arch. Southwell* the S.C.F. of IVth Army back with me from Querrieu but on the way I took a confirmation at Arras. We had to produce a special permit from time to time as all the roads were guarded for miles. When we entered Arras – all was quiet and silent – like a city of the dead save now and then a soldier and very few civilians. Our Confirmation was held in a Soldiers club in some back street, part of the town was being shelled during the service. After the service I visited the Divisional Gen. of the XIV,[31] Gen. Capper[32] who was most kind and gave us tea.

---

[23] General Herbert Charles Onslow Plumer, commander Second Army.
[24] General Sir Charles Monro, Bt, commander First Army.
[25] Possibly Major W. H. Daubney.
[26] Possibly Major A. A. Goschen.
[27] General Edmund Henry Hynman Allenby, commander Third Army.
[28] Possibly Major General Hugh Clement Sutton.
[29] Unidentified.
[30] General Sir Henry Seymour Rawlinson, commander Fourth Army.
[31] He should have written XXIV.
[32] Major General Sir John Edward Capper, commander 24 Div.

I intended calling for Harry[33] and taking him home with me but we had a bad time getting back and did not reach GHQ until 9.30.

24 March

I had a big accumulation of letters to go thro' this morning. The Archdeacon[34] and I had a long walk in the afternoon – and in the Evening at 5 we had our first meeting of S.C.Fs. of Armies, Southwell*, Day*, Blackburne* and Anderson*. I read out my instructions to them one by one after wh. we discussed the spiritual part of the work – C.E.M.S.[35] – Confirmations, etc. They all dined with me in the Evening.

25 March

Two confirmations in the Hospitals at GHQ. A long interview with the A.G. and settling up my work with Drury* and Thorold* took up most of my time. I also saw Carey* at lunch who seemed very depressed about his move from Rouen.

I motored to Boulogne by 7.30 and had dinner at the officers' mess with Balleine* and Abbott* and had a long talk with Masters* afterwards.

26 March

Celebrated at S. Johns at 7.30 am and took a Service at the Destructor, also held a confirmation at 11 after visiting the cemetery.

I lunched with the Harwoods[36] at me and walked out to one of the Docks to see the *Sussex* – which was torpedoed in the bow on Friday but managed to crawl to the harbour at Boulogne. 140 were missing amongst wh. was the Secretary of the American Legation in Paris and about 10 other Americans. The whole of the front of the boat to the companion ladders was blown away. How they managed to get the boat in beats me. I managed to get a place on the boat by 4 but at 5 we all had to come away as the voyage was postponed owing to mines or submarines.[37]

27 March

Prayed. Read and filled up to date my diary in my room at the Officers Club. Attended the short intercession services at the office. Found Heath,[38] my old friend from the Sudan and gave him lunch at the club. After doing a little work at the office got the boat about 4 and crossed over in pouring rain at 4.30 wh., thank God

---

33 Possibly Harry Gwynne.
34 The Venerable A. K. Southwell*.
35 Church of England Men's Society.
36 The Rev. R. C. Harwood*, minister at Holy Trinity, Boulogne.
37 The SS *Sussex* was a cross-channel ferry en route from Folkestone to Dieppe on 26 Mar. 1916 when she was torpedoed. Although at least fifty were killed she continued to Dieppe, where she was beached.
38 Unidentified.

we reached safely about 6. Well looked after on the way by torpedo Destroyers and Sweepers after the terrible experience of the *Sussex* torpedoed on Thursday by a German submarine. Stopped the night at the Grosvenor.[39]

28 March

Went to the Service at Westminster Abbey at 10. Called at the War Office and saw the C.G., did business. Lunched at the S. James' Club[40] with him. Called on the Archbishop[41] at 3.30 asked him to come out to the B.E.F. Fixed on May 16. Called on Connell[42] had tea with him in the Bath Club.[43] Dined and slept with Canon Pearce[44] at the Abbey. C.G. also stayed, did work together.

29 March

Holy Communion in the little chapel at 8. Did more work together, Prayer Book – Establishments, etc. Saw Ward[45] of the Navvy Mission at the W.O. had lunch with Edie[46] at 7 Collingham Gardens.[47] Had a talk with Lord Salisbury[48] at 20 Arlington Street.[49] Shopped. Wildsmith[50] and Hawkes[51] had teas with Canon Pearce and dined with the Moncks[52] at 109 Eaton Sq. Stopped at the club- did not good by stopping up late and reading papers.

30 March

Wrote the last of the tract, 'Finding God.'[53] Spent the morning at the W.O. – seeing the Church Army representative and talking over things with the C.G. Lunched with Dick at the Norfolk Hotel and saw Howell and Harry afterwards at the *Morning P.*[54] office.[55] Interviewed 'Burrough'[56] of Hertford Coll. Oxf. Went down for the night to the C.G.'s at Northwood.

---

39   The Grosvenor Hotel, Victoria.
40   The St James's Club was at 106 Piccadilly. It offered special terms to diplomats who wished to be members. It would have been convenient for the chaplain general's office.
41   The archbishop of Canterbury.
42   Unidentified.
43   The Bath Club was at 34 Dover Street.
44   The Rev. Canon Ernest Pearce, canon of Westminster.
45   The reference might be to John Ward MP who had raised several 'navvy' battalions for service in France.
46   The wife of Howell Gwynne.
47   SW5, the area in south-west London between the Cromwell and Brompton Roads.
48   James Gascoyne-Cecil, 4th marquess of Salisbury
49   W1, the area in London on the south side of Piccadilly, between St James's Street and Green Park.
50   Wildsmith were a firm of shoe retailers.
51   Hawkes & Co. were a firm of tailors.
52   Possibly Brigadier General (Retired) C. S. O. Monck.
53   This has not been traced.
54   The *Morning Post*, of which Howell Gwynne was editor.
55   All three members of the Gwynne family.
56   Possibly the Rev. E. A. Burroughs.

31 March

Very early start this morning and caught the 8.10 to Folkestone. Crossed on a smooth sea and lunch with Balleine* and Thorold* and held a confirmation of 5 Railway R.A.M.C. men of the Princess Mary's train[57] prepared by a young Theo student named Knox.[58] Motored up by 7. Found GHQ away.[59]

---

[57] There was no Ambulance Train with that name. There were Queen Mary's and Princess Christian's trains which were numbered 14 and 15 respectively. Gwynne would appear to have conflated the names.

[58] Unidentified.

[59] It is not clear what he meant by this comment.

April 1916

Gwynne makes several references to the decentralization scheme for control of chaplains that he had created. In general, it appeared to be working well. His references to Easter devotions are of interest. Normally considered a Low Church bishop he appears to suggest that his preparations included auricular confession. At the end of the month he paid another visit to the WO, partly to ensure that the arrangements for the visit of the Archbishop of Canterbury were in place.

1 April

Walker[1] who had been home to be trained as a Staff Chaplain to Day* of the 3rd Army rode in the car with me as far as S. Pol on my way to Gosnay (en Artois) where I confirmed 170 of the 55th Division in a large barn. I had not time to see the Divisional General so came away after tea and did not get back at S. Omer until 9.30

2 April

Celebrated Holy Communion in the small church at 7.30 and as all GHQ except ourselves have moved only two besides ourselves were present. At 9.30 I preached to the Artists[2] in the Monro Institute and worked in the office. After lunch I motored to Hazebrouck for a confirmation – walked out with Griffiths[3] and held a service in the Town Hall at 6.30. Milner[4] and Charles[5] of the Glasgow Highlanders dined with me.

3 April

Drury* moved my office today from the lower part of the square of the Salle de Musique. I worked there until 1 and was driven to the new office after a good walk in the Clairmarais woods. It was a glorious spring day and everything in bursting into new life.

4 April

The new decentralization is beginning to work and the S. Chaplains of Armies are functioning and so fewer papers have come through this office the last few days. I motored to my old Division in the afternoon and held a confirmation in the

---

[1] The Rev. F. J. Walker*.
[2] The Artists' Rifles who acted as security for GHQ.
[3] There were several chaplains with this surname.
[4] Unidentified.
[5] Unidentified.

Reformed Evangelique Church[6] at Bruay. Some the confirmees were my old lads from the Oxfords and Bucks.

5 April

Interviewed (by an interpreter) the landlady of a house with a view to taking new rooms. This present arrangement is very expensive and our new cook a robber. So instead of bandying a few weak French words in return for a volume of indistinguishable scorn and abuse, our Madame has a very bad temper! – we are moving our 'cuisine' privately. These are Thorold's* tactics, the house keeping being his department. At 12.30 I motored to Montrieull (T. Atkins 'Montreal'[7]) and saw the Commander in Chief[8] mainly about the visit of the Archbishop of Canterbury also about the work of the chaplains. He was very kind and evidently took a keen interest in our work. On my return I had a confirmation service in my own house and did some work in the office before dinner at wh. I entertained Hump. Bowman* and Gordon*.

6 April

After posting two chaplains to their new work[9] and doing other work in the office, I left for Treport and confirmed a nurse and two soldiers and had tea with Finnimore*, Stather Hunt* and Clissold* from Dieppe. John Macmillan* motored with me to Dieppe by 6.30 and I had a walk with Alfred Acland[10] into the town before dinner. His daughter Cicely[11] who is working in the French Hospital and a Miss Wild dined at the mess.[12]

7 April

Soon after 8 Acland and I made our way through St. Pol to Bethune and lunched at Hotel de France.[13] With great difficulty we found Harry Lewis's[14] Brigade was still at La Brebis[15] but found him out inspecting part of the line. However the young adjutant took us up to the guns and to an observation post from wh. we saw the enemy lines, Hill 70 and cross pits, wh. was the scene of terrible fight. I only caught a sight of Harry Lewis before I came away.

---

6 The Baptist church in Bruay was founded in 1833.
7 Montreuil.
8 General Sir Douglas Haig.
9 SAD 28/1/21 noted one chaplain posted on 6 Apr., the Rev. J. G. Tyson*, to Boulogne.
10 Colonel A. D. Acland.
11 Possibly Clemence M. Acland, Voluntary Aid Detachment.
12 There were several nurses with the surname.
13 Hotel in Bethune.
14 Brigadier General F. G. Lewis.
15 Location is uncertain.

8 April

Alfred Acland[16] stayed all the morning and had lunch and went on to Boulogne. Ellison* came in from the P. Schools Batt, to talk over a change. After lunch I motored down to the IV Army and called at Querrieu on the way and talked over matters before I went on to Ribemont to the 21st Div. HQ. where I find Troyte[17] in company of Alfred Acland whom I had met before and Col. Paley[18] the great grandson of Paley's 'Evidences.'[19]

9 April

I had a blessed Sunday. Holy Com. at 7.30. Services at 9.30, 10.30, 11.45 and lunch with my dear old friend Wilkinson[20] of Khartoum and with whom I had a short but glorious talk about old days. A confirmation was held in RIBEBONT School room at 3.30 where about 40 were present. After confirmation tea at H.Q. Archdeacon Southwell* and I motored back to Querrieu where I dropped him. Went on alone to S. Omer where all the fiends of hell seemed let loose to my undoing. Masters* dined with me.

10 April

My spirit was calmed within me while I prayed in the garden and quiet reigned in my heart all day. I walked with Masters* towards the woods from 2.30 – 5. I confirmed a young fellow in our own little chapel at 5.30 and spent some time in the office before dinner. Bagshaw* and Hare* of the Fusiliers dined and slept and I turned in about 11.

11 April

I had breakfast in our new quarters today with Hare* and Bagshaw* and worked in the office until 12.

Masters* then drove me in his car to Calais where I was entertained to lunch by the chaplains – Smithwick*, Ninis*, Sam Ryan,[21] Harvey[22] and another. I held a confirmation in the English Church at 3[23] – did some work until 6 pm had tea with Ninis* and dined with Colonel Nicholson[24] the Base Commander.

---

[16]   Colonel A. D. Acland.

[17]   Possible Captain C. J. A. Troyte.

[18]   Possibly Lieutenant Colonel A. T. Paley.

[19]   W. Paley, *Natural theology or evidences of the existence and attributes of the deity* (London, 1802.) This is famous for the use of a watchmaker as an analogy for the nature of God.

[20]   Possible Major Ernest Bedoe Wilkinson.

[21]   Possibly the Rev. F. Downland Ryan*. A Ryan was mentioned in SAD 28/1/15 when, on 11 Nov. 1915, he was posted from 12 Div to Calais.

[22]   Unidentified, but SAD 28/1/7 mentions a Harvey as posted to the Duchess of Westminster's Hospital

[23]   Holy Trinity, Calais where the minister was the Rev. W. P. Parker.

[24]   Colonel John Sanctuary Nicholson, base commandant Calais, promoted brigadier general in 1916.

12 April

In the driving rain I was shewn over the great workshops at Calais by General Nicholson[25] and was then driven by Masters* in his motor to S. Omer. After an hours work in the office and a short time for lunch went off the Welsh Division and held a confirmation for about 55 Welshmen. I met, in Wills[26] the A.Q.M.G. of the Div. the brother of two friends of mine Mrs Staunton[27] and Mrs Buchan,[28] and had tea with the Divisional General Philipps.[29] One of the sons of Lloyd George[30] had tea with us. Goudge* stayed the night with me.

13 April

Worked in the office all the morning and in the afternoon walked with Geoffrey Gordon* in the woods – Neville* and Ted* Talbot[31] came to stay the night.

14 April

Started for the Southern Armies, ii and iii, soon after 10.45. With Ted Talbot* lunched with Gen. Snow[32] at Pas and found him not only willing but keen and insistent about a Corps Chaplain for his Corps. Drove back into Doullens picking up Ted Talbot*and proceeded to the 49th Division near Talmas. Confirmed more than 200. Gower Rees* bringing 170 gunners. After tea at HQ the Archdeacon,[33] Ted Talbot* and self, motored to Querrieu where I stayed with the Army Commander, Rawlinson[34] and talked over the question of Corps Chaplains and cars.

15 April

Stopped to talk to the Archdeacon[35] and made for S. Omer with a short break for business with Day* at S. Pol. Worked for a couple of hours in the office. Had a short walk with Thorold* and motored to Popperinghe having dinner with John Ponsonby[36] at his mess.

16 April

Holy Comm. at 8 am at wh. there must have been about 30 present. I preached to a large number of units in one of the Church Huts at 10 and addressed the 1st

---

25 It is not clear exactly when Colonel Nicholson was promoted.
26 Unidentified.
27 Unidentified.
28 Unidentified.
29 Major General Ivor Philipps, commander 38 (Welsh) Div.
30 Major G. Lloyd George was ADC to General Philipps.
31 The Rev. N. S.* and the Rev. E. K.* Talbot.
32 Lieutenant General Sir Thomas D'Oyly Snow, commander VII Corps.
33 The Venerable A. K. Southwell*.
34 General Henry Seymour Rawlinson, commander First Army.
35 The Venerable A. K. Southwell*.
36 Brigadier General J. Ponsonby.

COLDSTREAMS at 11, Geoffrey Fielding[37] and John Ponsonby being present. The band of the COLDSTREAMS played. I interviewed Stanley[38] of the Ch. Army and Avery[39] of the Navvy Mission,[40] had lunch with Geoffrey Fielding[41] at the Guard's Mess and confirmed in the cellar of the prison in Ypres. Had tea with the 3rd COLD-STREAMS and motored back after 6.

17 April

In the office all morning. Took Shipman* out in the woods. Stone* and Ogden* came to stay. Confirmed 5 in our private chapel at 165 Rue Dunkirk.

18 April

On the way to the confirmation at Bethune today I lunched with Harry Black-burne* and met a Major Nicholson[42] at lunch. There were more than 100 candidates confirmed from the various divisions. Callender[43] of the CCS afterwards entertained myself and a few of his friends to tea and I afterwards saw the little chapel provided for his CCS.

19 April

My spirit was calmed in looking over the addresses I propose to give on Good Friday. The Picture of our Lord on the Cross sunk into my inner consciousness with the thoughts it produced, a longing to be better. I walked a long way with Thorold* this afternoon and Boyd* of the Cavalry and Tanner*, a newly joined [the word 'Chaplain' would appear to be missing here] dined with me.

20 April

Another quiet day, thank God. I walked in the woods in the afternoon and prepared some of my sermon for tomorrow. The woods are beginning to be dressed. Nature always dresses from the foot so the ground is carpeted with beautiful flowers and fresh young grass, the primroses and cowslips are strewn lavishly in our woods. After two hours work in the office I had dinner alone and tried to prepare address for tomorrow, but was too sleepy.

---

37 Lieutenant Colonel G. P. J. Fielding.
38 Stanley was the commissioner for the CA in France.
39 Unidentified.
40 The Navvy Mission was one of the organizations that came together to form the Industrial Christian Fellowship.
41 Lieutenant Colonel G. P. J. Fielding.
42 Unidentified.
43 Possibly Lieutenant Colonel E. M. Callender.

21 April

Good Friday – My preparation for the one hour service was all too scanty and with the exception of the Introduction I had to fall back on the labour and inspiration of other days. I was dissatisfied worse than usual with my address to the Artists at the Monro Institute this morning. After an hours work in the office and a slight lunch I motored to ROUEN stopping at Neufchatel for half an hour.

I attended a sacred concert in the Theatre des Artes where Studdert Kennedy* delivered spoken helpful and inspiring words on the meaning of the Cross.

22 April

It poured with rain all day long. I spent the morning with Tuckey* looking into the business of Rouen Base and lunched with one of the hospital messes and confirmed at No. 2 Stationary[44] where Gutch* is attached. I had tea with the Matron and had a short walk before dinner. After which I prepared for Sunday and heard my own and the confession of another chaplain.

[23 April] EASTER DAY

Holy Communion at 7.45. A large number attended. Altogether there must have been 350 during the morning at the Echelon Chapel. I preached to a large Parade Service at the Reinforcement Camps at 11. Had confirmations in the hospital and had lunch with Colonel Gideon[45] and Romney Hadow.[46] I visited No. 2 Red Cross and confirmed one of the officers after wh. I went to tea at No. 9 Stationary Hospital where I met a large number of doctors and nurses I preached to a crowded congregation at the Echelon Chapel (it only holds 200) held a confirmation afterwards and dined with Capt. and Mrs Cooper[47] who entertained our Church Committee to dinner.

24 April

Nearly all the clergy at the Base received Holy Communion with me at the Echelon Chapel. I spoke a few words to them about the magnificent chance of work before us. We breakfasted together. I had a few interviews with some of them afterwards and I came away directly after lunch. Stopped at S. Pol and did work with Day* and Walker[48] and had lunch [Gwynne probably meant to write 'dinner'] at their mess and drove home in the motor by 11.5.

---

44 Hospital.
45 Probably Colonel J. H. Gideon, commandant, lines of communications.
46 Unidentified.
47 Unidentified.
48 Probably the Rev. F. J. Walker*.

25 April

In the office most of the day, except from 1 – 5 in wh. I had a walk with Smith[49] in the woods. The monthly meeting of the SCF Armies at 5 pm in our new office and Stanley[50] of the Church Army attended to produce his scheme.

All dined with me afterwards.

26 April

Worked in the office until 1. All the SCFs departed this morning. I picked up Harry Blackburne* on the way to Bruay where I confirmed for the 23rd and 47th Divisions. I saw my old friend O'Conner[51] at S. Omer and Oxley[52] at Bruay. O'Kell* dined with me afterwards and I saw Gordon* on my short walk after dinner.

27 April

Was able to go out into the gardens and pray before breakfast. We had quite a good number of chaplains at intercession at 11.45. Moved off from S. Omer for Corbie near Amiens. The day was a beautiful warm spring day and the roads dusty. Excellent for view and pleasant to travel except for the leaking of the tyres. Twice I had to stop, at Doullens a stop of ¾ hour wh. threw me late. I did not reach Corbie until nearly 4. About 60 were confirmed for the 31st Division of wh. Canon Linton Smith* is the SCF. I confirmed an officer at Bonnay on my way to Hailles where I had a most pleasant evening and stopped the night.

28 April

After breakfast motored to Sir John Keir[53] and interviewed him on the subject of Corps Chaplains, then returned back to the 31st Division and held a confirmation near Bus where I saw John Thornton* amongst the other chaplains. I had tea with General Hunter[54] afterwards and motored back to S. Omer. After dinner I worked until 12.30

29 April

Up at 5.30, I started with Gordon* to Boulogne where I caught the boat to Folkestone. Sea smooth, easy crossing, and safe arrival at 2. Saw the C.G. at St. Stephen's Club.[55] Hair cut at Victoria and worked at my sermon after a light dinner. Stopped at St Stephen's Club.

---

49 There were several chaplains with this surname.
50 Stanley was Commissioner for the CA in France.
51 Unidentified.
52 Possibly Brigadier General R. S. Oxley.
53 Lieutenant General Sir John Lindesay Keir, commander VI Corps.
54 Possibly Lieutenant General Sir Aylmer Gould Hunter-Weston, commander VIII Corps.
55 St Stephen's Club was on the corner of Bridge Street and the Embankment.

30 April

Holy Comm. at W. Abbey. Saw Sir W. Robertson[56] and Mrs at the service. Worked at my sermon all the morning, lunched with Canon Pearce and attended the Shakespearian Service[57] at the Abbey where Boyd Carpenter[58] delivered a most eloquent and moving address. I preached for Dick Shepherd[59] at S. Martin's in the Field at 6.15 and supped with him afterwards.

[56] Adolphus Cambridge, 1st marquess of Cambridge
[57] Service to mark 300th anniversary of the death of William Shakespeare.
[58] The Rt Rev. William Boyd Carpenter, bishop of Ripon between 1884 and 1911.
[59] The Rev. H. R. L. Sheppard.

May 1916

The month started with Gwynne in England. Whilst he was planning for the visit of the archbishop of Canterbury to the BEF, he also took the opportunity to spend some time with family in the Wirral. Much of the middle of the month was taken up with the visit of the archbishop. Gwynne was conscious of the continuing battle taking place between the French and Germans at Verdun.

1 May

Worked at the War Office part of the morning. Lunched with the Archbishop of C. at Lambeth and talked over the arrangements for his visit. Went back to the W.O. Saw Howell at 5 at his office. Dined with Bland Sutton,[1] Howell and Edie.[2] Slept at the Club.

2 May

Worked at my letters, visited the War Office, visited the Academy, lunched on sandwiches at Lyons.[3] Spent the night at Northwood with the C.G. London much interested in the Compulsion Bill.[4] Walked out before dinner and spent a quiet evening.

3 May

Came to town by 10 having breakfasted with the C.G. Saw Dick at the W.O., took him to lunch and caught the 2.35 train to Neston.[5] Arrived with Charlie soon after 7 pm.

4 May

Went out all day with Charlie. Train to Hope Village,[6] walked up Ffrith valley had tea at Caergwrle[7] and caught the 5.40 train back. Col and Mrs Dobby[8] dined and we spent a very pleasant day. It literally poured with rain all day, C and I came in drenched. However I managed it thoroughly.

---

[1] Sir John Bland-Sutton, surgeon at the Middlesex Hospital.
[2] Brother and sister-in-law.
[3] A branch of Lyons Corner Houses, a chain of teashops.
[4] Presumably the Military Service Act (1916) that introduced conscription was discussed. One issue was the exemption from compulsory military service that was to be granted to ministers of religion. The Act was passed in Jan. and came into operation in Mar. 1916.
[5] A parish in the Wirral.
[6] A small village in Flintshire with a direct rail route from Neston.
[7] The village south of Hope with the next station on the route.
[8] Unidentified.

5 May

A very unpromising outlook in the way of weather kept us in until 12. Part of the time I employed in writing up the Diary and writing letters. At 12 we faced the dreary weather and walked through Burton – Puddington – Shotwick[9] where we ate our sandwiches in the Porch of the church which dates to the 11th Century and whose stones were ribbed where the spear heads were sharpened.[10] We walked back thro' the rain and reached Neston before seven. The Staffords dined with us.[11]

6 May

Notwithstanding all efforts to show itself the sun failed to pierce the clouds, so C and I essayed forth in gloomy weather and walked through Heswall[12] and along the sands towards West Kirby.[13] We returned to tea at 5 and spent a quiet evening at home.

7 May

I celebrated and Harris[14] the curate helped at the 8 am service. C had a cold and stayed in. I preached at the morning service on, 'the victory that overcometh the world, even our faith.'[15] I slept soundly in the afternoon being tired after more walking that I had done for a long time. I preached again in the Evening on 55th Chapter of Isaiah, 'Seek ye the Lord.'[16] Mr Harris, the Curate, came to dinner but I felt so tired and sleepy that I contributed very little towards the conversation after dinner. I had a very blessed day, surrounded with the love and affection of my 'own' and God was with me teaching me in this atmosphere perhaps more valuable lessons than in the stormy conflict of work in France.

8 May

Took Charlie, Nellie, Lewis and the girls for the day to Liverpool, had lunch at Lime St. Station[17] and saw the Cinema display, 'Birth of a Nation'[18] in the Olympia.[19] In

---

9   Villages to the south of Neston.
10 St Michael's Shotwick has a Norman porch with slots for sharpening weapons.
11 Possibly the Rev. Albert Stafford of Bromborough, Birkenhead, and his wife Kathleen. They had a son, Albert Miles Gwynne Stafford.
12 A village to the north of Neston
13 A community on the north-west corner of the Wirral.
14 The Rev. H. M. Harriss.
15 'This is the victory that overcometh the world, even our faith.' 1 John chapter 4 verse 5, The Bible (Authorized Version).
16 'Seek ye the Lord.' Isaiah chapter 55 verse 6, The Bible (Authorized Version).
17 The main station in Liverpool.
18 *The Birth of a Nation* is a 1915 American silent epic drama film directed and co-produced by D. W. Griffith and starring Lillian Gish.
19 The Olympia Theatre in West Derby Road opened in 1905. Although not converted into a cinema until 1925, it was showing films before that date.

the evening Anderson, the Therapeutic Specialist[20] came in to dine and Charlie and I had a very interesting talk to him about the state of Religion.

The Rebellion in Ireland is being stamped out and the leaders shot.[21] The Irish members are very restive.[22]

9 May

Travelled to London by the 9.15 train with Mr. Gladstone[23] in the same Department [presumably means 'compartment'] Charlie coming as far as Chester. After lunch at Euston I went to the W.O. and spent the night at the Cloisters with Canon Pearce.[24]

10 May

Had a walk in the Park before the work in the office. Had Howell and Edie[25] to lunch at the Norfolk Hotel and worked at the office again until 4.30 after wh. I had a walk in the park and caught the 6.53 to Northwood.

The rebellion in Ireland is the chief topic in the papers – and the answer of Germany to Wilson's note – yielding to America's demands, suggesting conditions.[26]

11 May

Crossed over to France this afternoon. Howell and Edie coming to see me off by the train. We had a very easy crossing. Owen[27] of the Oxfords crossed with me and came up to S. Omer with me, Drury* and Thorold* after dining at the Louvre. Owen stayed the night. The class of chaplains now joining is excellent, I am glad to say, being [loosed] after Easter.

Peace has been mooted by Germany perhaps for America's good will.[28]

Germany is still bringing her forces against Verdun.[29]

---

[20] Unidentified.
[21] The reference is to the events in Dublin at Easter 1916. Ninety were tried by courts martial and fifteen had a sentence of death confirmed. The executions began on 2 May and ended on 12 May.
[22] Presumably the Irish members of the House of Commons.
[23] Possibly Henry Neville Gladstone who had taken over the family property in Apr. 1915 following the death, in action, of his nephew.
[24] The Rev. Canon Ernest Pearce lived at 3 The Cloisters, Westminster Abbey.
[25] Wife of Howell Gwynne.
[26] Following the attack on 24 Mar. 1916, on the SS *Sussex* by a German submarine in which four United States citizens had been killed, President Woodrow Wilson made demands that the German Imperial Navy restrict their attacks on unarmed ships. Gwynne had seen the *Sussex* in Boulogne harbour.
[27] Captain R. M. Owen.
[28] The reference is presumably to the exchange of notes between the United States and German following the attack on the SS *Sussex*.
[29] The German attack at Verdun had begun on 21 Feb. 1916. It was to last until Nov.

It is significant that the German communiques up to the battle of Verdun were accurate and truthful discounting the minimising of defeats and magnifying of victories.

12 May

Started again in the office this morning and began to take the reins. Walked out in the Forest in the afternoon with Thorold*, dropping Owen[30] on the way to Cassel. Askwith[31] has gone over to Ireland.

13 May

Working hard in the office at the Archbishop's visit. Chaplains Tyndall* and one[32] other to duty at the Bases on the 12th.[33]

Buxton* arrived and stopped the night and went on to his unit today.

Thorold* and I walked through the Forest on to the Road and because it was rather wet took cover in an Estaminet, returning about 6. Aisbitt* dined with me alone at 8. There are peace rumours in the papers but only in connection with the Wilson note.

One reason for the great attempts and losses of the Germans at Verdun, in the opinion of high authority, is to use up the French reserve and stop an offensive this year if possible.

God be praised for all his mercies and goodness. These I have placed on record. They are daily and hourly. Let us not forget Thy Benefits.

14 May

Sunday. I celebrated the Holy Communion at the little chapel of the Munro Institute at 7.30 – only 5 in all were present and preached to about 200 men at the 9.30 service. I felt the Spirit of God moving in me making me yearn for the awakening of souls and the regeneration of our race.

Major Courage[34] the AAG[35] came and lunched with me and looked over our office. He is in the 15th Hussars and was wounded severely at Ypres part of his jaw being shot away. He now has a gold piece in the place of the bone and except for the skin over the jaw being a bit scarred his face looks quite normal.

---

[30] Captain R. M. Owen.
[31] The reference is to a visit paid to Ireland by H. H. Asquith, the prime minister, that began on 12 May.
[32] Possibly a chaplain named Newcombe*. There were several chaplains with this surname.
[33] SAD 28/1/23 indicated that Tyndall* was to go to Boulogne and Newcombe (unidentified) to Etaples.
[34] Probably Major A. Courage.
[35] Assistant AG

I preached at XI Corps HQ at 6 in a small hut. Arthur Smith[36] and Ben O'Rorke*.

The Germans won about 500 yards of Trench near Vermelles wh. is not very serious.

May 15

A great deal of my time in the office this morning was taken up with preparing for the Archbishop's visit and knowing what little exercise I should have in the coming week I took Drury* out for a walk in the woods.

After office work on my return John MacMillan* came and dined with me – sleeping at 6 Rue Carnot to be ready for the Archbishop tomorrow.

The woods looked its loveliest and the new life of spring seems to bring new hope and faith – that nothing is dead that, 'nothing walks with aimless feet and not one life shall be destroyed.'

Russia seems to be pushing on with great vigour in Mesopotamia. France is taking the offensive at Verdun and seems quiet along our line.

May 16

Archbishop arrived at Boulogne at 12.15.[37] After lunch at the Club held a meeting at Etaples, for the chaplains. Had tea with Col. Harris[38] and drove to St. Omer. Drury* and Thorold* dined.

May 17

The Archbishop and John MacMillan* went off to visit the Guards Division where his nephew is CRA.[39] He was taken to Ypres and visited the dug-outs on the Canal Bank.

I motored in the afternoon by 3 in time for a short conference – a service and a confirmation by the Archbishop at 5.30 – The Conference produced two important subjects wh: are much in the minds of the chaplains – the question of suitable men for ordination, and the mission of repentance and hope.[40]

Dr Simms* and Avent* dined at 8. The trial [of] Casement the Traitor[41] was reported

---

[36] Unidentified.
[37] Details of the archbishop's visit are in LPL, Davidson papers, vol. 583.
[38] Possibly Major A. E. F. Harris.
[39] Commander Royal Artillery (CRA).
[40] This is the first reference to the National Mission of Hope and Repentance. It had been launched by the archbishops of Canterbury and York in Mar. 1916 and was intended to take place in Oct. and Nov. of that year.
[41] The trial of Sir Roger Casement for treason following his involvement in events in Ireland began in London on 12 May. Gwynne was correct as Casement was hanged on 3 Aug.

today in London Papers – the evidence against him was too damning and there is very little chance of his escaping a cheap martyrdom.

May 18

The Archbishop, John MacMillan* and I journeyed in the motor to Querrieu today starting soon after nine. We arrived just on the stroke of one. Rawlinson[42] the Army Commander gave the Archbishop a great welcome. At 3 pm the Archbishop held a conference and spoke to the chaplains of the Fourth Army. I stupidly did not seek out one or two of the disaffected ones who had misunderstandings. Archdeacon Southwell* gave all the clergy tea in Gen. Congreve's[43] chateau grounds after wh: we drove along to Albert Road to a point overlooking Albert from whence we could see the whole battle area in front of Albert and the German and British trenches. We drove into Amiens by 7.50 the Archdeacon joining us afterwards at dinner. The Germans dropped bombs about 11 and again at 12.

The Fourth Army now has five Corps, and will probably overflow into another Army.

May 19

The Archbishop had a look round the Cathedral while John MacMillan* and I settled up at the hotel. We stopped at Doullens and Trevant on then to S. Pol where we lunched with the Army Commander and his staff. In the afternoon we met the chaplains for a short service where the Archbishop preached and held a conference afterwards. The subjects discussed were (1) preparing for the National Mission (2) What kind of services men may need after the war – we had tea in the Hotel de France where Humphrey Snow[44] came to tea with the chaplains. We drove off about 6 via Lillers but had a bad break down on the way keeping Harry Blackburne* and Gen. Franks[45] waiting dinner until 9.

Allenby[46] had a long talk with the Archbishop and showed interest in the chaplains. The Lancashire Fusiliers are still holding Vimy Ridge[47] wh: they took from the Germans a few days ago.

May 20

The Archbishop had a quiet time until 12.30 when we drove into [Dove?] and lunched with the acting Army Commander Sir Henry Wilson[48] before meeting the chaplains in Bethune. Wilson thought the Germans were particularly lively just now

---

42 General Henry Seymour Rawlinson.
43 Lieutenant General Walter Norris Congreve, commander XIII Corps.
44 Lieutenant General Sir Thomas D'Oyly Snow, commander VII Corps.
45 Major General George McKenzie Franks, commander Royal Artillery, Second Army.
46 General Edmund Henry Hynman Allenby, commander Third Army.
47 The 11th (Service) Battalion of the Lancashire Fusiliers were involved in the fighting on Vimy Ridge in May 1916.
48 Lieutenant General Henry Wilson, commander IV Corps.

and showed not the slightest sin of weakening. He thinks the French have done splendidly but are using up some of their resources.

The Archbishop spoke to the men after the intercess[49] service in Bethune were we afterwards met about forty generals to [at] tea in the garden with a large number of the clergy of the 1st Army. The Archbishop was taken by Sir Henry Wilson to the Loretto Ridge from wh: he saw the German Trenches, while I returned to S. Omer whilst taking Blackburne* as far as Aire.

May 21

I celebrated at 7.30 in the upper Military Church and at 9.30 we motored to Hesdin where the Archbishop addressed about 1500 troops out in the open under the trees. McNutt*, Edwards* were on duty and officers were introduced after the service amongst them Prescot Roberts[50] and Blamy[51] It took half an hour to get to Montreuil where we interviewed the AG had lunch with the CinC and visited the QMG in his garden. I had a long talk with Cavan[52] after lunch and he was most optimistic about the war, thinking it might be over before the end of the year. We had two good pushes and took about 1000 Germans.

We visited Ames and had tea with Cooper[53] from whose garden we saw the great bombardment on Vimy where the Germans afterwards attacked. The Archbishop addressed about 100 officers and men in a school room.

May 22

It is interesting to notice the variety of opinion about the length of the war. We have seen all the Army Commanders now, Plumer[54] and Munro[55] today Allenby[56] and Rawlinson[57] when we held conferences in their armies. They frankly don't know, they are agreed that the foe is as virile and determined as ever in his trenches [which] are splendidly made, his wire entanglements superior to ours, his artillery excellent and his ammunition almost miraculously abundant. Plumer thinks the war will last another year. So does Munro. Allenby expresses no ideas and Rawlinson thinks the Germans may, 'tho he has no proof', crumple up any minute.

After lunching with Sir Charles Ferguson[58] at Ballieul we visited the Bantams,[59]

49 Service of intercessions.
50 Probably Lieutenant Colonel P. A. Prescott Roberts, assistant director Signals and Telegraph, GHQ troops.
51 Possibly 'Blamey'. There were several officers with this surname.
52 Major General Frederick Rudolph Lambart, 10th earl of Cavan, commander XIV Corps.
53 Unidentified.
54 General Herbert Charles Onslow Plumer, commander Second Army.
55 General Charles Monro.
56 General Edmund Henry Hynman Allenby, commander Third Army.
57 General Henry Seymour Rawlinson, commander First Army.
58 General Sir Charles Fergusson, commander II Corps.
59 These were battalions which comprised men who did not meet the standard height for the army of 5 feet 3 inches.

two Batallions of wh: were inspected by the Archbishop. One of the Bantams was pointed out as 49 around the chest. On duty as a policeman a few days ago he astonished some gigantic Australians by attacking and thrown on the ground one of them who refused to leave an[d] Estamanet[60] at closing time.

May 23

The Archbishop's last day was spent quietly in the morning not starting until 11 to visit Abbe Le Meyer the Mayor of Hazebrouck who is a priest – inhibited by Rome because he is a deputy in the French Senate. He had a long talk with the Archbishop when I was present about the state of Religion in France. He said the present anti-clerical feeling did not prevent the French from seeing that their religion was taught in the schools.

We lunched with Plumer[61] at Cassel after which we drove to S. Omer and visited the 3rd Coldstreams in their Barracks and were shown over the Munro Institute. Crawford[62] and John Campbell[63] came to tea and General Munro[64] dined with us at 8 bringing with him his ADC. The Archbishop was most interesting telling us of his experiences of the Kaiser at the funeral of the Queen.[65]

May 25 [date may be 24 May]

On the way to Boulogne and England the Archbishop stopped on the way to see General Pitman[66] a friend of his who is in charge of the Cavalry Brigade. The Archbishop addressed a meeting of the chaplains in Boulogne about 12 and lunched with Goudge* – Col. Lister[67] – and Col. Wilberforce[68] CO of the Base.

The Archbishop left about 3.30 and after tea I motored to S. Omer, full of gratitude that the Archbishop's visit had been such a great help and inspiration to our chaplains, and that everything had gone without a hitch.

We had a break down once or twice on the road, but they were times when it did not matter very much. Kiltermaster* stopped the night with me.

May 26

One special mercy I wish to record. On our return from Arras to the XIV Division HQ there was a sudden drop on one side of the car – the side nearest to the Archbishop wh: I thought meant a bad tyre burst. The next thing I saw was a tyre rushing

---

60 An estaminet was a local French place where light refreshments were served.
61 General Herbert Charles Onslow Plumer, commander Second Army.
62 Possibly Captain B. J. Crawford.
63 Possibly Major J. V. Campbell.
64 General Charles Munro.
65 Queen Victoria.
66 Brigadier General T. T. Pitman.
67 Possibly Colonel W. T. Lister.
68 Colonel H. Wilberforce.

past on the right of the car and climbing up into a field. It seemed almost like a bit of your own inside flying off. The chauffeur with real presence of mind and great skill kept charge of the car wh: slowed down without accident. It appears that the nut of the hub came off and wheel escaped free leaving the car to stand on the steel plate round the hub.

I spent the day in the usual way at S. Omer in office – a walk and office in the Evening.

May 27

Another long motor drive to the IV Army picking up Archdeacon Southwell* on the way to Albert where I confirmed about 30 lads of VIII Division. Blencoe* was in charge of an Institute for soldiers where they have a very nice chapel as well as rooms for the soldiers.

I had a long talk with the Archdeacon[69] about the work on the way back to Corbie. Gordon* came to see me before I started. I motored on to S. Pol – was very late in arriving but spent a very pleasant evening Sillem[70] and Logan[71] being present.

At Albert the leaning virgin and child on the top of the ruined tower was still leaning. The local French say that falls the war stops.

28 May

I worked in Drury's* office until 11 and then motored out to see the 3 Casualty Clearing Stations around Aveluy, Kelly[72] the brother of the CO of the El Fasher[73] Expedition was in charge of one of them. Most of the cases had been cleared but there were a few badly wounded left. One man had a piece of shrapnel lodged just above his heart where it could not be touched. They shewed me part of a bomb taken from a man's buttock – bit of chalk thrown up by a shell wh: had punctured a lung and a piece of knuckle from one man extracted from another, It was all so terrible and yet so grand that men should still go one with the fight. I motored to Hesdin in time for a concert at 6 at wh: I opened the new CEMS and CA hut after which I dined with the officers of the HAC.[74]

May 29

I stayed at the Hotel de France,[75] but could not get much of a move on for hot water or clean boots until nearly eight. I celebrated Holy Communion in the new chapel adjoining the hut at 9.30. I preached to the Northumbrians[76] and other details and at

---

69   The Venerable A. K. Southwell*.
70   Major General A. Sillem, deputy adjutant and QMG.
71   Possibly the Rev. V. Logan, British Red Cross Society.
72   Unidentified.
73   Possibly Al-Fashir in south-west Sudan.
74   The Honourable Artillery Company.
75   Not clear in which town this was.
76   The Northumberland Fusiliers.

11 addressed the Artists. At 12 I confirmed nine in the new chapel and lunched with the Artists afterwards.

At 3 I moved on towards Montreuil and stopped on the way to see a view from some high ground. The scenery in this part is excellent and attracts a large number of painters of all nationalities who make Montreuil their centre. After tea with Carey* walked round the ramparts and preached in a small room wh: Carey* has furnished in the theatre and started back about 7.30 reaching S. Omer about 8.30 where I dined at 6 Rue Carnot.

May 30

I entertained to tea in the Monro Institute some of the men of the 3rd Coldstreams who were in Egypt and the Sudan. There are one hundred and forty seven men at present in the Batallion about 100 came to tea and I chatted with them about the Sudan and reminded them each of the quiet restful days. We all felt we could pray 'Oh for the wings, for the wings of a dove…In the wilderness build me a nest',[77] after tea I spoke to them about the old days and of the loss of many of our pals in this war and spoke of the future and the hard fighting before them and begged that they would make it alright with God our Father and come to him for Pardon, Peace and Power.

Hanks* came and stayed the night. Robertson[78] of *The Times* also stayed.

May 31

The sergeants [*sic*] of the 3rd Coldstreams did me the great honour of having tea with me in the Monro Institute – sixty five came to tea and forty five of these were with me out in Egypt and the Sudan. Of course most of them were privates in the Batallion in those days. Before tea I journeyed to Aire and spoke on spiritual equipment for successful work to the School of Instruction for chaplains of the 1st Army. This is a most interesting attempt to instruct chaplains for their special work in the field and papers on such practical subjects as – Method what messages to deliver – are read by experts and discussed while devotional services of the deepening of spiritual life and also held.[79] These days were very full and very helpful and the Hand of God can be traced in it all. Would that my heart were purer that I may see clearer His Hand.

---

[77] 'Oh for the wings, for the wings of a dove…In the wilderness build me a nest', Psalm 55 verse 6, The Bible (Authorized Version). The text was made famous by its use by Mendelssohn in his anthem '*Hear my prayer*'.

[78] Possibly Henry Perry Robinson who was an accredited war correspondent for *The Times*.

[79] This initiative of the Rev. H. Blackburne, ACG First Army, was the first attempt to set up a training centre for chaplains serving with the BEF. It was the precursor to a force wide Chaplains' School that was to be established at Blendeques, near St Omer.

June 1916

During June 1916, the British army was preparing for its great offensive to be mounted around the River Somme. Gwynne referred to the artillery barrage that was to lead up to the assault. That would eventually take place on 1 July 1916. The elaborate planning detailed the rôle of all arms and services during the battle. Gwynne was concerned that the planning of the rôle of the chaplains was taking place without the agreement of the AChD chain of command. That was a direct challenge to the system that he had created. He was also concerned about the over-sight of chaplains serving with the Dominion forces. He referred to meetings with Australian, Canadian and New Zealand (NZ) chaplains.

June 1

Ascension Day – I attended and celebrated Holy Communion at our Small Garrison Church at 8 am and held a confirmation at Merville CC Station for about 40 candidates. Some of them were of the Welsh Division. I heard a quite delightful story from the Canadian Division a few days ago. One of the Presbyterian chaplains is a dear old boy but very long and prozy in prayer at the Parade Services. The Senior Corps Chaplain chatting with some of the men of his flock asked how they liked their chaplain, 'a very nice old boy,' said one of them, but he prays too long – he asks for the King, country, Empire, the Allies, victory by land and sea, the breaking up of the Turkish Empire, the entire destruction of the German Army and fleet – the speaker was continuing his list, but was interrupted by a pal who said quite seriously, 'In fact Sir he indents for too much.'

June 2

I made a mistake today and was late for my confirmation at Ballieul because I got out of my car to eat my lunch and take a little exercise – but missed the lane and fetched up far from my rendezvous. I had good exercise but was late for the Confirmation. Mellish* the chaplain VC was at the service and brought some of his men to be confirmed. I saw my old friend Potter[1] after the service and had a long talk with him. He gave me a very interesting account of the attack his Brigade made on the German trenches at S. Eloi. He also told me that Mellish* was a most natural and unassuming hero. It is a habit of his to be heroic out of pure unselfishness and willingness to sacrifice with never any idea that he is doing nought else but his simple duty.

---

[1] Lieutenant Colonel H. C. Potter.

June 3

One of the drawbacks of my work is that I have very little time for preparing my sermons and putting down the thoughts wh: are pressed on my mind from the sights I see. Tomorrow I am preaching to my old friends the 3rd Coldstreams and am most anxious to give them a message from God my Father. However I feel at times that God himself knows all about it. Crawley* the chaplain to the 1st Guards Brigade came to dinner and spent the night with me. He was one of the Archbp. of York's chaplains and is brother in law to Lord Cavan[2] whom I consider to be the best all round General in this army, because of his disinterestedness he is the most outspoken and fearless of any in stating his views.

June 4

I had a truly blessed Sunday today wh: began with a celebration at 9.30, after wh: I motored out to the village of Quelmes where I spoke to the 2nd Coldstreams. At 11 am I preached to the 3rd Coldstreams in the Monro Institute on the Fatherhood of God. It moved me greatly to speak to my dear old friends from the Sudan or rather to the Batallion wh: was so well known to me. Alas now only a fifth of the number is known to me though the spirit of the Batallion goes on. 'Hasn't the old Batallion done well' was the remark of one of the men. He thought not of the hundreds who had fallen – the honour of the Batallion shone bright. I motored to Boulogne in the afternoon and took confirmation preaching at Kensiville Camp[3] at 6.00 I saw some of the Conscientious objectors afterwards.[4]

June 5

After intercessions with the chaplains at Boulogne I made my way to Montreuil to interview the AG and spent some time waiting in his office. I had only a short time with him before lunching with Turner[5] in his mess.

I had a stroll round the ramparts with Turner and saw magnificent scenery and picturesque bit of the old walls wh: attracts so many artists to live and paint here.

Motored back to S. Omer in the afternoon and worked at the office.
Ben O'Rorke* who is now working with me in place of Thorold* is doing very well.

---

2 Major General Frederick Rudolph Lambart, 10th earl of Cavan, commander XIV Corps.
3 He may have been referring to Henriville Camp.
4 Conscientious objectors were those who refused to serve under the Military Service Act 1916. The group at Boulogne included the 'Richmond Sixteen'. These were a group of men who had been held in the castle at Richmond in North Yorkshire before being sent to France. Once there, they were court martialled as being subject to military discipline and disobeying orders as they refused to accept any military discipline. The sentence, passed on 14 June, was that they were to be shot. It was subsequently commuted. It is of interest that if Gwynne met that group he should have made no comment on the stance they were taking. However, there were other conscientious objectors, who accepted work not directly in support of military activities and who worked in local quarries, and it might have been these that he met.
5 Possibly Colonel E. V. Turner.

I prepared him for confirmation years ago in Nottingham when I was in charge of my Bible Class of wh: he was a member.

June 6

We had our monthly meeting of the Council of ACGs of Armies at 5 this afternoon. I managed to get a short walk before the meeting. The important matters of this Conference were the positions of chaplains in time of action – Schools of Instruction for chaplains and further decentralising by giving the ACGs powers to send the names of their Confirmed straight to England to their several parishes. There was no more complaint about cars though each ACG felt their work could not be well done without a car especially set apart for them. We all dined together at No. 6 Rue Carnot and talked over the latest news from the Army.[6]

June 7

After office Ben [O'Rorke*] and I had a walk in the gardens for an hour. I then motored to THEROUANNE where I took a confirmation in the School for the Ninth Division wh: is mainly Scotch. The poor old Scottish Divisions find it very hard to keep up their strength and so they are no made up of one Brigade South African. John Kennedy[7] turned up at the gunners[8] mess where I had my tea and we had all too short a chat about Khartoum and the old days.

I stopped the night with Bill Furze[9] the brother of Bishop Furze of Pretoria.[10] He is the Divisional General of the 9th Division (Scotch). He is a most amusing fellow and yet so genuine.

June 8

Came back from the IXth Division early and walked part of the way to get some exercise. Dexter,[11] Australian Corps Chaplain, Mitchell[12] of the Cavalry and Anderson* came to lunch which was amusing chiefly because of Dexter's* condemnation of the 'Singe Tax' wh: Drury* thinks is going to bring in the millennium.[13] I tried to

---

6   The issue of where a chaplain was to be located at the front was of considerable importance. The existence as to whether there were rules governing it has been debated at length. It was of importance because of the understanding as to how far the military chain of command had the authority to tell a chaplain what he should be doing as a clergyman.
7   Unidentified.
8   Members of the Royal Regiment of Artillery.
9   General William Thomas Furse commander 9 (Scottish) Div.
10 The Rt Rev. Michael Bolton Furse, bishop of Pretoria since 1909. His visit to the BEF in the spring of 1915 had been significant for the changes that were to be made to the structure of the chaplaincy and thus to Gwynne's appointment as DCG.
11 The Rev. W. E. Dexter*.
12 Probably the Rev. C. W. Mitchell*.
13 A tax on land following the principles of the American economist Henry George (1832–97) which had gained some popularity in Australia.

straighten out the Canadian chaplains entanglement and understand their point of view. Succeeded to some extent.

We had a confirmation for the XVII Div in our Church Room at the Monro Institute and entertained the candidates to tea afterwards.
It was very impressive to see mem so earnest before their march south where they are taking part in the great push.[14]

June 9

I lunched with an old friend at Bethune General Landon[15] and found one of my old flock there, Strickland[16] who used to be in the Sudan with me and we talked with evident pleasure of the old days there. I confirmed about a hundred and fifty from the 33rd Division and visited a new Institute established by Stone* of the 33rd Division.

The confirmation was very impressive and I met most of the candidates at tea afterwards.

In one of our trenches in the [front?] trenches was installed in a dug out over which was printed on a board 'The Rectory.' Two men marching up the trench were struck all of a heap by the sight, one said to the other, 'Fancy Bill 'eres a bloody Rectory', and the next moment a chaplains head emerged saying, 'And 'eres the bloody Rector.'

June 10

Cavanagh[17] who was V Divisional General is now commanding 1st Corps and I quite expected to see him this afternoon when I travelled down south of Bethune to his Head Quarters but unfortunately he was away on leave and one of his Divisional Generals, a very nice fellow named Scott[18] entertained me instead.

June 11

I had a very busy and happy Sunday. Webb Peploe* took me to six services. Harry Lewin turned up at the morning service and came with me to St. Omer where we had a long talk and a [buck][19] together before tuning in. Webb Peploe* seems to be doing very good work amongst the Corps Troops. It was my birthday and I asked for a sense of His Presence – a Passion for Christ and more faith in Him.

---

14   The first comment about the forthcoming battle to take place on the Somme.
15   Major General Herbert Landon, commander 33 Div.
16   Brigadier General E. P. Strickland.
17   Lieutenant General Charles Kavanagh, commander I Corps.
18   Possibly Major General A. B. Scott.
19   The word is unclear.

June 12

Boyd* of the Cavalry came in the afternoon, but I had to run away to one of our Chaplains Schools of Instructions now well established in the 1st Army by Harry Blackburne*. My lecture was on 'The Taking of Services', and I gave a few hints from my experience. General Hobbs[20] the AG of the 1st Army gave an excellent address on the duties and manners of chaplains from an army point of view.

June 13

Simultaneously with the memorial service for Lord Kitchener in S. Pauls we held services all over the field. I took a service at Montreuil the Head Quarters of the Army and said a few words about Kitchener before a distinguished company. His greatness consisted, to my mind, of 5 great powers, Concentration – Indefatigable work – Knowledge of men – Foresight – Made an aim and made a determined bid for it.[21]

June 14

After Holy Communion and work in the office I started for Corbie doing the distance between S. Omer and S. Pol in 1½ hours and Amiens in another 1½. I was turned back at the Amiens Barrier being a closed day when they catch spies dressed in British Officers uniform when the real British Officers are not allowed in the city. I held a confirmation at Corbie for [number is unintelligible] Division there were about 40 present. I then motored to Lucheux and stayed with Hales*.

June 15

Motored with Hales* into Pas[22] and saw some of the clergy and Walkey* the Corps Chaplain. After praying for them I made for S. Pol where I interviewed Walker[23] and before coming to S. Omer I confirmed for V Division in Agnes when I saw Pym* and Geoffrey Gordon*. I reached home just before 8 pm.

June 16

When I had finished certain amount of work in the office I proceeded to Havre via Abbeville were I saw and talked to Fox.[24] Then I motored through Neufchatel and S. Saéns to Havre by the lower road, had dinner after 8.30 and dined quietly with Parry Evans*.

---

[20] Major General P. E. F. Hobbs.
[21] Field Marshall Lord Kitchener, secretary of state for war, was drowned on 5 June 1916 when HMS *Hampshire*, in which he was travelling to Russia struck a mine off the Scottish coast. Gwynne had first met him when he arrived in Khartoum as Kitchener then was still in the Sudan.
[22] Pas-en-Artois.
[23] There were several chaplains with this surname.
[24] Possibly the Rev. H. S. Fox*.

June 17 [this appears *after* entry for June 18]

Service for Chaplains at 8 am and gave an address. 9.30 – 12 Interviews with chaplains. 12 – 1 walked. Lunched with Gibbons[25] – tea at Le Treport with nurses and Red Cross drivers. Parry Evans* gave a dinner a dinner at Continental. Hills[26] and Asser.[27] [last part squeezed on bottom of page]

June 18 Sunday

A blessed and happy Sunday was spent in preaching to the Venereal Hospital patients[28] and a large service in the Ordnance Stores where they must have been 800 voluntarily on parade.

I spoke at both places of Nicodemus and the spiritual insight.[29] I then touched on the spiritual war. I had lunch at the Transport Camp, had a short walk and tea at Miss Blakely's Hospital[30] though she was not there and held a confirmation in the Church at the Reinforcement Camp. Asser gave me dinner in the evening.

June 19

Motored with Whinny[31] to Abbeville, though we had punctures on the way Wh: kept us back and made us late. I then proceeded to Querrieu the other side of Amiens where are the Head Quarters of the IVth Army wh: was supposed to move against the Germans on Tuesday morning. I arrived late and stopped with DMS[32] of the Army where Masters* messes.

June 20

The Archdeacon[33] and I motored out this morning to see Ted Talbot* but found him not yet returned from leave. In the afternoon we lunch with Colonel Bridges[34] of the 19th Division and held a confirmation in the field afterwards – of about 80 candidates.

I then called on Tom Tillard[35] at the Flying Corps and had a walk with him and the Archdeacon.[36] Dined at the mess at 8 and had a long talk with MacIntosh[37] afterwards.

25   Possibly the Rev. H. H. Gibbons*.
26   Unidentified.
27   Major Verney Asser.
28   No. 9 Stationary Hospital.
29   John chapter 3 verses 1 to 21, The Bible (Authorized Version).
30   Miss Maud Blakely was a matron in the Queen Alexandra's Imperial Military Nursing Service.
31   Major G. S. Whinney.
32   Director of medical services.
33   The Venerable A. K. Southwell*.
34   Possibly Lieutenant Colonel G. T. M. Bridges.
35   Lieutenant T. A. Tillard, Norfolk Regiment, was seconded to the RFC on 14 May 1916.
36   The Venerable A. K. Southwell*.
37   Unidentified.

June 21

No sign of the bombardment or attack appearing I returned to S. Omer stopping on the way at S. Pol. Two pieces of information I gleaned during the stay at Querrieu. One from the German aviator who descended in our lines and disclosed it at dinner to our officers – that four days ago the German knew we were to attack. The other was that out men are so fit and keen to attack that, one of our chaplains declared – they would be disappointed if the attack were postponed – arrived in time for the opening of the hut at Wisk.

June 22

Worked in the office all the morning. John MacMillan* came out for a walk with me in the woods in the afternoon after wh: I worked in the office. I saw Hawkins[38] of the Newzealanders and tried to understand their position and difficulties. The Dominions are very jealous of their power and do not like being under any other authority than their own government.[39]

June 23

Still no news of the bombardment. Our people postponed the attack as the Somme divided the French and British forces weakening our attack so the French have been brought across and are astride the Somme.[40] I visited one of our Cavalry chaplains – Timmins* – in hospital damaged from a bad throw off a Bicycle. I took Ben O'Rorke* and Drury* down to the stream when Drury* fished and Ben [O'Rorke*] and I walked. It poured with rain. Colonel Boscowen came to dinner.

June 24

I visited the Anzac Corps Head Quarters this afternoon and saw Gen. Birdwood.[41] Almost the first person I met was Butler of Khartoum.[42] From him I learned that another of my flock 'Skinfaced' Newcombe[43] was with the New Zealand contingent. The Army Commander Plumer[44] was also at tea. After attending to some letters in hospital I motored to Cassel and spent the night with dear old Franks.[45]

---

[38] The Rev. H. A. Hawkins* was an Anglican chaplain with the NZ Expeditionary Force.
[39] The arrangements made for the oversight of chaplains differed between the various Dominion forces. They were all different from the arrangements in the BEF.
[40] Gwynne had limited knowledge of the tactical position.
[41] Lieutenant General William Riddell Birdwood was commander of the 1st Australia and New Zealand Army Corps (ANZAC) Corps.
[42] Unidentified.
[43] Major Edward Osborn Armstrong Newcombe, traffic manager Sudan Railways 1906–26, apart from service in the war.
[44] General Herbert Plumer was commander Second Army.
[45] Major General George McKenzie Franks, commander Royal Artillery, Second Army.

June 25

There were only four persons at Holy Comm: this morning at 7.45 General Franks[46] came with me. At the II am service the Army Commander with a large portion of the Staff came to the Service where I took special intercessions for the war and preached on the subject of 'Interview with Christ,' imagining as reverentially as I could what Christ would say to us about the war.

I had an interview with Plumer the Army Commander before lunching at Archdeacon's Mess[47] and I discussed with him the subject of Corps Chaplains – Australian and New Zealand Chaplains and that of a lecture at the Army School. I preached at one of the army aerodromes at 3 and motored to Ballieul where I had tea with Fenshaw[48] the Army Commander and spoke to a good congregation at 6 pm in the Theatre. I then motored home by 8.30.

June 26

These are days in which one is grave doubt what is best to be done. One hears the long roll of the guns like muffled drums (They must be bombarding nearly 50 miles off) but I never know when the attack is coming off. Rumour has it that there are to be days and days of Bombardment before we attack, and somehow it does not seem fair to my office to motor down so far on the off chance of an attack.

I worked in the office in the morning getting up to date with correspondence and other business. I took out in the car a young officer named Liddel[49] and Drury* to see the woodpecker's nest and to watch the herons feeds their young, stopping in the forest quite a long time. I tried to pick up my correspondence when I returned to the office and wrote home to some of those whom I owed letters. Rostrum[50] and Brown[51] came to dinner.

June 27

Heavy rain fell today – probably the result of Bombardment further south. There is expectance of some great move in the very air. Rumour says that 18,000 tons of ammunition were expended in 3 hours – troops are gradually moving south gathering for the great assault. I wait for marching order from God and try to keep out all inquisitiveness and restraining all impatience to be near the place of assault that I may have a clear guidance to go where I am needed. Potter[52] came into see me for a short time this morning and in the afternoon I went out into the woods with Ben

---

46 Unidentified.
47 The Venerable A. K. Southwell*.
48 The reference may be to Lieutenant General Hew Dalrymple Fanshawe, commander V Corps at the time.
49 Unidentified.
50 Probably the Rev. S. N. Rostron*.
51 There were several chaplains with this surname.
52 Lieutenant Colonel H. C. Potter.

O'Rorke* for a stroll and worked again in the office before dinner. Aisgith[53] one of our local chaplains came to dinner with me and talked over many things.

June 28

I motored out to Potter[54] who has come back with his Brigade to rest – which means to work hard practicing over ground prepared from aeroplane photographs of the German Trenches. Potter is a splendid specimen of a Xtian British Officer – clean-earnest and indefatigable worker and a great lover of his fellow men. I brought him into lunch and shewed him some of the sights of S. Omer St Bertin's Tower – the old picturesque houses along the canal – then a walk through the gardens and a visit to the Cathedral. A very friendly priest shewed us round all the objects of interest and amongst others the tombs of an Irishman and an Englishman with his mother and sister – whose portrait was depicted in white and black stone – once slabs over the graves now placed on the walls.

June 29

Drury* the Staff Officer is an odd man in many ways. He was appointed to help Dr Simms* at the beginning of the war and was such a help in putting the Department into some sort of shape for working in the field. Strange to say he was supposed to be against law and order and continually gave trouble to his Seniors who is now a great stickler for keeping others in order. It is the case of setting a thief to catch a thief or making the bad boy at school a monitor to look after other boys. He works very well and gets on well with me. He is a very keen fisherman – so today on the way to Etaples where I journeyed to take confirmations, I dropped him near a stream and picked him up on my way back after seeing nearly all the chaplains – taking 3 confirmations and having tea with Col. Harrison[55] at No. 23 Hospital.[56] Drury* took 9 fishes out of the stream but had to use an artificial minnow.

June 30

A Bishop of the Canadian Church arrived amongst the other chaplains to be posted. I had to alter the place originally chosen for him and hope to make great us of him by putting him at Etaples one of our largest Bases. The Canadians, like all young Dominions and young children just learning to walk, are very jealous of their young powers and resent the paternal assistance on learning to walk. So I took the Bishop de Pencier[57] to the Corps Commander of the Canadians (Julian Byng an old friend of mine) and to the Corps Chaplain Canon Almond* also a friend of mine and settled the whole thing without a hitch. Grateful to God for another Bishop to help and that everything was arranged in love and harmony.

---

53   Possibly the Rev. R. Aisbitt*.
54   Lieutenant Colonel H. C. Potter.
55   Possibly Colonel C. E. Harrison.
56   No. 23 General Hospital was at Etaples from June 1915 to Nov. 1916.
57   The Rt Rev. Adam de Pencier* had been bishop of New Westminster since 1910. In 1915, he was appointed chaplain and honorary captain in the Canadian Chaplain Services, attached to the 62nd Overseas Battalion of the Canadian Expeditionary Forces, by Militia Orders dated 14 Aug. 1915.

July 1916

The entries are dominated by the battle of the Somme. The infantry attack began at 7.30 am. Among the battalions to advance was 1st Battalion of the Newfoundland Regiment. Attacking at Beaumont Hamel at about 8.45 am the unit had suffered 90 per cent casualties within fifteen minutes. On 17 July Gwynne paid a visit to the unit whilst it was in the process of being reformed. It would appear that he had known the commanding officer (CO), Lieutenant Colonel Arthur Lovell Haddow in the Sudan. Gwynne also visited the Ulster Div which had suffered a high casualty rate on 1 July. Gwynne was aware of the casualties and spent much of the early part of the month visiting various medical units. He noted that there was an expectation of 250,000 casualties during the battle. He made no comment about the scale of the casualties. At the end of the month he paid another visit to London.

July 1

Over the parapets, or trenches as they are here, went our lads this morning. The French and our right accomplished their objective and our left did well up to a point but were held up by a strong point. Rumour has it we have advanced two miles on some part of our front. The IV Div had to meet the strongest opposition and lost about 4000 men. Our casualties up to yesterday afternoon were about 20,000. The French are said to have captured 2000 and we 1000 prisoners. An airman in the CCS saw the German lines full of Germans who were suffering badly from our shell fire.[1]

I travelled down from S. Omer this afternoon bringing Gen. Kentish[2] the Army Officer Schools Expert as far as Auxi-le-Chateau Brought ACG to dinner at Amiens and called on CCS.

July 2

The Casualty Clearing Station expected such a full influx of wounded that the little chapel was also used as a hospital ward. Consequently I had no place to celebrate our Holy Communion. I did not get up early as I sat up late reading, 'The Soul of the War', by one 'Gibbs.'[3] I motored to Querrieu and picked up the Archdeacon[4] and proceeded to Daours where we saw some of the wounded – one man showed us his helmet with a hole 1½ inch long which received the ragged bit of shrapnel wh: only cut his skull instead of braining him. Another a boy of the Berkshires

---

[1] This entry marks the opening day of the battle of the Somme. Gwynne's estimate of casualty figures would be shown to be significantly below the total number.

[2] Brigadier General Reginald Kentish, GOC 76 Bde (3 Div), Apr. to Sept. 1916. He had commanded an infantry training school and then been the advisor on such schools in the BEF.

[3] P. Gibbs, *The soul of the war* (London, 1915). A description of the fighting in 1914.

[4] The Venerable A. K. Southwell*.

originally now of the Service Bat of Dorsets[5] – shot in the arm by a German officer with is revolver – 'I did my duty, Sir', he said, 'with my bayonet but I brought away a souvenir showing us a brand new Iron Cross. Another showed me a bent range finder wh: saved his life. Boulby,[6] who seemed to think that we lost about 15,000 in killed and wounded since yesterday but feared that the badly wounded had yet to come in because of their inability to help themselves.

I visited two more Casualty Clearing Stations near Heilly and found one of my old friends named Thompson[7] from the Sudan in charge of the CCS nearest the front. We lunched at Heilly in a restaurant chateau run by a Belgian lady and her two daughters.

After lunch I saw the fight from the Army Commander's Observation Post from wh: we could see the terrific bombardment of our trenches wh: we had lately taken from the Germans. We saw our men under a sandy bank waiting to attack the enemies lines. There were about 19 of our balloons up in the air, while three of the enemies were visible. While we looked two had been withdrawn. Every now or then a rocket soared up, we thought from the German Trenches, evidently a signal that they still held them and warning to their artillery not to shell them. We said our Evensong outside the trench and watched the bombardment and heard the roar of our heaviest gun called 'Grand Mother' cough her heavy shells into the German lines.

While we were there we heard news of our advance along our right and that a place called Bottom Wood had been taken by one of our Divisions and that the German were holding up their hands in some quarries. We visited an Ambulance in Albert and saw two of our chaplains, Broadbent* and Robertson*, the first named of the 19th Div., and the latter of the 34th. It appears that the 34th and 29th Divisions ran over the first line of the German lines and omitted to search the deep dug outs from wh: emerged German with machine guns which mowed down some of our men from behind. On our way back we caught sight of a Batallion on the brow of a hill behind Albert. The Archdeacon[8] and I made our way over to them and found their chaplain [Force?][9] who had once called the men to gather together to the number of about 800. We sang, 'Jesu, lover of my soul',[10] then I spoke to them on the greatness of our Cause. What we fight for – the Fatherhood of God. After the last verse of 'O God our help in ages past',[11] I gave them the Blessing: To the Gracious Mercy and Protection I commit you.

A young officer named Rutherford[12] met me [crossed through] came up to me as we broke up and told me he was one of the congregation of Emmanuel, Nottingham,[13] a

5 Service Battalion of the Dorset Regiment.
6 Possibly Major General Sir Anthony Alfred Bowlby, RAMC.
7 Possibly Major Douglas Stokes Brownlie Thompson, RAMC.
8 The Venerable A. K. Southwell*.
9 Name is unclear.
10 The hymn was written by Charles Wesley.
11 The metrical setting of Psalm 90.
12 Unidentified.
13 Gwynne had been vicar of Emmanuel Nottingham between 1892 and 1899. The church no longer exists.

great friend of Paul the Vicar and had heard me preach on occasions when I visited Nottingham.[14] We then motored back to Amiens.

July 3

I said my prayers in the Cathedral before going to Querrieu. In the office I met Gibbs[15] and Barclay[16] and sent off a few telegrams.

Dive's Croft[17] is an ambulance of the 30th Division wh: is turned into a kind of collecting station and named after a Major who is now in charge and has done excellent work. It is a new link between the CC Station and Ambulances. Between two and three thousand wounded passed through from Saturday midday and when I saw it this morning there were only about 25 in the place. A Church Army hut as arrived at a station near – lying unused when Chadwick* the Corps Chaplain took the thing in hand, put two chaplains on the job and were hard at it while I was there.

Chadwick* the Corps Chaplain seemed to be doing excellent work with the Divisions in his Corps. All the chaplains had maps showing their posts and those of others around them.

Dire[18] very kindly showed us the plan of his camp and how expeditionaly [presumably he meant expeditiously] he unloaded and cleared in 10 places at a time.

From there we went to Bouzincourt to NNW of Albert in the hope of seeing Waggett* but missed him, the chaplains of XVII Div[19] seemed to be all over each other in the village.

I intended to visit another casualty clearing station at Warloy but time fled.

One of the Manchesters at the Ambulance in Bouzincourt church amused me. He had been wounded in the arm in the morning and was very excited after all his experiences. 'My opinion is, Sir, is that the war will be over in a week, they were only waiting for this to give in. I saw them throwing up their arms all over the place. I 'eard a million and a 'arf have already surrendered.' This was too much for a Corporal standing near who smiled at the number of prisoners but was too kindly to cast doubts on his veracity. A smart young Sergeant of the Gunners also wounded in the arm by a spent bullet said that his Battery which crept up on Sunday afternoon

[14] The Rev. F. W. Paul was curate at Emmanuel 1883 to 1886 and vicar between 1886 and 1892, and again between 1904 and 1907. Gwynne had preached at the church in 1908.
[15] There were several chaplains with this surname.
[16] There were several chaplains with this surname.
[17] Dive Copse was a concentration of FAs which became the XIV Corps Main Dressing Station. It was named for a small wood and after one of the COs. It is north of Sailly-le-Sec between Amiens and Albert.
[18] Unidentified but presumably a member of the RAMC.
[19] 17 (Northern) Div was a New Army Div raised in Northern Command and sent to France in 1915. It took part in the battle of the Somme.

and were bombarding the wood, Fricourt Wood, in wh: a large number of Germans were surrounded.

On our way back to Querrieu we suddenly alighted on 'a cage for prisoners' which belonged to the XXI Div and was under the charge of one Godfrey,[20] once a Staff Officer at Etaples. He let us inside the cage where about 150 Germans were interned. An elderly officer was in a cage by himself under suspicion of murdering the man to whom he surrendered. The charge against him was that he put up his hands to his Captor, one of our soldiers, who beckoned this prisoner to follow and when he turned his back was blown to bits by a bomb flung by the Prisoner in his hut who fled back into his dug out.

Godfrey was only prevented from shooting him by the Pro Marshall.[21]

I felt very sorry for the man and wondered whether he was really guilty of such an act.

The cage was on the floor of a kind of amphitheatre around which our soldiers sat and gazed. I saw some of them give cigarettes.

I had tea at Querrieu and proceeded to the Head Quarters of the 3rd Army where I learnt all their doing, did some business with the ACG and dined at his mess.

The 3rd Army had made demonstrations and lost heavily – the 46th[22] in wh: are the Derby, Notts had two Batallions either cut up or taken prisoners. Good news came in from 3rd Army – Batteries taken – La Boiselle – the wood behind Fricourt, 10,000 prisoners in all. After dinner worked my way back to S. Omer by 12.

July 4

Managed to get through a great deal of accumulated work in the morning, after a short night. In the afternoon I visited General Godley[23] the Corps Commander of the New Zealand Division and the two Australian Divisions and talked with him about the chaplains of the CofE in the Corps. He explained the relationship between the NZ and AI[24] forces and how that he was Officer Commanding the New Zealand army as well as Corps Commander of the 2nd ANZAC Corps. I arrived back about seven and finished off all the pressing work. Good news continues to arrive from the IVth Army. The French have now taken more prisoners and are advancing north of Péronne. It appears that the Germans put most of their forces against us never expecting that the French had left much of a kick after their severe losses before Verdun.

---

[20] Possibly Captain F. Godfrey.
[21] Provost marshal.
[22] 46 (North Midland) Div was one of the fourteen Territorial Force divisions formed after the 1908 reorganization of the Volunteers. It was the first complete TF to arrive in France in 1915. Mounted a diversionary attack at Gommecourt on 1 July 1916.
[23] Lieutenant General Alexander John Godley commanded II ANZAC Corps and was also the senior NZ officer.
[24] Australian Imperial Force was abbreviated AIF.

July 5

Up to now only two new chaplains are reported from home.[25] Worked at the office until one and motored to Boulogne to see Howell[26] passing through from Paris. The powers that be could not allow him to stop the night with me at S. Omer so I spent the night with him at Boulogne. Lady Bathurst[27] also met him and came to tea with us at the Dervaux.[28] Howell had interesting stories to tell of Joffre[29] and the French Government whose guest he was in Paris. Joffre was very optimistic. His Head Quarters was very modest about a quarter of the size of our GHQ with the same proportion of staff. He was loud in his praise of our British Infantry but said we lacked leadership and our Artillery was not properly handled. He thought our General Gough[30] was the most promising of our leaders: he also said the Germans had locked themselves to Verdun and could not unlock. We stopped the night at the Dervaux.

July 6

Arrived back from Boulogne at 11.30 Found the office full of chaplains lately arrived from England and excellent men they seem to be for the most part. Rogers* came in from the Guards Division for some advice about West Ham[31] and accompanied me to Bruay where I had a confirmation. Harry Blackburne* joining me on the way at Arques. We had a blessed time at the confirmation and interviewed some of the chaplains afterwards. I came back with Rogers* to tea at Arques and worked at my office for an hour. Rogers* and I had a stroll after dinner and talked over some of the lessons the war was teaching us. Lack of fellowship and in consequence the losing of the idea of communion and fellowship in the Holy Communion service we thought one of the reasons of our weakness. Please God common suffering and common sacrifice may being about a stronger desire for fellowship.

July 7

Six more chaplains turned up this morning[32] and Studholme the Military Secretary of the NZ contingent to talk over the work of his chaplains.[33] Griffiths[34] also turned

---

[25] SAD 28/1 does not indicate whom these two chaplains were.

[26] Gwynne's brother.

[27] Lady Lilias Margaret Frances Bathurst, wife of the 7th earl. The Bathursts owned the *Morning Post* of which Howell Gwynne was the editor.

[28] Hotel at Boulogne.

[29] Marshal Joseph Jacques Césaire Joffre was commander of the French army between 1911 and late 1916.

[30] General Herbert Gough, commander Fourth Army which had been created from the Reserve Army and separated from Third Army on 3 July 1916.

[31] Location has not been identified. It might refer to the area of east London.

[32] SAD 28//1/28 lists seven names under 7 July. Horsley-Smith (the Rev. C. J. Horsley-Smith*) to go to 56 Div, Reid (the Rev. E. Reid*) to go to 4 Div, Jameson (unidentified) to go to 2 Cav Div, Winter (unidentified) to go to 61 Div, Boorman (the Rev. H. Boorman*) to go Etaples, Griffith (unidentified) to Auxi-les-Chateaux (unidentified) and Davenport (unidentified) to Calais.

[33] The military secretary was the staff officer responsible for the posting and appointment of officers. Studholme has not been identified.

[34] There were several chaplains with this surname.

up who had been invalid home some time ago from Bailleul. We had a short walk in the afternoon and I returned to the office for a couple of hours work.

A large number of prisoners are being brought in from different parts of the line by night parties. We saw some of them being drilled in a Barrack yard in S. Omer. The news of the war is again excellent. The French have taken more than 60 pieces of heavy artillery and a large number of machine guns and we have repulsed all attacks on our new positions and advanced slightly. Colonel Sprott[35] dined with us tonight and Griffiths,[36] Sprott and myself had an argument about the question of how much the war was really costing. It arose out of a statement of Howell,[37] 'There will be very little extra taxing after the war.'

July 8

After working in the office until 12.15 I motored to Amiens stopping to say prayers at Fruges. I called on the 4th Army HQ; had tea in his mess and motored to try to catch Tom Tillard[38] who had unfortunately been sent on leave a few days before. I then visited Gen. Gough[39] at Toutencourt who has now organised a reserve Army. I have arranged that Southwell* should still manage the new Army from IVth Army HeadQuarters. Gough explained on the map his hopes during the next few days. He seemed to me to be the embodiment of energy and skill. He gives me great confidence for he is a real man of God who believes in prayer. I brought into Amiens to the [name of hotel is indecipherable]. Masters* and the Archdeacon[40] to dinner after wh: we had a long talk about many things and the state of the war. The French, and our own troops are pushing ahead gradually.

July 9

I celebrated the Holy Communion in the South Midland CC Station at Amiens at 7 am. I then visited the Cathedral and said my prayers as well as I could with all the noise of the various services and sight seer. It is a beautiful building in wh: to say one's prayers if there were some quiet. I took up Archdeacon Southwell* on the way to Heilly where we called on Thompson[41] my old friend from the Sudan. We visited Baumens Clearing Station and walked round amongst the wounded for a short time, and lunched with Thompson. We then viewed the battlefield from above Albert and saw a terrific bombardment wh: we thought was a counter attack on our trenches but we found that we were also bombarding their just as much. We lost Contalmaison or part of it, by sheer weight of men, but we shall take it back again, please God, before long. I hear that the Army Commander told the press men that the British Public were not to expect anything very sensational, but that our Military situation was satisfactory.

35 Lieutenant Colonel A. Sprot, commandant St Omer.
36 Unidentified.
37 Howell Gwynne, editor of the *Morning Post.*
38 Lieutenant T. A. Tillard.
39 General Sir Hubert de la Poer Gough, commander Reserve Army.
40 The Venerable A. K. Southwell*.
41 Possibly Major Douglas Stokes Brownlie Thompson, RAMC.

We entered Albert and visited the Field Ambulance we saw last Sunday. The place was crowded with troops, some going up into the fight and others coming away. I saw 3 Welsh Fusiliers and made one of them beam when I addressed him in Welsh.

Southwell* dined with me at Amiens. During dinner Arthur Lee[42] from Nottingham made himself known and talked with me after dinner.

I also saw … Howell's correspondent amongst the press men[43] and also came across Beech Thomas[44] of the Daily Mail.

July 10

I only had time to visit Dive's Croft and Heilly CC Stations[45] before returning to S. Omer via S. Pol. The battle was still going on and we saw heavy shelling on one part of the road. The Cavalry were all along the road – evidently close up some of them hoping for a gap to break through. On all sides I hear our chaplains have done well so far, two wounded and an RC chaplain killed in a dug out.[46] I had tea at S. Pol with Day's* mess and heard that the 33rd Division were also well on the way to the fray. We seem to be moving all our best troops southwards.

The French are now quite close to Péronne and have brought up some of the very pick from Verdun.

I reached home about 7.40 and worked in the office before dinner.

July 11

I spent the day as usual at my Quarters, out in the afternoon with MacMillan* in the woods and office in the morning and afternoon after 5. I dined with Colonel Boscowen[47] of the Hampshires stationed here and met a good many of men at his mess. We are still pegging away at the Germans on the Somme and making some headway. I do not suppose we shall hear of any great advance until Friday or Saturday. I mean no chance of the Cavalry breaking through. The Irish Question is very much muddled by the present Government and all here seem to think the Government is making a great mistake. We are sending down more and more troops

[42] Unidentified.
[43] Name is unclear.
[44] William Beach Thomas was war correspondent for the *Daily Mail* in France throughout the First World War.
[45] A village near Albert where 36, 38 and 2/2 London CCSs were located during the battle of the Somme.
[46] The Rev. Donal Vincent O'Sullivan chaplain to the forces (RC) was killed in action on 5 July 1916 and is buried in the Bouzincourt Communal Cemetery.
[47] Lieutenant Colonel Sir A. Boscowen MP.

into the 4th Army and so it is evident that we are going to get through this time. It is sad to think that we may lose 250,000 men in this great effort.[48]

July 12

Back again in the office one hears very little news except through the papers. In recreation in the afternoon I took Drury* down to a very pretty valley where I walked along the river bank while Liddle[49] and Drury* fished. Canon King*, the Senior Chaplain of the Ulster Division came to see me and told me of the doings of the Ulster men. They too the three lines of the Trenches very quickly on the first rush but those on their flanks failed and unfortunately the 38th had to come back without any other result that taking about 700 prisoners and slaying a large number of Germans while the Division through forests of maxims[50] lost about 5000 men. Thank God many of these were lightly wounded but a large number were killed.

July 13

Canon King* who told me these things today and not yesterday also told me how one of the men who was brought back with a severe shell shock unconscious, on being told by an orderly that he was coming round [and] that he would soon be alright, pulled himself together and refused to go further back to a Casualty Hospital saying if he couldn't be sent out with the fighting men he could carry a stretcher and from that moment until the stress abated flung himself into the work of carrying the wounded.

My tooth was troublesome today and an absess which would have hindered my work had I allowed it to go on was stopped by a skilful doctor at No 10 Stationary.[51]

Drury* went home on 14 days leave and Fleming* came and stayed the night.

July 14

Anderson* was the first to tell me the good success in the Somme fighting. We have made a great advance and put in the Cavalry by his account. This news he told me when I picked him up at Cassel on my way to a confirmation at Nieppe, after my mornings work at the office. No fewer than seven postings were made of new men to their posts today. There was only one weak man amongst the lot and three outstanding chaplains, of whom I expect great things. The candidates for confirmation were from the New Zealanders and the 41st Division about forty in

48 The casualty figures are the subject of debate. It has been calculated that the British and Empire casualties on the whole Western Front between July and Dec. 1916 (inclusive) were 513,289. This was about twice Gwynne's estimate. The totals for the Somme were over 400,000. It is to be noted that Gwynne expresses no feelings about this casualty figure.
49 Unidentified.
50 The maxim was a form of machine gun.
51 No. 10 Stationary Hospital was at St Omer between Oct. 1914 and May 1918. Dental surgeons were members of the RAMC during the First World War.

all, and they seemed very earnest and keen. We all had tea together afterwards and I made a speech to them after tea, telling them of the good news from the south and encouraging them to make good the great confession they had witnessed today.

July 15

An hour was enough to do the necessary in the office. So I started at 11 and moved Southwards in the car, through S. Pol, Doullens and Amiens reaching the 4th Army HQ at Qui soon after 3 pm. We drove into Albert and found on the way Macready* and Griffin[52] who invited us to tea with the 48th Transport near Albert. The CO gave us a hearty welcome and was most cheery about things. He gave us the head of a shell as a souvenir.

Griffin showed me over one section of his ambulance in Albert, where the wounded were passing through in great numbers and a wonderful sunk garden belonging to the chateau the HeadQuarters of his Division.

Dropping Southwell* on the way into Querrieu I branched off towards Varrennes and reached Acheux at 7.45 Malcolm Peake[53] one of my flock from the Sudan kindly put me up. He is CRA of the Division.

July 16

In the YMCA we had about thirty to a celebration of Holy Communion at 7.30 I preached in the same building to the H. Quarter Staff composed of signallers and ASC and the Officers attached on the Epistle, 'I reckon that the sufferings of this present time are not to be compared to the Glory wh: shall be revealed hereafter.'[54] I then walked up to the woods and reached to Lucas' Brigade[55] wh had been badly cut up in the recent fighting. I visited Sewell[56] of the 49th Division and had tea with Jack Brand[57] who is staff officer to Lucas. I preached in Mailly woods to one of the Brigades whose Brigadier was Caley.[58] After a most picturesque confirmation wh: was held in the woods with just a canopy. Malcolm Peake and I dined with the General at night.

[Small pen drawing of the open air confirmation service.]

July 17

After breakfast I motored up to Mailly and walked into the Trenches of the

---

52 There were several chaplains with this surname.
53 Brigadier General Malcolm Peake.
54 Romans Chapter 8 verse 18, The Bible (Authorized Version).
55 87 Bde was commanded by Brigadier General Cuthbert Henry Tindall Lucas.
56 Unidentified.
57 Possibly Major J. C. Brand.
58 This was probably Brigadier General Douglas Edward Cayley, commander 88 Bde.

Newfoundland to find Hadow.[59] Campbell[60] led the way and took me to his dug
out and I had a long talk about the Sudan. His Batallion had a terrible time. They
charged magnificently but were badly mawled only very few coming back again.
He and the Adjutant were the only two left out of the Batallion. There were lines
cut in the wire but the machine guns of the German were evidently untouched and
the part of the line they attacked was called 'the fort' by the Germans themselves. I
wished I had time to stay and look round, he was very anxious I should not go away
but I had to motor to S. Omer the same day and work in the office before dinner.

July 18

John Macmillan* accompanied me this afternoon to the river near Lumbres where
we walked along the river bank and talked out what could be done for the new child
to be born into this world as a result of the war.

I am convinced that unless we become more comprehensive and extend our borders
we as a child shall be unworthy and unable to mother spiritually our Empire after
the War.

My tooth was stopped by the local Dentist attached to No 10 Stationary and gave
me some pain. Harry Blackburne* came over. Fleming* came and stayed the night
and we talked over the old days in the 2nd Division. The news from the south is still
good. We are still advancing to gradually work behind Thiepval.

July 19

The Ulster chaplains[61] came to tea at 6 Rue Carnot. I gave a short address at the
intercession service afterwards on the Epistle for Sunday. The chaplains have worked
wonderfully well with the men during their trying time when they lost about 5000
men at their attempt at Thiepval. We cannot get at the truth of things until after their
fighting, but it is easy to see that the Ulster men feel they were let down badly by
Division or Divisions on both sides of them. There is no doubt that the men of Ulster
fought like tigers and won great praise, but had to come back from the Trenches
they won because of the failure of those on each side of them.

Canon Hannay 'George Birmingham'* came to dinner and brought his son from the
Irish Guards. Cols Sprott[62] and Boscowen[63] came to dinner to meet them.

59 Lieutenant Colonel Arthur Lovell Haddow, CO of the 1st Battalion of the Newfoundland Regi-
    ment. On the morning of 1 July 1916, the unit suffered extreme casualties, with 22 officers and
    over 650 men put out of action. The battalion was reformed and returned to the line on 13 July
    1916.
60 Unidentified.
61 38 (Ulster) Div endured hard fighting on 1 July 1916 and had many casualties. The division is
    commemorated by the Ulster Tower on the Somme battlefield.
62 Lieutenant Colonel A. Sprot, commandant St Omer.
63 Lieutenant Colonel Sir A. Boscowen MP.

July 20

Worked in the office all the morning and took out for a drive in the woods Neville Talbot* whom I brought in to see his brother Ted*. They still seem to fight in the 4th Army and good news arrive of the gradual advance. We were warned that there was to be a demonstration of air guns as the inhabitants had been growing rather slack about lights etc. At 11 pm the anti aircraft guns fired into the air and brought out many of the population into the streets.

July 21

Strange to say the German aeroplanes did come over and dropped bombs on one of our ammunition stores, and half the people were out in the streets again from 3 – 5.30 this morning. The noise of the explosions was exactly like a bombardment. I visited Heilly taking Southwell* to stay with Thompson of the 38 CCS.[64] I slept in a tent.

July 22

The Archdeacon and I paid a visit to Fricourt past Albert and saw some of the ground our men had fought over for the past fortnight. Fricourt was no longer a town but a heap of ruins. On reaching the spot we were asked by a Scotch soldier, 'Are ye looking for the Town Major?'[65] I answered by asking, 'What town?' he grinned and pointed to a hole in the ground where the Town Major held court. At 12 I motored through Amiens to Rouen where I preached at the dedication of the new church of S. George.

The ceremony brought together a large number of people from the French people of Rouen and attracted crowds from the street.

It was a great success and the band made the service go with a swing. Tuckey* came and dined with me at the hotel afterwards.

July 23

There was a celebration of Holy Comm. At 7 am wh. I did not attend, but I celebrated at 7.45. Capt and Mrs Cooper[66] and others attended.

In the morning I confirmed some of our wounded in Hospitals and saw Richards[67] and Colbeck* and lunched with Tuckey* where he has his own rooms, and confirmed in the new chapel of S. George at 5. The French people were so keen on seeing what manner of people we were that they thronged our church and it very awkward to speak with such a noise. In the Evening I preached to a crowded congregation on the

---

[64] Major Douglas Stokes Brownlie Thompson, RAMC.
[65] The town major was an officer responsible for non-operational military activities in a location.
[66] Unidentified.
[67] Possibly the Rev. W. D. Richards*.

messages of the Epistles in the midst of the war. The French people say our church looks like a Swiss or a Norwegian wooden church. It holds about 600 comfortably and 750 in a push. God be praised for the good work of all who helped in the good work and have given us a building in wh: to worship.

July 24

I visited the Hospital of the Red Cross[68] interviewed some of the clergy and called on the General of the Echelon with Tuckey* in the morning and moved off for S. Omer at 2 pm. After going hard the whole time I reached S. Omer at 8 and found Burroughs[69] with Ben[70] sitting down to dinner.

July 25

After working in the office I took Burroughs lurching in the car as far as Noeux-les-Mines where he saw the grave of one of his friends and called on the place where Harry was. We then motored as far as Mazingarbe, Haisnes and Philosophe where Dicky Dunn[71] and Ensor[72] picked us up in their car and took us to a dressing station at Vermelles wh. was being shelled by the enemy, a piece of shell was brought to Burroughs. Harry Blackburne* and I had tea with Cavanagh[73] where I saw Potter[74] and called on General Monro[75] with the HQ at Chocques and had a chat with him on the way back to S. Omer.

July 26

Burroughs[76] accompanied me to Lucre beyond Bailleul today to hold a confirmation of about 40 lads in the Northern Division, the 50th. After confirmation the Divisional General and some of his staff came to tea in the Convent where our confirmation was held. Crawhall* the SCF of the Division seemed to have the chaplains well in hand. Drury* came back today.

July 27

Baines* our new ACG for Etaples came with me as far as Montreux where I had a confirmation of candidates prepared by Carey*. I missed seeing the QMG as lunch was put to an earlier hour and returned to S. Omer by about 7. Not much news from the south except that we are pushing steadily ahead.

---

[68] A number of British military hospitals included 'British Red Cross' in their title although none we sited at Rouen.
[69] Unidentified.
[70] The Rev. B. G. O'Rorke*.
[71] Unidentified.
[72] Possibly Colonel H. Ensor.
[73] Possibly Lieutenant General Charles Kavanagh, commander I Corps.
[74] Lieutenant Colonel H. C. Potter.
[75] General Sir Charles Monro, commander First Army.
[76] Unidentified.

July 28

John Macmillan* went across to England with me today. We crossed in perfect weather and I sat up most of the voyage in Sir Chas Fergusson's[77] cabin and talked over my message to the troops wh: I finished on the boat. We only arrived in London about 4 pm when I went at once to 15 Albermarle Street,[78] the new HQuarters for Chaplains. I spent the night at Northwood.

July 29

All day part in the garden and part in my room I spent writing and thinking out my sermon for the Abbey.

As a matter of fact the only time I turned out was to walk to the station to buy a paper. I never had such a peaceful quiet day, so full of thoughts of God. Mrs Butler[79] and Mary[80] were most kind.

July 30

I attended early Communion with Mr & Mrs Lewick[81] at Emmanuel Church[82] at 8 and breakfasted with them afterwards. I spent all the rest of the time with my sermon until I went up to London at 3.50. During the service in the Abbey I kept thinking of mother who worshipped as a girl in the Abbey, and my prayer was that Christ should mount the steps of the pulpit, use me for His message.[83]

July 31

I stopped the night with the Pearces[84] at the Little Cloisters. After work in the office in the morning I lunched with Howell and Dick at the Norfolk Hotel. Had a long talk with the Archbishop at 6 and dined with the Moncks[85] at 8 where I also met Mrs Julian Steele.[86] I returned to roost at the Cloisters.

---

77 Lieutenant General Sir Charles Fergusson Bt, commandeer XVII Corps.
78 W1X 3HA. The expansion of the WO required the taking over of many additional buildings in London.
79 Mrs Elizabeth Butler, housekeeper.
80 Miss Mary Gladwell, general domestic servant.
81 Unidentified.
82 Emmanuel Church Northwood.
83 The evening service was at 7 pm. The hymns used that Sunday were 'Three in One, and One in Three', 'Jesus where'er thy people meet' and 'Saviour again to thy dear name we raise'. The litany was said with one lesson and an anthem by Walmisley, 'Father of Heaven in whom our hopes confide'.
84 The Venerable Canon Ernest Pearce, canon and archdeacon, who lived at 3 The Cloister.
85 Possibly Brigadier General (retired) C. S. Monck.
86 Wife of Major Julian Steele.

List of clergy mentioned in the diary entries

Anglican chaplains

These names have been identified from the pages of the diaries. Information is given as to their status within the AChD, whether Regular, Acting or Territorial Force in August 1914, or subsequently appointed as a temporary chaplain. Details of the regular chaplains are taken from Appendix 1 to Howson, *Muddling through.* Details of interviews are taken from a card index held by the Museum of Army Chaplaincy and accessed at www.chaplains-museum.co.uk/. Additional information can be obtained from those records. Where entries are annotated 'Blackburne', the notes and comments come a list maintained by the Rev. H. Blackburne, sometime ACG of First Army, and now at the Museum of Army Chaplaincy. Some additional information has been obtained from *Crockford's.* Some details have been taken from the *Army List* for 1918. Some information has been obtained from the Medal Card index in TNA, WO 339 series. Some information has been added from other entries in the Gwynne archives, notably SAD 28/9 and SAD 28/10 in the Special Collection of Durham University. The former is a manuscript book that would appear to have been entries about individual chaplains made by Gwynne in the months after he was appointed DCG. SAD 28/10 is an alphabetically indexed volume that contains entries in various hands. The entries contain additional information about the clerical history of individuals. It would appear to have been an attempt to maintain a record of those chaplains serving with the BEF. Neither is a complete record. No details of, for instance, the Reverend B. G. O'Rorke were entered into either volume.

In the case of some common surnames it has been impossible to identify which chaplain is the correct one.

Name	Details
Rev. W. H. Abbott	The Rev. Wilfred Henry Abbot was listed in the *London Gazette* for 8 Sept. 1914 as commissioned on 9 Sept. 1914.
Rev. H. W. D. Ainsworth	The Rev. Hubert Ainsworth was interviewed on 3 Aug. 1915. SAD 28/1/6 indicated that Ainsworth was posted to 2 Indian Cavalry Division (Cav Div) on a temporary basis. SAD 28/9/2 indicated that he was commissioned as a temporary chaplain in the last week of Aug. It also noted that he was 'A useful sort.'
Rev. R. Aisbitt	The Rev. R. Aisbitt was interviewed on 6 Mar. 1916.
Aisgith	See 'Aisbitt'

Rev. C. C. Adderley	Interviewed on 28 Sept. 1915. Posted on 7 Oct. 1915 to No. 8 CCS at Bailleul.
Rev. C. C. Aldred	Interviewed on 22 Sept. 1915. Posted to Boulogne on 7 Oct. 1915.
Rev. F. L. Anderson	Regular chaplain. He was not among the first group of chaplains to be mobilized in August 1914.
Avant	See 'Avent'
Rev. E. Avent	Rev. E. Avent a regular chaplain in Aug. 1914.
Rev. A. G. Bagshaw	Possibly the Rev. A. G. Bagshaw interviewed on 19 Dec. 1915. SAD 28/10/7 includes this chaplain but with no information as to his postings.
Rev. F. A. Baines	Regular chaplain mobilized in Aug. 1914. Appointed ACG at Etaples base in July 1916.
Rev. A. H. Balleine	The Rev. Austen Humphrey Balleine became a temporary chaplain to the forces in 1914.
Bamell	See 'Burnell'.
Rev. H. G. Barclay	Temporary chaplain to the forces. Served as chaplain to 1 Cav Div. SAD 28/9/3 noted that he was a 'Nice Gentlemanly fellow', and that he had worked for the Missions to Seamen.
Rev. E. Y. Bate	Acting chaplain at the outbreak of war and mobilized in Aug. 1914.
Beresford	Probably the Rev. J. R. Beresford.
Rev. H. Blackburne	Regular chaplain mobilized in Aug. 1914. Appointed ACG of First Army.
Blakeston	Possibly the Rev. R. B. Blakiston, temporary Royal Navy chaplain 1914–19.
Rev. J. W. Blencowe	Probably the Rev. J. W. Blencowe who was a temporary chaplain to the forces between 1915 and 1920. SAD 28/9/5 noted a 'Blencoe' as strong and fit. It also indicated that he was posted to 8 Div on 11 Apr. 1915.
Blucoe	See 'Blencowe'.
Rev. H. Boorman	Interviewed on 22 June 1916. The Rev. H. Boorman was posted by Gwynne on 7 July 1916 to Etaples.
Rev. W. Bowden	Temporary chaplain to the forces commissioned on 30 Sept. 1914. SAD 28/10/4 noted him as having been posted from 8 Div to Le Havre on 23 Aug. 1916.
Rev. H. Bowman	'An excellent chaplain. Served with Corps Reinforcement Corps.' Blackburne.

Rev. A. H. Boyd	Temporary chaplain commissioned on 3 Feb. 1915. Served with 3 Cav Div SAD 28/9/3 noted that he was a 'Good stamp of man'.
Rev. W. H. Bray	The Rev. W. H. Bray was interviewed on 30 Dec. 1915. Posted by Gwynne on 18 Feb. 1916.
Rev. H. S. Broadbent	The Rev. H. S. Broadbent was interviewed on 3 Dec. 1914. Serving in July 1916 with 19 Div.
Rev. T. Brook	Regular chaplain in August 1914
Rev. A. H. Broughton	The Rev. A. H. Broughton was interviewed on 11 Dec. 1914.
Browne	A 'Browne' was posted, on 7 Oct. 1915, temporarily to B Echelon Cavalry FA in 2 Div. There were several chaplains with the surname Browne. SAD 28/1/13 referred to a P. F. Browne posted to Etaples on 6 Dec. 1915.
Rev. M. Buchanan	The Rev. Malcolm Buchanan was interviewed on 2 Dec. 1914. SAD 28/2/13 has an entry for 6 Dec. 1915 which would appear to refer to this chaplain. He was posted to 3 Div.
Rev. H. B. Burnaby	The Rev. H. B. Burnaby was posted to 33 CCS on 3 Feb. 1915. SAD 28/9/3 noted 'Would like to get to the front.'
Rev. E. R. Burnell	Interviewed on 1 Dec. 1915. Mistakenly entered as 'Bamell' in the list of new chaplains posted by Gwynne on 18 Feb. 1916.
Burrows	Possibly the Rev. Hedley R Burrows, listed in the *London Gazette* of 9 Sept. 1914 as having been commissioned on that day.
Rev. A. Buxton	The Rev. Arthur Buxton was interviewed on 6 Jan. 1916. SAD 28/10/3 noted that he arrived in the BEF on 2 May 1916 and was invalided out on 20 Sept. 1916. It also indicated that he then returned in 1917 and was posted to 24 Div.
Rev. E F. Campbell	Regular chaplain mobilized in August 1914. Criticized by Gwynne for his comments about the CG. In SAD 28/9/7 he was noted a, 'A sharp, bright sort of man.'
Rev. D. F. Carey	Regular chaplain.
Cass	Possibly the Rev. A. W. Cassan who was a temporary chaplain to the forces 1915–19.
Rev. A. M. Cave	Possibly the Rev. A. M. Cave who was interviewed on 15 Dec. 1915. His card was confusing as to his dates of service.

Rev. C. R. Chadwick	The Rev. C. R. Chadwick had been an acting chaplain at the outbreak of war and had deployed to France with 1 Cav Div FA. In July 1916, he was serving as senior chaplain of a corps.
Rev. P. T. B. Clayton	Temporary chaplain from 1915. Better known as 'Tubby' Clayton and famous for work with TocH. Posted from Etaples in October 1915.
Rev. C. H. Clissold	Temporary chaplain to the forces 1914–20. Serving at Dieppe in Apr. 1916. SAD 28/10/0 noted that he was posted from GHQ to England on 8 Oct. 1916.
Rev. G. H. Colbeck	Regular chaplain in Aug. 1914. 40 Div. Posted to base on 17 June 1916 as 'too old'. Blackburne. SAD 28/8/7 noted that he was senior chaplain 7 Div.
Rev. H. L. Connor	Temporary chaplain to the forces 1915–19. '5 Div' Blackburne.
Rev. M. W. T. Conran	Temporary chaplain to the forces 1914–16.
Rev. A. M. Cook	Interviewed on 28 Sept. 1915. Posted to North Midlands FA on 7 Oct. 1915.
Rev. D. S. Corkey	The Rev. David Sloane Corkey was a temporary chaplain. He does not appear in the Museum of Army Chaplaincy card index.
Rev. T. E. Crawhall	Temporary chaplain to the forces. In July 1916, he was senior chaplain 50 Div.
Rev. A. S. Crawley	The Rev. A. S. Crawley was interviewed on 1 Sept. 1915.
Rev. W. J. Crick	Possibly the Rev. W. J. Crick interviewed on 18 Aug. 1915. Posted to 3 Div.
Rev. E. C. Crosse	Temporary chaplain to the forces 1915–19. SAD 28/9/8 noted that he was with 20 Bde, and 'Very happy with the Devons' (the Devonshire Regiment).
Rev. W. L. S. Dallas	The Rev. William Lorraine Seymour Dallas was interviewed on 29 July 1915 and accepted for immediate service. WO 95/1337/2, the war diary of 5 FA noted, on 9 Aug. 1915, that the Rev. W. L. S. Dallas had become chaplain in place of Bishop Gwynne. A further entry on 11 Sept. 1915 noted that he, together with his horse and groom, had been stuck off the strength of the unit. He was to be killed in action on 20 Sept. 1917 and is commemorated on the Tyne Cot Memorial to the missing. Blackburne commented, 'Keeps a moustache but looks as if he ought to be a good fellow. Came to stay night, a very good fellow in every way and a perfect Sahib.'

Rev. R. A. Davenport	A chaplain with this surname was posted by Gwynne on 7 July 1916 to Calais. The medal card index at TNA has only one chaplain with this name, the Rev. Rowland Ashley Davenport. It also indicated that he had served in the RAMC. The Museum of Army Chaplaincy card index noted only the Rev. Francis Davenport, interviewed on 16 Aug. 1915. However, his card was marked, 'For Home Only.' SAD 28/9/10 noted that the Rev. R. A. Davenport was seen at GHQ on 9 Nov. 1915 and that he had served for six months in the RAMC.
Rev. G. A. Davies	A Rev. G. A. Davies was interviewed on 26 Sept. 1915. Posted to Boulogne on 7 Oct. 1915. SAD 28/9/9 noted that he had been a combatant in the Leicesters and that he was posted to 30 Div. SAD 28/10/17 indicated that it was 3 Leicesters. It also has a reference to an entry in 'Vol. 1 p. 115' which has not been traced.
Rev. E. R. Day	Regular Chaplain mobilized in August 1914.
Dent	Possibly the Rev. E. Dent. His entry in *Crockford's* 1921 has no information for the period 1915–16. There is no entry under this name in either the Museum of Army Chaplaincy card index or the medal index at TNA.
Rev. H. A. Dibben	The Rev. H. A. Dibben was interviewed on 5 May 1915.
Rev. W. Drury	Regular chaplain mobilized in Aug. 1914. Served as a staff chaplain. Originally assisted MacPherson and was then transferred to Gwynne's staff.
Rev. H. C. Eddowes	The Rev. H. Cyril Eddowes was interviewed on 16 Oct. 1914.
Rev. N. W. A. Edwards	The Rev. N. W. A. Edwards was interviewed on 27 Oct. 1915. SAD 28/9/11 includes him but with no details of postings.
Rev. H. B. Ellison	33 Div. 'A good and capable organiser.' Blackburne.
Rev. C. S. Ensell	Regular chaplain in Aug. 1914.
Rev. A. K. Finnimore	Temporary chaplain to the forces 1915–16. Serving at Dieppe in Apr. 1916.
Rev. J. C. Fitzgerald	The Rev. J. C. Fitzgerald was interviewed on 17 Nov. 1914. A Mirfield Father.
Rev. H. J. Fleming	Regular chaplain mobilized in August 1914. Serving in Sept. 1915 as senior chaplain to the Guards Div.
Rev. E. A. Forbes	Serving with 15 Div. 'Rather old and pig headed. Returned to UK on 10 July 1916 at end of contract.' Blackburne.
Rev. J. R. Foster	The Rev. J. R. Foster was interviewed on 10 Sept. 1915.

Rev. H. W. Fox	Temporary chaplain to the forces 1914–19. Serving at Le Havre.
Rev. H. H. Gibbons	The Museum of Army Chaplaincy card index noted a Rev. H. Gibbon as available after Nov. 1914. The medal card index at TNA has an entry for the Rev. Henry Hensman Gibbon. Noted by Gwynne as serving at Le Treport in June 1916. It is likely that this is a spelling error. However, SAD 28/10/23 contained two entries,one of which was crossed through. There was some confusion about this chaplain in the records.
Gibbs	There were several chaplains with this surname.
Rev. F. S. P. L. Girdlestone	The Rev. Frederick Stanley Pears Lynn Girdlestone was interviewed on 11 Nov. 1914.
Gittens	The Rev. O. E. Gittens was noted in SAD 28/1/18 on 10 Feb. 1916 as posted to 5 Div. His card in the Museum of Army Chaplaincy card index does not record the date of his interview. The Rev. Edw. Gittens was interviewed on 6 Apr. 1915, These may be the same person.
Rev. F. G. Goddard	The Rev. F. G. Goddard was interviewed on 14 May 1915.
Rev. G. Gordon	Temporary chaplain to the forces 1915–19.
Rev. T. S. Goudge	Regular chaplain mobilized in Aug. 1914.
Rev. H. P. Gower Rees	'Bishop thinks highly of him.' Blackburne. (Presumably Bishop Gwynne.) SAD 28/9/33 noted that he was at GHQ for two months had then three months at Le Havre with 2 General Hospital. It noted that he could ride well and suggested 'West Riding, DLI or Cavalry.'
The. Rev. J. W. K. Griffin	The card in the Museum of Army Chaplaincy card index indicates that he reached the upper age limit for Reserve Service in 1940. He was serving as an 'acting chaplain' at Shorncliffe in Aug. 1914.
Griffith	There were several chaplains with this surname.
Rev. J. W. Griffiths	The Rev. J. W. Griffiths was interviewed on 27 Aug. 1915. He had served as a chaplain with the Australian Forces. SAD 28/1/3 indicated he was posted to No. 2 CCS in Sept. 1915.

Rev. R. Griffiths	SAD 28/1/4 noted that a R. Griffiths was to be moved from 8 Div to the base at Etaples. SAD 28/9/4 noted that he was 'Rather overstrung after ten months at the front', and suggested a move. There is no entry under this name in either the Museum of Army Chaplaincy card index or the medal card index at TNA. His published letters show that he was a TF chaplain who was commissioned as a temporary chaplain on 28 Sept. 1914.
Rev. P. W. Guinness	Regular chaplain mobilized in Aug. 1914. Posted to East Africa Command in Dec. 1915.
Rev. A. L. Gutch	The Rev. A. Leslie Gutch was interviewed on 23 Dec. 1915. In Apr. 1916, he was attached to No. 2 Stationary Hospital.
Rev. J. P. Hales	'A strong excellent chaplain.' Blackburne. He was commissioned as chaplain in the TF on 1 Mar. 13 and attached to the 8th Battalion of the Sherwood Foresters. He was interviewed by the CG on 31 Oct. 1914 and transferred to the status of a temporary chaplain to the forces. He remained with the battalion and accompanied it to France. His brother, also J. Hales, was a regular chaplain who had accompanied the BEF and had been one of the two chaplains taken prisoner during the withdrawal following the battle of Mons.
Rev. L. Hamilton	Possibly the Rev. L. Hamilton who was interviewed on 17 Feb. 1916.
Rev. W. P. Hanks	Temporary chaplain to the forces 1915–16. SAD 28/9/15 noted that he had worked amongst troops at home.
Rev. J. O. Hannay	The Rev. James Owen Hannay was interviewed on 29 Dec. 1915. He was a prolific author under the pen name of George A. Birmingham. He was a priest of the Church of Ireland. SAD 28/9/16 indicated that he was posted to Le Havre.
Rev. S. H. Hare	Temporary chaplain to the forces 1915–16.
Rev. H. C. Hargreaves	The Rev. Henry C. Hargreaves was interviewed on 12 Mar. 1915 for service from June 1915.
Rev. W. E. Harper	Posted to Le Havre on 7 Oct. 1915. SAD 28/9/16 noted that he had been seen at GHQ and posted to Le Havre.
Harvey	There were several chaplains with this surname.
Rev. F. J. Hazeldine	SAD 28/1/13 referred to a Rev. F. J. Hazeldine posted to 20 Div.
Rev. F. A. Hill	Regular chaplain mobilized in Aug. 1914.

Rev. W. Hogarth	The Rev. William Hogarth was interviewed on 17 Aug. 1915. Church of Ireland. SAD 28/1/3 indicated in an entry for 6 Sept. 1915 that he was posted to Boulogne. The entry for 7 Sept. 1915 posted him to No. 8 CCS.
Rev. P. G. Holden	SAD 28/1/5 noted 'Holden V Stationary Hospital, Abbeville, vice Watney.' SAD 28/9/16 noted that he liked working in hospitals.
Rev. B. L. Hope	Temporary chaplain to the forces 1914–19. Chaplain to hospital in Versailles.
Rev. H. L. Hornby	Temporary chaplain to the forces 1914–19.
Rev. C. Horsley-Smith	Interviewed on 6 Apr. 1916. Noted as available in July. Later, the card was annotated as BEF 'vice Staveley'. The Rev. C. J. Horsley-Smith was posted by Gwynne, on 7 July 1916 to 56 Div.
Horwood	SAD 28/9/16 noted that a chaplain with this surname was stationed at Calais. It further commented, 'Employs one of the CofE chaplains attached to the YMCA.' He was recorded as spending the night of 26 Aug. 1915 at Rue de Dunkirk. The diaries referred to this visit in terms of problems with the YMCA.
Rev. E. H. Hughes Davies	The Rev. E. H. Hughes Davies was interviewed on 3 Feb. 1916. He was posted by Gwynne on 18 Feb. 1916.
Rev. P. D. Irwin	The Rev. P. D. Irwin was commissioned on 14 Apr. 1915. SAD 28/9/18 noted that he was posted to Dieppe on 4 Sept. 1915 but that he would be glad to get up to the front.
Jameson	Jameson, unidentified, was posted by Gwynne on 7 July 1916 to Cav Div. There were two chaplains with this surname.
Rev. G. F. Johnstone	The Rev. G. F. Johnstone was interviewed on 28 Sept. 1915. The handwriting on the card suggests that in fact it was 'Johnston' Posted to Le Havre on 7 Oct. 1915. There is no entry under either name in the medal card index at TNA. SAD 28/9/19 indicated that he was posted to Boulogne on 8 Oct. 1915.
Rev. W. N. Kempe	Temporary chaplain. 46 Div. 'Splendid man in every way.' Blackburne. SAD 28/9/21 noted that he was attached to GHQ troops for work with the Parks (ASC). 'A very good sort.' 'Parks' was a military term for concentrations of equipment. In this case, it would have been mechanical transport of the Army Service Corps (ASC). He was later attached to the 7th Battalion of the Sherwood Foresters in 46 Div.

Rev. H. H. Kettlewell	The Rev. H. H. Kettlewell interviewed on 24 Nov. 1915
Rev. S. W. King	Most probably the Rev. S. W. King, a priest of the Church of Ireland who was interviewed on 11 June 1915. Served with Ulster Div.
Rev. D. B. Kittermaster	The Rev. D. B. Kittermaster was interviewed on 1 Sept. 1915. Chaplain to 2 Bde in Sept. 1915. Former master at Harrow School. Both Gwynne and Blackburne appeared to have had problems with the spelling of his surname.
Rev. A. E. B. Leahy	Temporary chaplain to the forces 1915–19. Sometimes appeared in the diaries as 'Leakey.' SAD 28/9/22 noted that he 'Would like to go up to the front.'
Rev. T. A. Lee	Possibly the Rev. T. A. Lee who was available from 5 Oct. 1915. Posted on 7 Oct. 1915 to Etaples. SAD 28/9/22 noted that he was from Southwell Minster.
Rev. F. T. O. Lewis	SAD 28/1/13 referred to a Rev. F. T. O. Lewis as posted to Boulogne on 6 Dec. 1915.
Rev. A. A. Liney	The *Army List* for 1918 shows him as commissioned as a temporary chaplain on 5 Nov. 1915. He does not have an entry in *Crockford's* 1921. Sometimes appeared in the diaries as 'Livey'. SAD 28/9/22 noted that he 'Would like to go up to the front as soon as possible.' It also noted that he was seen at GHQ and posted to Le Havre.
Rev. Canon M. Linton Smith	Temporary chaplain to the forces 1915–17. Appears in the diaries as 'Canon Linton Smith'. Appointed bishop of Hereford in 1920.
Rev. W. P. G. McCormick	The *London Gazette* of 9 Sept. 1914 recorded the Rev. W. Patrick G. McCormick as being commissioned on 9 Sept. 1914. A diary for the early months of his service is in the Imperial War Museum. SAD 28/9/3 noted that he was seen in the office on 24 Aug. 1915. There is an annotation that he was removed from Le Havre to the Guards Bde. It also commented that he was a 'Good all round man.'
Rev. J. V. MacMillan	The Rev. J. V. MacMillan was interviewed on 30 June 1915 and declared himself to be available three months hence.
Rev. C. T. B. MacNalty	Temporary chaplain to the forces 1914–17.
Rev. Canon F. B. Macnutt	The Rev. Canon F. B. Macnutt was interviewed on 4 May 1915.

Rev. E. G. F. Macpherson	Regular chaplain mobilized in August 1914. Appointed as senior of the chaplains of the Church of England in Dec. 1914. Gwynne superseded him when appointed DCG.
Rev. M. P. Macready	Regular chaplain mobilized in August 1914.
Rev. H. Maddrell	Interviewed on 14 Dec. 1915. The Rev. H. Maddrell was posted to 23 CCS on 3 Feb. 1916.
Rev. R. S. Marsden	Temporary chaplain to the forces 1915–19. Posted to 23 Div in Sept. 1915. SAD 28/1/5 contained entries for 26. Sept. 1915, posting him from 23 Div to 10 CCS and for 27 Sept. 1915, posting him to 33 CCS. SAD 28/9/24 noted that the CG said that he would like to see him posted to 70 Bde.
Rev. H. Marshall	SAD 28/9/24 noted that he had been in the AChD for seven years and that he was at Dieppe. WO 95/14071/1, the war diary of 8 FA noted that the Rev. H. Marshall joined the unit on 23 Nov. 1914.
Rev. H. G. Marshall	SAD 28/9/23 noted that he was a regular chaplain. He was seen on 16 Dec. 1915 and posted to 21 Div.
Rev. T. H. Masters	Possibly the Rev. T. H. Masters who was interviewed on 14 Oct. 1915 and expected to go to France after dental problems had been cured.
Rev. F. C. L. Matthews	Noted by Gwynne as serving with 7 Div.
Rev. E. N. Mellish	The Rev. E. Noel Mellish was interviewed on 28 Apr. 1915. He was awarded the Victoria Cross for his actions in rescuing wounded near St Eloi, between 27 and 19 Mar. 1916.
Rev. G. R. Milner	Posted to Le Havre on 7 Oct. 1915.
Rev. E. Milner White	The Rev. Eric Milner White was interviewed on 11 Nov. 1914 and departed for the BEF on 30 Nov. 1914. Served with 7 Div.
Rev. C. W. Mitchell	The Rev. Charles Wand Mitchell was interviewed on 1 Mar. 1915. He died of wounds on 3 May 1917 and is buried at Faubourg d'Amiens Cemetery, Arras
Rev. P. R. Mitchell	Regular chaplain at HM Tower of London in July 1915 and assisting CG at the WO.
Rev. D. Moir	The Rev. David Moir was interviewed on 15 June 1915 and originally posted to Aberdeen Hospital. His card is annotated, 'refused saying Church Commissioners required him to serve at the front'. He had already indicated his willingness to do so and apparently had his way. Episcopal Church of Scotland. In France by Sept. 1915.

Rev. H. B. de Mont-morency	The Rev. H. B. de Montmorency was interviewed on 14 Sept. 1915. A priest of the Church of Ireland. Posted on 25 Oct. 1915 to Etaples. SAD 28/9/25 noted that he 'Came out with the Ulster Division', and that he 'would like to go to the front'.
Rev. C. A. Mourilyan	The Rev. C. A. Mourilyan was interviewed on 21 July 1915. SAD 28/9/26 noted that he was posted to 8 Div.
Rev. R. T. Newcombe	SAD 28/9/27 noted that he was sent to Le Havre on 12 May 1916.
Rev. C. Ninis	The Rev. C. Ninis was interviewed on 20 Jan. 1915.
Rev. P. M. Northcote	Appointed a temporary chaplain on 14 July 1915. Serving at Calais in April 1916.
Rev. G. H. Ogden	SAD 28/9/28 noted that that he was, 'Attached to 36th Ambulance. Not too happy with the doctors. Complained about not having real charge of his own.'
Rev. F. J. Okell	Temporary chaplain to the forces 1915–1919. SAD 28/1/22 indicated, on 26 Apr. 1916, that he was to be posted to the Guards. SAD 28/9/28 noted that he 'Wanted to take his chance at the front.'
Rev. B. G. O'Rorke	The Rev. B. G. O'Rorke was a regular chaplain who had been taken prisoner in the withdrawal from Mons. He was repatriated in July 1915 and wrote of his experiences in *In the hands of the enemy*. He returned to serve as a chaplain in France. As a teenager, he had been prepared for Confirmation by Gwynne in the parish of Emmanuel, Nottingham. He had remained in touch with Gwynne and provided him, in Aug. 1914, with advice about army chaplaincy. His wartime service has been described in Howson, *Padre, prisoner and pen-pusher*.
Rev. F. G. J. Page	Joined BEF in August 1915.
Rev. R. Palmer	Posted on 18 Feb. 1916. SAD 28/9/30 noted that he was 'Strong, fit, had been in the South African war as a combatant and would like to serve with mounted troops.' He appears in TNA medal card index as the Rev. Reginald Palmer. There is no card in the Museum of Army Chaplaincy card index.
Rev. J. D. S. Parry Evans	Regular chaplain mobilized in Aug. 1914. Serving at Le Havre in October 1915.
Rev. S. B. Pelling	Temporary chaplain to the forces 1914–19.

Rev. A. E. Popham	The Rev. A. E. Popham was mentioned in dispatches on 18 June 1915 (*London Gazette*, 18 June 1915, p. 6009) and awarded a Military Cross (MC) on 22 June 1915 (*London Gazette*, 22 June 1915). Popham was previously the successor of Southwark Cathedral and the diocesan missioner. He was, in 1917, to be awarded a bar to his MC.
Rev. T. B. Pym	Temporary chaplain to the forces. 'A first rate chaplain. Quite the best.' Blackburne.
Rev. E. Reid	The Rev. E. Reid was interviewed on 22 June 1916. He was posted by Gwynne on 7 July 1916 to 4 Div.
Rev. W. D. Richards	Possibly the Rev. W. D. Richards who was interviewed on 8 June 1916 and was available from 11 July 1916.
Rev. J. D. S. Rider	SAD 28/1/13 referred to a Rev. J. D. S. Rider as posted to Le Havre on 6 Dec. 1915.
Rev. A. H. Robertson	The Rev. A. H. Robertson was interviewed on 15 June 1915. Serving in July 1916 with 34 Div.
Rev. P. F. Robinson	The Rev. P. F. Robinson was posted on 7 Oct. 1915 to Etaples.
Rev. V. R. Rogers	Temporary chaplain to the forces 1916–19. Noted as with 37 Div by Blackburne. Serving with the Guards in July 1916.
Rev. S. N. Rostron	The Rev. Sydney Nowell Rostron was interviewed on 29 Dec. 1915. He indicated that he would be available 'in a few months'.
Rev. C. R. Ryall	Joined the IEE in 1910 and served with the Indian Cav Div.
Rev. F. D. Ryan	The Rev. F. Downland Ryan was interviewed on 24 Sept. 1914. This is possibly the Ryan mentioned in SAD 28/1/15 when, on 11 Nov. 1915, he was posted from 12 Div to Calais. SAD 28/9/33 noted that he was an 'Outstanding man, will do well anywhere.'
Rev. R. Shipman	The Rev. Robert Shipman interviewed 10 Dec. 1915. SAD 28/9/34 noted that he 'Will take his chance. Recorded as posted to GHQ on 13 Jan. 1916.'
Arthur Smith	There were several men with this surname.
Rev. C. M. Smith	The Rev. Clarence M. Smith was interviewed on 16 June 1915. Posted to BEF in August 1915.
Rev. F. F. S. Smithwick	Regular chaplain mobilized in Aug. 1914. Serving at Calais in Apr. 1916.
Venerable A. K. Southwell	The Venerable A. K. Southwell was a chaplain to the TF.

Rev. H. O. Spink	The Rev. H. O. Spink was interviewed on 17 Dec. 1915. He was posted temporarily to 55 Div on 3 Feb. 1915. He was later killed in action on 9 Aug. 1916. SAD 28/9/35 noted that he was 'Strong and fit.'
Rev. D. J. Stather Hunt	The Rev. D. J. Stather Hunt was interviewed on 3 Nov. 1914. He was serving in Dieppe in Apr. 1916. SAD 28/9/14 noted that he was senior chaplain 46 Div. He recorded that he 'Will do well at any job, wishes to stay at the front.'
Stephenson	There were two chaplains with this surname.
Rev. J. R. Stewart	The Rev. James Robert Stewart had been a missionary in China with the CMS. He was interviewed in May 1915 and accepted for service. He was to be killed on action on 2 Jan. 1916 whilst serving with 2 WORCS, and is buried in Bethune Town Cemetery.
Rev. F. Stone	The Rev. Frank Stone was a temporary chaplain 40 Div. 'Excellent.' Blackburne. SAD 28/9/30 noted that he 'Will do well in the field.'
Rev. G. K. A. Studdert Kennedy	Temporary chaplain. Known as 'Woodbine Willie'. SAD 28/9/21 noted that he would 'Like to go up to the front.' It further noted that he 'Knows Hospital work. Knows 8th Worcs 48 Div.' (8 WORCS).
Rev. E. K. Talbot	Temporary chaplain to the forces 1914–20
Rev. N. S. Talbot	Temporary chaplain to the forces 1914–19.
Rev. E. V. Tanner	The Rev. E. V. Tanner was interviewed on 30 Dec. 1915. He was an assistant master at Weymouth College and indicated that he would not be available until the end of the Easter Term, hence his arrival in Apr. 1916. His diary was one of those quoted in M. Moynihan in *God on our side: the British padre in World War One* (1983). The original is in the Imperial War Museum collection.
Rt. Rev. J. Taylor Smith	CG throughout the First World War.
Thomas	There were a number of men with this name.
Rev. J. G. Thornton	31 Div CCS. 'Good and keen.' Blackburne.
Rev. E. H. Thorold	Regular chaplain mobilized in Aug. 1914. Later to become CG.
Rev. F. C. Timins	Temporary chaplain to the forces 1915–19. Served with the 2nd Cavalry Dismounted Div.

Rev. H. C. Townsend	The Rev. H. C. Townsend interviewed on 16 Dec. 1915. It was noted that he would be available in 1916. He was a priest of the Church of Ireland. SAD 28/10/57 noted that he was at 30 CCS on 15 Oct. 1915. This would appear to be an error and should have read 1916. It further commented that the Rev. Dr J. Simms had written saying that he had heard from Brigadier General Baird 'that he had knocked himself up thro' spending a fortnight in No Man's Land and would be better for a move'. It also noted that, 'Gen Baird wrote saying he will … to return and wanted him back, "He's not only a charming man and companion, but he is one of the greatest moral assets to Bde HQ. All the soldiers love him and will do anything for him."'
Rev. A. C. Trench	The Rev. A. C. Trench was interviewed on 20 Sept. 1915. Served with 7 Div. 'Transferred to Canadian chaplaincy.' Blackburne.
Rev. J. G. W. Tuckey	Regular chaplain mobilized in August 1914.
Rev. P. H. Turnbull	The Rev. P. H. Turnbull was interviewed on 24 Aug. 1915. Posted on 28 Oct. 1915 to GHQ troops. SAD 28/9/27 noted that he would eventually like to go to the front.
Rev. E. D. Tyndall	The Rev. E. Dennis Tyndall was interviewed on 8 Nov. 1915. He was judged to require some training and did not depart for the BEF until 10 May 1916. Served in Aldershot before being posted to the BEF. Posted to Boulogne by Gwynne on 13 May 1916.
Rev. Canon the Hon. L. F. Tyrwhit	Temporary chaplain to the forces appointed 12 Oct. 1914.
Rev. J. G. Tyson	The Rev. John George Tyson was commissioned on 5 Apr. 1916 (*London Gazette*, 9 May 1916) and see by Gwynne on 6 Apr 1916. His card noted that he was interviewed on 13 Feb. 1915, to be available for the BEF from 4 Apr. This would appear to be mistaken as to the year. Blackburne noted on 28 Oct. 1916, '5th Division. Quite good and keen, has much yet to learn.'
Rev. P. Waggett	The Rev. Peter Waggett, usually known as Father Waggett, had arrived in France in September 1914 to offer his services to the troops. He wrote to the archbishop of Canterbury (LPL, Davidson papers, vol. 343, fo. 39) on 30 Sept. 1914 asking him to assist in a challenge to an order from the CG requiring him to return to the United Kingdom. He was interviewed by the CG on 7 Oct. 1914 during which he apparently apologized for his behaviour. He was then granted a commission in the AChD.

Rev. S. Waldegrave	The Rev. Samuel Charles Waldegrave appears in the medal card index at TNA. There is no entry in the Museum of Army Chaplaincy card index. He appeared in the *London Gazette* of 9 Sept. 1914 as having been commissioned on that date. SAD 28/1/5 noted 'Waldegrave from Boulogne to 19 CCS.' SAD 28/1/9 noted on 3 Nov. 1915 'to 4 Div.'.
Rev. F. J. Walker	Regular chaplain who had been serving in Tienstin at the outbreak of war. He was posted to the BEF in Apr. 1916 to act as a staff chaplain but does appear to have worked in Gwynne's office.
Rev. J. M. S. Walker	SAD 28/1/13 referred to a Rev. J. M. S. Walker as posted to 21 CCS on 6 Dec. 1915.
Rev. J. R. Walkey	Regular chaplain mobilized in Aug. 1914. He served as senior chaplain 19 Div.
Rev. H. J. Watney	The Rev. H. J. Watney was interviewed on 12 May 1915.
Rev. H. M. Webb Peploe	Regular chaplain mobilized in Aug. 1914. SAD 28/9/42 noted that he had been posted to 41 CCS, but that he would 'Like to be with the fighting troops.'
Wilson	There were several chaplains with this surname.
The. Rev. E. S. Woods	Temporary chaplain to the forces commissioned in Oct. 1914. Serving at Woolwich in July 1915 then in France.

Clergy and ministers who were not commissioned as Anglican chaplains in the AChD

Name	Denomination	Details
Canon J. Almond	Anglican	Canadian chaplain.
Rev. G. Bennett	Church of England	The Rev. George Bennett served as an assistant chaplain at the British embassy, Paris, 1913–20.
Rev. A. S. V. Blunt	Church of England	Chaplain at the British embassy, Paris.
Rev. P. Dearmer	Church of England	Not a member of the AChD when Gwynne met him in France.
Rev. W. E. Dexter	Anglican	Australian chaplain.
Rev. R. C. Harwood	Church of England	Chaplain at Holy Trinity Boulogne from 1912.

Rev. H. A. Hawkins	Anglican	NZ chaplain.
Fr. A. E. McCabe	Catholic	Fr Austin England MacCabe was commissioned as a temporary chaplain to the forces class 4 on 19 Sept. 1914 and demobilized on 25 June 1919.
Rev. C. H. Merk	Anglican	Chaplain at All Saints Dieppe.
Rev. D. V. O'Sullivan	Catholic	The Rev. Donal Vincent O'Sullivan chaplain to the forces (RC) was killed in action on 5 July 1916 and is buried in the Bouzincourt Communal Cemetery.
Rt Rev. A. de Pencier	Anglican	The Rt. Rev. Adam de Pencier had been bishop of New Westminster since 1910. In 1915 he was appointed chaplain and honorary captain in the Canadian Chaplain Services, attached to the 62nd Overseas Battalion of the Canadian Expeditionary Forces, by Militia Orders dated 14 Aug 1915.
Rev. R. H. Pryde	Church of Scotland	Sometimes 'Pride'. Chaplain attached to 5 FA from 2 May 1915.
Canon F. G. Scott	Anglican	Canadian chaplain.
Rev. Dr J. Simms	Presbyterian Church of Ireland	Regular chaplain mobilized in Aug. 1914 as principal chaplain to the BEF. He served in that post until Feb. 1919.

Bibliography

ARCHIVAL SOURCES

Amport, Hampshire

Museum of Army Chaplaincy

Record cards of Church of England chaplains
Blackburne papers

Birmingham

Cadbury Research Library Special Collection of the University of Birmingham

CMS/ACC/18F1 Bishop Gwynne diaries
CMS/ACC/18Z1 'War Book'

Durham

Special Collection of Durham University

SAD 28/1 manuscript notebook with comments by Gwynne about possibility of becoming a chaplain
SAD 28/5 manuscript notebook with comments by Gwynne entered between 1 Aug. and 31 Oct. 1915
SAD 28/9 manuscript notebook with details of chaplains
SAD 28/10 indexed book with details of chaplains
SAD 34/10/1 – 120 diary of Bishop Gwynne for May 1915 to May 1916

London

Lambeth Palace Library

Archbishop Davidson papers

The National Archives

1911 Census returns

WO various series

WO 32/5636 Church of England chaplains
WO 32/6624 abolition of uniform for chaplains

WO 33/611 mobilization details
WO 106/49A/8 details of mobilization of medical units
WO 339 medal cards

WO 95 series: war diaries

WO 95/23/3 AG of the BEF, Nov. 1918
WO 95/27/3 AG of the BEF, Aug.–Dec. 1914
WO 95/25/7 AG of the BEF, July–Dec. 1915
WO 95/43/2 AG 3rd Echelon, Jan. 1915 – Jan. 1916
WO 95/1337/2 No. 5 FA 1915
WO 95/1342/2 2 COLDSTREAMS Aug. 1914 – July 1915
WO 95/1343/3 HQ 5 Bde July–Nov. 1915
WO 95/1347/22 HLI Aug. 1914 – Mar. 1919
WO 95/1347/3 9 HLI Nov. 1914 – Apr. 1916
WO 95/1348/2 2 Ox & Bucks 1915
WO 95/1351/1 2 WORCS Aug. 1914 – Dec. 1915
WO 95/1407/1 No. 8 FA Aug. 1914 – May 1919
WO 95/2023 18 Div Chaplains (Church of England) Aug.–Nov. 1916
WO 95/4043/2 Commandant Rouen base 1915
WO 95/4047/1 Commandant St Omer July 1915 – July 1917

National Army Museum

NAM 2006-12-65 minutes of the Presbyterian Advisory Committee to the WO

PUBLISHED MATERIAL

Church Times
Crockford's
House of Lords debates
Kings Regulations for the Army
London Gazette
Post Office Directories
The Scotsman
Tablet

Anon., *The Army List* (London, various years)
Anon., *Hart's Army List* (London, various years)
Anon., *Rough journal of army scripture reader H. Wisbey with the Suffolk Regi-
ment with the British Expeditionary Force in Belgium and France August–
September 1914* (Leyland, n.d.)
Anon., *A service of humble prayer to Almighty God on behalf of the nation and
empire at twelve noon on Wednesday, August 4th, 1915, after one year of the
war* (London, 1915)
Anon., *Statistics of the military effort of the British Empire, 1914–1919* (London,
1922)

Anon., *The Times history of the war 1914–1920* (22 vols., London, 1920)

Anon., *War establishment, Great Britain, army*, Parts I, II, IV and V (London, 1912)

Bell, G. K. A., *Randall Davidson: archbishop of Canterbury* (Oxford, 1952 edn)

Beresford, C., *The Christian soldier: the life of Lt. Col. The Rev. Bernard William Vann, VC, MC, and bar, Croix de Guerre avec palme* (Solihull, 1917)

Blackburne, H., *Trooper to Dean* (Bristol, 1955)

Blackburne, H. W., 'Existing organisation and work of the Royal Army Chaplains' Department', *RUSI Journal*, 67 (1922), 421–33

Blackburne, H. W., *This also happened on the Western Front* (London, 1932)

Crerar, D., *Padres in no man's land: Canadian chaplains and the Great War* (Montreal, 1995)

Doherty, S., and Donovan, T., *The Indian Corps on the Western Front: a handbook and battlefield guide* (Brighton, 2014)

Dow, A. C., *Ministers to the Soldiers of Scotland* (London, 1962)

Edmonds, J. E. (ed.), *The official history of the war military operations France and Belgium 1914*, I (London, 1933)

Edmonds, J. E. (ed.), *The official history of the war military operations France and Belgium 1915*, II (London, 1927)

Edmonds, J. E. (ed.), *The official history of the war military operations France and Belgium 1916*, I (London, 1932)

Gibbs, P., The soul of the war (London, 1915)

Gwynne, L. H., 'The Church of England organisation and work in the British Expeditionary Force', *Journal of the Royal Army Chaplains' Department*, 1 (1923), 185–8

Haigh, J. B., *Men of faith and courage: the official history of the New Zealand Army's chaplains* (Auckland, 1983)

Hill, R., *A biographical dictionary of the Anglo-Egyptian Sudan* (Oxford, 1951)

Howson, P. J., *Ministry to Saturday night soldiers: the formation of a Chaplains' Department for the new Territorial Army of 1907*, United Board History Project (n.p., 2016)

Howson, P. J., *Muddling through: the organisation of British Army chaplaincy in World War One* (Solihull, 2013)

Howson, P. J., *Padre, prisoner and pen-pusher: the World War One experiences of the Reverend Benjamin O'Rorke* (Solihull, 2015)

Jackson, H. C., *Pastor on the Nile* (London, 1960)

Johnstone, T., and Hagerty, J., *The cross on the sword: Catholic chaplains in the forces* (London, 1996)

Keable, R., *Simon called Peter* (London, 1921)

Keable, R., *Standing by* (London, 1919)

Langston, E. L., *Bishop Taylor Smith* (London, 1939)

Law, D., 'Frank Weston, the Kikuyu Controversy, and the necessity of episcopacy', *International Journal for the Study of the Christian Church*, 15 (2015), 214–43

MacDonald, D. R., *Padre E. C. Crosse & 'The Devonshire Epitaph'* (South Bend, IN, 2007)

Macnutt, F. B., *The church in the furnace* (London, 1917)

Madigan, E. *Faith under fire: Anglican army chaplains and the Great War* (Basingstoke, 2011)

Miles, W. (ed.), *The official history of the war military operations France and Belgium 1916*, II (London, 1938)

Moynihan, M. (ed.), *God on our side: the British padre in World War One* (London, 1983)

Oliver, F. S., *Ordeal by battle* (London, 1915)

O'Rorke, B. G., *In the hands of the enemy* (London, 1915)

Paley, W., *Natural theology or evidences of the existence and attributes of the deity* (London, 1802)

Parker, L. *The whole armour of God: Anglican chaplains in the Great War* (Solihull, 2009)

Pym, D., *Tom Pym, a portrait* (Cambridge, 1952)

Pym, T. and Gordon, G., *Papers from Picardy by Two Chaplains* (London, 1917)

Reid, D., *The kirk of the 93rd: a short history 1808 to 1968* (Plymouth, 1968)

Robinson, A. W., *God and the world: a survey of thought* (London, 1913)

Ryan, E. P., *Haig's medical officer: the papers of Colonel Eugene 'Micky' Ryan CMG DSO RAMC* (Barnsley, 2013)

Sherhod, N. A. and Allison, N. E. (eds.), *Bunyan history: Padre W. J. Coates' letters from the front* (Bedford, 2015)

Smyth, J., *In this sign conquer* (London, 1968)

Snape, M., *Clergy under fire: the Royal Army Chaplains' Department 1796–1953* (Woodbridge, 2008)

Snape, M., 'The First World War and the chaplains of British India', in *The clergy in khaki: new perspectives on British army chaplaincy in the First World War*, ed. M. Snape and E. Madigan (Farnham, 2013)

Snape, M., *The redcoat and religion: the forgotten history of the British soldier from the age of Marlborough to the eve of the First World War* (London, 2005)

Snape, M. (ed.) *The back parts of war: the YMCA memoirs and letters of Barclay Baron 1915–1919* (Woodbridge, 2009)

Spens, W., *Belief and practice* (London, 1915)

Talbot, N. S., *Thoughts on religion at the front* (London, 1917)

Tobias, M., *Collects for the British army* (London, 1930)

Watkins, O. S., *With French in France and Flanders* (London, 1915)

Wilkinson, A., *The Church of England and the First World War* (London, 1996 edn)

Winnifrith, D. F., *The church in the fighting line: experiences of an army chaplain* (London, 1915)

Youngson, D. T., *Greater love* (Hartlepool, 2008)

Websites

www.bl.uk
www.chaplains-museum.co.uk
www.cwgc.org.uk
Govt.nz
hansard.millbanksystems.com/lords
www.london-gazette.co.uk
www.nationalarchives.gov.uk
www.nls.uk
en.wikipedia.org

Dissertations and theses

Brown, A. M., 'Army chaplains in the First World War', Ph.D. thesis, University of St Andrew's, 1996
Thompson, J. H., 'The free church army chaplain, 1830–1930', Ph.D. thesis, University of Sheffield, 1990

Films

The Battle of the River Plate (1958)
The Birth of a Nation (1915)

Index

Titles for people mentioned in the diary entries are given as far as possible in the form that Gwynne have known them at the time. Where a position has been used frequently in entries, e.g. 'Chaplain General,' all references have been grouped under that heading.

PUBLICATIONS

1. Visitation Articles and Injunctions of the Early Stuart Church. Volume I. Ed. Kenneth Fincham (1994)

2. THE SPECULUM OF ARCHBISHOP THOMAS SECKER: THE DIOCESE OF CANTERBURY 1758–1768. Ed. Jeremy Gregory (1995)

3. THE EARLY LETTERS OF BISHOP RICHARD HURD, 1739–1762. Ed. Sarah Brewer (1995)

4. BRETHREN IN ADVERSITY: BISHOP GEORGE BELL, THE CHURCH OF ENGLAND AND THE CRISIS OF GERMAN PROTESTANTISM, 1933–1939. Ed. Andrew Chandler (1997)

5. VISITATION ARTICLES AND INJUNCTIONS OF THE EARLY STUART CHURCH. VOLUME II. Ed. Kenneth Fincham (1998)

6. THE ANGLICAN CANONS, 1529–1947. Ed. Gerald Bray (1998)

7. FROM CRANMER TO DAVIDSON. A CHURCH OF ENGLAND MISCELLANY. Ed. Stephen Taylor (1999)

8. TUDOR CHURCH REFORM. THE HENRICIAN CANONS OF 1534 AND THE REFORMATIO LEGUM ECCLESIASTICARUM. Ed. Gerald Bray (2000)

9. ALL SAINTS SISTERS OF THE POOR. AN ANGLICAN SISTERHOOD IN THE NINETEENTH CENTURY. Ed. Susan Mumm (2001)

10. CONFERENCES AND COMBINATION LECTURES IN THE ELIZABETHAN CHURCH: DEDHAM AND BURY ST EDMUNDS, 1582–1590. Ed. Patrick Collinson, John Craig and Brett Usher (2003)

11. THE DIARY OF SAMUEL ROGERS, 1634–1638. Ed. Tom Webster and Kenneth Shipps (2004)

12. EVANGELICALISM IN THE CHURCH OF ENGLAND c.1790–c.1890. Ed. Mark Smith and Stephen Taylor (2004)

13. THE BRITISH DELEGATION AND THE SYNOD OF DORT (1618–1619). Ed. Anthony Milton (2005)

14. THE BEGINNINGS OF WOMEN'S MINISTRY. THE REVIVAL OF THE DEACONESS IN THE NINETEENTH-CENTURY CHURCH OF ENGLAND. Ed. Henrietta Blackmore (2007)

15. THE LETTERS OF THEOPHILUS LINDSEY. VOLUME I. Ed. G. M. Ditchfield (2007)

16. THE BACK PARTS OF WAR: THE YMCA MEMOIRS AND LETTERS OF BARCLAY BARON, 1915–1919. Ed. Michael Snape (2009)

17. THE DIARY OF THOMAS LARKHAM, 1647–1669. Ed. Susan Hardman Moore (2011)

18. FROM THE REFORMATION TO THE PERMISSIVE SOCIETY. A MISCELLANY IN CELEBRATION OF THE 400TH ANNIVERSARY OF LAMBETH PALACE LIBRARY. Ed. Melanie Barber and Stephen Taylor with Gabriel Sewell (2010)

19. THE LETTERS OF THEOPHILUS LINDSEY. VOLUME II. Ed. G. M. Ditchfield (2012)

20. NATIONAL PRAYERS: SPECIAL WORSHIP SINCE THE REFORMATION. VOLUME I: SPECIAL PRAYERS, FASTS AND THANKSGIVINGS IN THE BRITISH ISLES, 1533–1688. Ed. Natalie Mears, Alasdair Raffe, Stephen Taylor, Philip Williamson and Lucy Bates (2013)

21. THE JOURNAL OF BISHOP DANIEL WILSON OF CALCUTTA, 1845–1857. Ed. Andrew Atherstone (2015)

22. NATIONAL PRAYERS: SPECIAL WORSHIP SINCE THE REFORMATION. VOLUME II: GENERAL FASTS, THANKSGIVINGS AND SPECIAL PRAYERS IN THE BRITISH ISLES, 1689–1870. Ed. Philip Williamson, Alasdair Raffe, Stephen Taylor and Natalie Mears (2017)

23. THE FURTHER CORRESPONDENCE OF WILLIAM LAUD. Ed. Kenneth Fincham (2018)

24. THE HOUSEHOLD ACCOUNTS OF WILLIAM LAUD, ARCHBISHOP OF CANTERBURY, 1635–1642. Ed. Leonie James (2019)

25. THE FIRST WORLD WAR DIARIES OF THE RT. REV. LLEWELLYN GWYNNE, JULY 1915 – JULY 1916. Ed. Peter Howson

Forthcoming Publications

THE PAPERS OF THE ELLAND SOCIETY 1769–1818. Ed. John Walsh and Stephen Taylor

NATIONAL PRAYERS: SPECIAL WORSHIP SINCE THE REFORMATION. VOLUME 3. Ed. Philip Williamson, Stephen Taylor, Alasdair Raffe and Natalie Mears

THE CORRESPONDENCE OF WILLIAM SANCROFT. Ed. Grant Tapsell

THE SERMONS OF JOHN SHARP. Ed. Françoise Deconinck-Brossard

THE RESTORATION OF THE CHURCH OF ENGLAND: CANTERBURY DIOCESE, 1663. Ed. Tom Reid

THE CORRESPONDENCE AND PAPERS OF ARCHBISHOP RICHARD NEILE, 1598–1640. Ed. Andrew Foster

BIRKENHEAD, ALL SOULS, AND THE MAKING OF HERBERT HENSLEY HENSON: THE EARLY JOURNALS, 1885–1887. Ed. Frank Field and Julia Stapleton

PROCEEDINGS AGAINST THE 'SCANDALOUS MINISTERS' OF ESSEX, 1644–5. Ed. Graham Hart.

THE 1669 RETURN OF NONCONFORMIST CONVENTICLES. Ed. David Wykes

THE CORRESPONDENCE OF FRANCIS BLACKBURNE (1705–1787). Ed. G. M. Ditchfield

THE LETTERS AND PAPERS OF WILLIAM PALEY. Ed. Neil Hichin

THE CORRESPONDENCE, DIARIES AND PERSONAL MEMORANDA OF CHARLES SIMEON. Ed. Andrew Atherstone

THE DIARY OF AN OXFORD PARSON: THE REVEREND JOHN HILL, VICE-PRINCIPAL OF ST EDMUND HALL, OXFORD, 1805–1808, 1820–1855. Ed. Grayson Carter

THE CORRESPONDENCE OF ARCHBISHOP LANG WITH BISHOP WILFRID PARKER. Ed. Garth Turner

Suggestions for publications should be addressed to Dr Grant Tapsell, General Editor, Church of England Record Society, Lady Margaret Hall, Norham Gardens, Oxford OX2 6QA, or at grant.tapsell@lmh.ox.ac.uk.